Praise for *Global Search Engine*

"If you're planning on having a web presence outside your country, then this book is absolutely essential to have on your desk/e-reader. Kennedy and Már Hauksson have done a fantastic job detailing the intricacies of marketing online to the people of different nations around the world. Whether you're planning on selling your products in Prague, Pretoria, or Patagonia, or if your plan is to become the worldwide leader in online news, this book gives you the tools you need to succeed."

—Simon Heseltine, Director, AOL Inc.

"With today's continued spiral into complexity of search marketing around the world, and the huge opportunity that global markets represent, large enterprises and aspiring small companies alike cannot afford to get multinational, multilingual search engine marketing wrong.

There have been clear examples of websites and companies ignoring multinational factors with dire results from lack of visibility to compete reversal of fortune.

What Anne Kennedy and Kristján Már Hauksson have given us in this seminal book is the first real roadmap and guide as to how to *get it right*. The detail and accuracy of the strategies presented are both proven and critical to your success across the globe. Whether you are a website manager or CEO, 2 people or 200,000, in America, Austria, or Australia, you need to know the intricacies and value of a multinational search strategy that can both conquer unknown competitors, and propel you into online success. This book is your must-have manual to monetize that huge opportunity."

—Crispin Sheridan, Senior Director, Global Search SAP

"Great resources for digital marketers and business owners, especially if you need a bit more convincing, or are afraid of going global. This book will clear the concerns and help you making the right business decisions."

—Motoko Hunt, President & Search Marketing Strategist, AJPR

"Finally! A must-have book for everyone who uses international search engine optimization and advertising as part of their online marketing plan. *Global Search Engine Marketing* is the definitive guide for anyone who is serious about creating effective multilingual and multicultural websites."

—Shari Thurow, Author of *Search Engine Visibility* and *When Search Meets Web Usability*

"*Global Search Engine Marketing* is the most comprehensive theoretical and practical application manual on the subject. Steeped in years of the solid international search marketing success of the authors and supported with thorough statistical research, this book guides you from strategy to implementation and analytics."

—Gillian Muessig, Founding President, SEOmoz

"There's only one marketing expert on the planet like Anne Kennedy. She has literally circled the globe to gain global search marketing knowledge and delightful tidbits, and shares it in a highly consumable format. You don't have to be a search marketing genius before you read the book, but you'll definitely feel like one after you finish it!"

—Dana Todd, Co-founder of Search Engine Marketing Professional Organization (SEMPO) and SVP Marketing, Performics

"No book I know of comes close to the detailed information that Anne Kennedy brings readers in *Global Search Engine Marketing*. She surveys search engines in various regions and outlines both SEO and PPC strategies to implement in each region, sometimes all the way down to the country and language level.

If you're planning to expand globally, you'll need this book!"

—Dr. Ralph F. Wilson, Editor, *Web Marketing Today*

GLOBAL SEARCH ENGINE MARKETING

Fine-Tuning Your International
Search Engine Results

Anne Kennedy

Kristján Már Hauksson

800 East 96th Street,
Indianapolis, Indiana 46240 USA

Global Search Engine Marketing
Fine-Tuning Your International Search Engine Results

ISBN-13: 978-0-7897-4788-4

ISBN-10: 0-7897-4788-X

First Printing: March 2012

Library of Congress Cataloging-in-Publication data is on file.

Trademarks

Warning and Disclaimer

Bulk Sales

Que Publishing offers excellent discounts on this book when ordered in quantity for bulk purchases or special sales. For more information, please contact

U.S. Corporate and Government Sales
1-800-382-3419
corpsales@pearsontechgroup.com

For sales outside of the U.S., please contact

International Sales
international@pearson.com

Editor-in-Chief
Greg Wiegand

Acquisitions Editor
Rick Kughen

Development Editor
Rick Kughen

Managing Editor
Sandra Schroeder

Project Editor
Seth Kerney

Copy Editor
Chuck Hutchinson

Indexer
Larry Sweazy

Proofreader
Paula Lowell

Technical Editor
Chris Sherman

Publishing Coordinator
Cindy Teeters

Book Designer
Anne Jones

Compositor
Mark Shirar

CONTENTS AT A GLANCE

TABLE OF CONTENTS

About the Authors

Anne F. Kennedy has been covering fast-changing Internet trends since the 1990s, especially international marketing. She has been a guest blogger for Microsoft AdCenter, Searchcowboys, and Web Marketing Today. She lectures at online marketing events worldwide.

Anne is a marketing veteran of more than 40 years. She founded Beyond Ink in 1997. Beyond Ink has offices in Portland, Maine, and Portland, Oregon, and is partnered with Nordic eMarketing in Reykjavik, Iceland.

She serves as an advisor to the SES global industry conference series. She was a founding member of the board of directors of Helium.com, a writer's community acquired in 2011 by publishing giant R.R. Donnelly. From 2001 to 2006, she published SEONews.net to explain the finer points of search engine optimization to business people who were new to it.

She holds a B.S. in radio, television, and film from Northwestern University, and was certified an Internet Professional by Novell, Inc.

Kristján Már Hauksson's company, Nordic eMarketing, specializes in multilingual online communications, organic search engine optimization, and marketing through several verticals such as technology, tourism, finance, government, and pharmaceuticals. Nordic eMarketing assists companies in gaining international visibility online and using the Internet as a communication channel; in addition, it provides consultation in web content management systems and analytics solutions.

Kristján is on the board of directors for the Search Engine Marketing Professionals organization (SEMPO), the founder of the Iceland SEO/SEM forum, and a published author on the topic of digital marketing. He is also a contributing author at such blogs and industry sites as Optimizeyourweb.com, Multilingual-Search.com, State of Search, and Search Engine Watch. On top that, he organizes the annual Reykjavik Internet Marketing Conference.

Kristján studied electrical engineering at Reykjavik Technical College in Iceland and has a degree in systems analysis from the Computer and Engineering Schools of Iceland and an Internet marketing degree from the University of British Columbia.

Dedication

We dedicate this book to all the pioneers who invented this still-young industry called search engine marketing. What a fascinating ride.

Acknowledgments

First, we must thank our families for their endless patience, especially Kristján's lovely wife, Guðbjörg Magnúsdóttir, and all our children (and grandchildren!) for their endless patience, and our past and present coworkers who have been supporting us with material, insights, and not least, time away to work on it.

We have been blessed with a great team at Pearson to help launch this first book on global search marketing, starting with our editor Rick Kughen, whom we thank for his patience, persistence, and continued faith in our project. We also want to make a BIG thanks to Chris Sherman, who not only was the technical editor of this book, but also has been instrumental in each of our careers, the great line of work that is international marketing.

A book of this scope would not be possible without the help of many colleagues in search marketing, among them Andy Atkins Kruger, Motoko Hunt and Bill Hunt, Shari Thurow, Andrew Goodman, Olafur Kr. Olafsson, Preston Carey of Yandex, Kathy Qi at Baidu, Elisa Jatho, Raúl Sáenz, Jan Murtomaa, Diemut Haberbusch, Malcolm Fraser, Monica Arthurson at Kvasir/Enrio and Jens Hilmersson, Rosemary Lising at GroupM, Fady Ramzy at Interact, Bas Van de Beld, Joost de Valk, Migueal Zabludovsky, and especially our man in Rome, Sante Achille, for his extensive contributions to the chapter on Italy. We are also grateful to our friends at comScore, Experian Hitwise, and, though we've never formally met, Internet World Stats, for providing loads of data to back up our opinions.

There, many others we should be mentioning. You know who you are, and Kristján says the first beer is on him.

Cheers,

Anne and Kristján

Find More of This Book Online!

In addition to the book you're now holding (or reading on screen), we have painstakingly assembled an appendix that details Internet and search engine usage by country and placed it online for free download from the Que website. This appendix is a treasure trove of valuable information for marketers who are looking to expand their search engine marketing efforts outside their home countries. Get your free copy of this exhaustive and valuable appendix by visiting www.quepublishing.com and clicking Register Your Product. You will be asked to either create a Que account or enter your existing login credentials. You will be asked for the book's ISBN. Enter "078974788X" and follow the on-screen prompts.

We Want to Hear from You!

As the reader of this book, *you* are our most important critic and commentator. We value your opinion and want to know what we're doing right, what we could do better, what areas you'd like to see us publish in, and any other words of wisdom you're willing to pass our way.

As an Editor-in-Chief for Que Publishing, I welcome your comments. You can email or write me directly to let me know what you did or didn't like about this book—as well as what we can do to make our books better.

Please note that I cannot help you with technical problems related to the topic of this book. We do have a User Services group, however, where I will forward specific technical questions related to the book.

When you write, please be sure to include this book's title and author as well as your name, email address, and phone number. I will carefully review your comments and share them with the author and editors who worked on the book.

Email: feedback@quepublishing.com

Mail: Greg Wiegand
           Editor-in-Chief
           Que Publishing
           800 East 96th Street
           Indianapolis, IN 46240 USA

Reader Services

Visit our website and register this book at informit.com/register for convenient access to any updates, downloads, or errata that might be available for this book.

Introduction

With nearly 90 percent of the world's Internet population outside the United States, you may already be tempted to expand your search engine marketing with pay-per-click advertising campaigns in other countries or by optimizing your website to attract foreign visitors. The Internet has erased borders and made geography irrelevant in many ways, easing the flow of information from one people to another. Just as the political unrest in Northern Africa in 2011 was facilitated by the ease of sharing information online, so it has become harder to make clear delineations between domestic and international markets in online commerce. Marketers from outside the United States are likely to compete on your home turf, and you can just as certainly find opportunities in markets outside the United States.

This book is the first guide to multinational, multilingual search engine marketing (SEM)—using both search engine optimization (SEO) and pay-per-click (PPC) advertising. In this book, you find out how to adapt your search marketing campaigns to different languages, cultures, and countries. We profile 25 top U.S. trade partners, detailing their Internet use, popular activities online, and factors unique to each market that equate to opportunities online.

This is a must-have book for marketing executives who intend to penetrate markets outside the comfort zone of their own languages and cultures. It's a book that explains in as simple language as possible how multilingual/multicultural search engine optimization works. It will help you at least avoid known pitfalls and at best conduct more successful organic and paid search campaigns. We illustrate from our own experience with approaches that produced significant returns on investment (ROI).

This book draws on the co-authors' broad global experience in multilingual/multicultural SEM, working with clients such as Actavis, Fujitsu, Google, HostelBookers, Icelandair, Orbitz, Philips, Toshiba, Nordic Store, and many more. After helping hundreds of clients realize better ROI from search engine marketing around the world, we know what works and what is a waste of time...and what is downright dangerous.

Kristjan Mar Hauksson authored a popular Icelandic book on search engine marketing and organizes the annual Reykjavik Internet Marketing Conference, which draws speakers from throughout Europe. Anne F. Kennedy has published articles and white papers on global online media and speaks frequently on successful search engine marketing.

There are a lot of geeky books on search marketing with a lot of jargon and probably more technical detail than most business readers need. This book is not one of those. Instead, it is a clearly written introduction to the opportunities waiting to be realized by a more culturally sensitive approach to search engine users in countries outside the United States. This book also points out the perils and pitfalls of poorly planned and executed global search marketing.

This is the first book on global search engine marketing in multiple countries, cultures, and languages. This book explains how international search marketing works and how to do it effectively. It is an authoritative guide marketing executives and product managers can turn to and learn what to do...and what not to do. It will serve as a reference against which marketers and other stakeholders can benchmark their global marketing plans.

In this book you find out how to select keywords in languages other than English and how to use them in website copy, online press releases, and paid advertising campaigns; in addition, you learn how to measure the success of your efforts. You also find the most complete and up-to-date review of Internet and search engine use around the globe, as well as a handy guide to resources to help you stay up to date in the ever-changing practice of search engine marketing.

If the success of your business depends on appealing to customers in other countries, you need to understand the principles, methods, and country-by-country details we present in this book.

Can You Afford *Not* to Think Globally?

Global search engine marketing (SEM) is unquestionably more complex than marketing via search engines in the USA alone. This is why you will find few marketing professionals willing to run a global campaign, and even fewer who have the knowledge and tools to execute it well. Keep in mind that you need to reach customers in languages other than English, often using different character sets and sometimes using multiple dialects. It is fairly well known that Chinese natives speak one or more of at least four different versions of Chinese, but did you know that the Japanese language has four different character sets? This matters because the algorithms that search engines use to sort information are literal and mainly capable of matching up only sets of data that actually match. Exactly.

But linguistic variations are only the beginning of the complexity of global search engine optimization (SEO). Besides needing to communicate in a different language, your website needs to appeal to the individual culture in each country you want to reach. We have years of experience working with a variety of multinational clients; we have learned that even within Europe, website use varies. Germans respond to different designs and content than French searchers, who behave differently online from Norwegians as do they, in turn, from Italians.

What's more, although Google may dominate search engine use in the United States and Europe, in some of the most promising markets—for example, Russia, China, and South Korea—Google lags behind local favorites. In these countries, optimizing content for Google or buying advertising on Google pages produces little measurable return on your investment. Instead, you need to learn to work with Yandex, Baidu, and Naver, respectively.

Last, there is much technical complexity in executing multilingual campaigns, including how your site's directory structure is set up, and sometimes even where you host your site. Indeed, multicountry search engine campaigns are so complex, you might well ask, "Why bother?" Can't you grow your web business to success in the United States alone? Possibly, but why wouldn't you want to try to capture a larger market? More importantly, will your competitors stick with a U.S.-only approach? Global opportunities abound, so to not look outside the United States is somewhat like leaving money on the proverbial table, isn't it?

Search Engine Use Is Globalizing on a Grand Scale

One of the net effects of the rise of the Internet for use as a business medium is that your competition may well come from outside the United States, and your customers surely will. According to Internet bellwether comScore, one of the more surprising revelations in June 2011 was that the once-dominant U.S. Internet population comprised only 11.6 percent of Internet users worldwide. Think about it: 88 percent of the people using the Internet around the world are outside the United States—almost a complete reversal from 1996 when two-thirds of the world's Internet users were U.S. based. Indeed, even if you include Canadian and Latin American web visitors, Europe is home to more of the world's online population than all the Americas combined.

As we write this, Asia-Pacific has more people on the Internet than any other region, at 44 percent—between one-third and one-half of the world's Internet population. The next largest is Europe at 23 percent, with North America far behind at 12 percent, followed by Latin America at 10.3 percent, and the Middle East at 3.3 percent. To be sure, most of the world's Internet "commerce" continued to be U.S. based in 2011, but with more than 8 in 10 Internet users elsewhere, the opportunity for growth looks greater beyond our borders.

Given that your next customers—and competitors—may well come from across the oceans complicates your marketing effectiveness enormously. Much of your overseas competition is already experienced in global trade. Global business has doubled in 20 years, according to the United Nations. The UN estimated that there were more than 60,000 multinational companies in 2010, compared to about 30,000 in 1990. Meanwhile, the average size of global companies is decreasing from the large multinational corporations of the previous 50 years. Many of the new businesses are "micronationals" whose success is both enabled by and dependent on the Internet. This can be a huge opportunity for Internet companies to grow business...and can often lead to a huge gap in marketing strategy for sites targeting U.S. customers only.

In total, 30 percent of the world's population is now online, and nearly everyone online uses search engines such as Google, China's Baidu, and Russia's Yandex. Increasingly, people (around the world) use social media to find what they want. Social media network use is catching up fast and in some countries even overtaking search engines as the most popular media. For example, in 2011 Facebook grew in size to nearly three-quarters of a billion members worldwide. Compare that to the 308.4 million people in the United States (according to the 2010 Census), and you can see just how enormous Facebook really is. In addition, some countries have millions of people engaged on local favorite social media sites, such as GREE in Japan and Hi5 in South America.

Clearly, marketing to people who search and socialize online is globalizing on a grand scale. Yet, fewer than 10 percent of U.S. companies engaged in international trade in 2010, and even fewer use global search engine marketing to find and retain customers.

Why? From our own experience using search media for marketing around the world, we conclude the genuine complexities of properly executing multicountry search engine marketing are holding many companies back from realizing huge opportunities in global business. We wrote this book to decipher these complexities for you, using what we have learned from working with many companies with customers in multiple countries and languages, such as Lufthansa, Fujitsu, Hitachi, the National Football League, and many more...even, Google itself.

The online world in which twenty-first century businesses operate is beginning to level the marketing playing field. No longer can any company that seeks to succeed ignore global opportunity or competition that results directly from global Internet access. In short: The Internet is quickly dissolving borders for business.

> The Internet is quickly dissolving borders for business.

For example, in Singapore, a large proportion of online shoppers go to U.S. ecommerce sites to find what they want.

Your Next Customer May Well Find You Online— from *Outside* the USA

According to comScore, the number of searches worldwide grew 46 percent in 2009 and an additional 22 percent year on year to October 2011. That month there were:

- 185 billion searches worldwide
- Nearly 6 billion searches per day
- 248+ million searches per hour
- 4 million searches per minute

Not only is the United States no longer the largest search market in the world, but since 2009 U.S. search engine user base growth has been slower than other countries, expanding only 18 percent to 2010 and another 12 percent to 2011. Meanwhile, in 2009 China was growing 32 percent; Korea, 34 percent; and Brazil, 38 percent. The biggest gainer was the Russian Federation with a whopping 40+ percent year-on-year growth.

Despite the evident opportunity, global search media marketing is not broadly understood, judging from many of the campaigns we authors have observed, and in many cases corrected. Doing business in a foreign language is challenging enough, but what's more, many multinational marketers fail to take into consideration critical cultural differences in how searchers gather and process the information they seek. Without addressing these differences individually, companies risk losing brand equity, traffic, and conversion, and often suffer wildly inefficient spending on their campaigns.

If businesses are to succeed in countries foreign to them, they had better know what things affect how potential customers respond in different cultures; it is most certainly not uniform. For example, Icelanders will search on Google but will not shop online. A campaign that targets Icelanders and counts only online purchases will appear to be a failure if success isn't measured according to the searchers' cultural behavior.

One size does not fit all for doing business online worldwide. To be successful in individual countries, you need to be aware of what factor is the most important to people online in each. Top concerns vary from country to country, and so should your marketing approach. Here are a few of the different aspects online shoppers look for according to their culture:

- In the United Kingdom, Brits look at delivery options and are repeat buyers.

- In Germany, privacy policies and local payment options need to be clear on the site to convince them to buy.

- In France, product pictures are as essential as local language to get their attention.

- In Spain, return options need to be clear, as does access to customer services to process those returns.

- In Italy, brand equity plays the most important role.

- Netherlands searchers need clearly secure transactions.

- Swedes care about reviews and recommendations.

Most of all, using translated keywords and content without also localizing them for idiom and culture just doesn't work. For example:

- Online businesses selling laptop computers in Sweden need to know that more than 40 percent of Swedes use local words when searching for a PC. That's a big chunk of market to miss if they use only "PC" or "Laptop" or even the Swedish translations.

- More than 50 percent of searches for Brazil in the world are spelled wrong (Brasilians actually spell their country name as "Brasil"). How can businesses help customers find your Brazilian site in those markets?

- A company that sells soccer cleats in the United States will not get much traffic in the United Kingdom without targeting the phrase "football boots."

Foolish and expensive mistakes are made because multinational advertisers fail to accommodate differences among searchers in foreign markets without thinking through what the target customers might actually be doing or seeing on their sites. For example:

- Although 83 percent of Germans shop online and spend an average of €520 online every six months, they do not use search engines to buy airline tickets as much as those in other European countries. Advertisers depending on PPC to attract German air travelers will realize low return on their investments.

- English-speaking kitchen remodeling customers in the United Kingdom might be attracted to kitchen appliance vendor results in Google. Imagine their dismay when a site on a .com or .net domain they click through to is entirely in Italian. This could happen if the site were hosted in Italy, because hosting is one of the signals that

Google uses to gauge which language to display if the site's domain is not country specific (for example, ending in .com instead of .co.uk). Without addressing such technical details, businesses will miss potential customers.

To make your website show up on search engines in foreign countries, cultures, and languages, you must pay attention to many, many details—and in languages not native to you. Following are some critical factors:

- **Local culture**—Even with a single country, such as Germany, there can be different regional cultures. Many companies ignore important cultural differences among their different markets, executing their multilingual marketing poorly and ineffectively. For example, French users search differently than Italians, as you will see in the following country chapters. You would need to take this into account when preparing to enter those markets.

- **Media selection**—It is critical to understand search media in different countries. Outside the United States, Google is not always the most prominent. Even where it is the biggest, there may be regional options that can play a major role when promoting in a foreign market. This book points out options that can either complement Google or replace it altogether. Our book's examples range from giants such as Yandex in Russia, Yahoo! in Japan, and Baidu in China to smaller but strong players, such as Kvasir in Norway, Leit in Iceland, and more.

- **Web analytics**—Tracking Key Performance Indicators (KPIs) is a must for any business. We explain how to apply effective analytic methods to multilingual campaign tracking, starting with the basic premise of how you can set key performance indicators even if you don't speak the language.

This book is for anybody who needs to incorporate these factors in multicultural and multilingual search engine marketing campaigns, including staff in foreign countries who are charged with executing marketing strategy for multinational companies. As they undertake search marketing in their own countries, this book provides better guidance for them than any of the ones written about search engine marketing methods in the United States.

It's true using search engines for marketing has always had a steep learning curve. Expanding into multiple languages and cultures turns this into more of a vertical ascent. As with mountain climbing, success with SEM depends on detailed preparation, careful attention to technique, the right equipment, and supportive teamwork. In this book, we intend to help you understand the techniques you need to increase your worldwide presence and revenues with better results in search

engines around the world. To get the most out of it, you need to be familiar with
the basic methods of search engine marketing. If you are not, we recommend you
find out more about it before tackling it in foreign languages and cultures. You can
find our favorite books, blogs, and other sources of the most up-to-date information in Appendix A, "SEO/SEM Resources." The publisher of our book, Que, has a
number of books on the topic as well.

 Note

Pearson offers a variety of excellent books covering search engine optimization. We suggest picking up a copy of one or more of these books if you are
new to search engine optimization, such as *The Truth About Search Engine
Optimization,* by Rebecca Lieb.

In this book, we do not provide a basic guide to Google AdWords or Facebook
advertising. There are many good books available on those topics. What we show
you in the following chapters are country-by-country tips on how to attract customers using search media in those specific countries. Like all things in SEM,
questions often lead to more questions. Moreover, data changes almost as fast as it
is published, and results often vary as each source measures differently. What we
expect to do in the book is point you in the right direction. Then you will have to
do your own homework.

Let's get started with a look at some examples of what NOT to do in Chapter 2,
"Common Territory: Search Marketing Without Borders."

2

Common Territory: Search Marketing Without Borders

Before we start talking about search marketing in specific countries, we think it's important to tell you about the elements of search marketing that we have found to be common around the world. We also think it's important to share some general strategies you should employ when you target foreign markets. And before we get into anything too deeply, let's look at the most common mistakes we see marketers making when it comes to marketing outside the United States.

Common Mistakes

It pains us to say so, but some of these errors and misfires are just plain careless search engine marketing (SEM), whereas others stem from lack of familiarity with or respect for local usability issues, missed opportunities caused by using the wrong keywords, and the omission of important indicators to help search engines correctly identify your intended market.

As we surveyed markets for this book, and based on our own experiences introducing companies to markets in multiple countries and languages, we found that the first and most serious issue was that marketers simply translated English campaigns and strategies and expected them to work in different, often very different cultures. We cannot make this point too often: When you go into another country, create unique content for that market and find a local, native speaker to guide you. Even better, locate a native speaker who has at least a rudimentary knowledge of search marketing and the vocabulary associated with it.

The other big mistakes we see marketers making fall into large categories for international search marketing:

- Having a single page for "international" customers...in English.
- Having a single page for multiple countries that speak variants of the same language (for example, using Mexican Spanish for all Spanish-speaking countries).
- Using the same content for a single language across a number of country sites—for instance, using the same Spanish content on your sites for Mexico, Argentina, and Spain. Doing this can put you at risk of tripping Google's duplicate content filters. We discuss ways to avoid this situation later in this chapter.
- Using only a U.S. or European keyword set.
- Using mechanized translations.
- Using literal translations of your English keywords, without taking local usage into consideration.
- Developing links only to your .com site instead of to your individual country sites.
- Neglecting to obtain links to each of your individual country sites from sites in each of those countries. While linking extensively between your many different country domains' sites will enhance search visibility for large global companies, your individual country sites need in-country links to do well in search results in each country.
- Designing sites for broadband, high-speed, and/or smartphone access only.

- Launching campaigns without regard for local holidays or setting the time for display of your ads (*dayparting*) for the time where you are based rather than the ideal time where your target customers are found.

None of these techniques impress search engines sufficiently to display your site in results for the country you are targeting, and even more to the point, none of them enhance your ability to appear in front of the right customers in your target countries.

You need to approach each country as a separate and unique market, and treat it with the same respect as your home market. Although global search marketing is nothing to be afraid of, it is also not to be thought of as effortless. There are no silver bullets in search engine marketing and most assuredly none in global search marketing.

Setting Goals and Measurements

Before we go any further into the multilingual marketing process, we want to stop and ask two important questions:

- What do you want your foreign language or international search marketing to accomplish?
- How will you know whether your marketing is succeeding?

To be sure, these questions are Marketing 101, and should be considered long before you get down to tactics for marketing your website in any language, even your own. However, we see this essential step omitted over and over again. We feel compelled to get on our soapboxes and point it out. Loudly. If setting and measuring goals come naturally to you, and you wouldn't dream of engaging in any marketing campaign without a fistful of Key Performance Indicators (KPIs), we wish there were more of you out there. You may be excused to skip down to the next section "ultilingual Keyword Research."

We continue to be dismayed at the number of companies that come to us with multilingual search marketing campaigns launched without clearly defined goals or clear-cut means for quantifying progress. This reminds us of the

"If you launch your campaign without clear goals and KPIs, you are pretty much shooting in the dark, and it's hard to hit even the broad side of a barn that way."

early days of web marketing, when companies would say, "We need a website," without having any idea what their website was to accomplish for their businesses. When you seek a market in foreign countries, your task is complicated by the differences in language and culture, and this adds to your scope and cost. As with any marketing effort, you can waste a lot of time and effort if you don't set KPIs and a method to establish a baseline for them and then measure performance from that point. All too often, we have seen plans developed based on assumptions instead of built around relevant qualitative and quantitative data, resulting in costly issues at a later date.

So begin with this question: What do you want your foreign language search engine marketing to achieve? Brand lift? Leads? Sales? All these responses are valid, but the one you select will lead to different decisions about how to proceed, as well as different KPIs to measure. The point is—and we cannot say this too firmly—you need to determine the goals of your multilingual marketing effort and select the KPIs that apply to them. If you launch your campaign without clear goals and KPIs, you are pretty much shooting in the dark, and it's hard to hit even the broad side of a barn that way.

To be sure, your goals for your online presence are unique to your business, and should be derived from the overall goals for your business online and off, and should be combined with your knowledge of what factors contribute to reaching those goals. For example:

- If you sell a product or service on your website, measuring the Return of Investment (ROI) of your advertising expense is pretty straightforward, although precise attribution is sometimes difficult as many online shoppers visit a site four or five times before they purchase, or even research online and purchase on the telephone or in a store.
- Is your website intended to generate leads for your sales team? In that case, one KPI would be inquiries to them. Another might be downloads of white papers, if you have them on your site.
- If you are seeking increased awareness of your brand, you might measure brand lift by whether searches for your brand name increased, or increased traffic, page views, and time on site, indicating greater interest.

The point is to set up a way of assessing the success of your effort that is meaningful to your company's performance. Only you know know what that should be.

Okay. Got your goals and KPIs and your measurement set up? Great, let's get started with what you need to do to succeed in global search marketing.

Multilingual Keyword Research

In search marketing, meticulous keyword research can move you ahead of your competitors. This is even more true for global search engine marketing, in both paid and organic results. If you use the right techniques for multilingual keyword research, you can get your website to the top of Google and any other search engine in the target language version. Although people in some countries such as Denmark, Sweden, and the Netherlands are as likely to use English as much as they use their own language, people in countries such as Russia, France, and Spain are less likely to do so.

Indeed, most of your potential customers will prefer online shopping and information on websites that have content in their native language and display their currency units. Not as many people as you might think speak or understand English very well (see Figure 2.1). According to Internet World Stats, only 26.8 percent of Internet users worldwide in May 2011 preferred to use English online. Chinese was a close second at 24.2 percent. If you are using only English, you are missing nearly three-quarters of the world's online market, as well as a single market—Chinese— that is nearly as large as English. Optimizing your websites in languages other than English is important to reach the widest pool of searchers and to pull traffic.

| Top Ten Languages Used in the Web | | | | | |
| (Number of Internet Users by Language) | | | | | |
TOP TEN LANGUAGES IN THE INTERNET	Internet Users by Language	Internet Penetration by Language	Growth in Internet (2000 - 2011)	Internet Users % of Total	World Population for this Language (2011 Estimate)
English	565,004,126	43.4 %	301.4 %	26.8 %	1,302,275,670
Chinese	509,965,013	37.2 %	1,478.7 %	24.2 %	1,372,226,042
Spanish	164,968,742	39.0 %	807.4 %	7.8 %	423,085,806
Japanese	99,182,000	78.4 %	110.7 %	4.7 %	126,475,664
Portuguese	82,586,600	32.5 %	990.1 %	3.9 %	253,947,594
German	75,422,674	79.5 %	174.1 %	3.6 %	94,842,656
Arabic	65,365,400	18.8 %	2,501.2 %	3.3 %	347,002,991
French	59,779,525	17.2 %	398.2 %	3.0 %	347,932,305
Russian	59,700,000	42.8 %	1,825.8 %	3.0 %	139,390,205
Korean	39,440,000	55.2 %	107.1 %	2.0 %	71,393,343
TOP 10 LANGUAGES	1,615,957,333	36.4 %	421.2 %	82.2 %	4,442,056,069
Rest of the Languages	350,557,483	14.6 %	588.5 %	17.8 %	2,403,553,891
WORLD TOTAL	2,099,026,065	30.3 %	481.7 %	100.0 %	6,930,055,154

Figure 2.1 *Internet World Stats figures as of May 31, 2011: English was spoken by barely more than a quarter of the world's Internet visitors, and only slightly more than Chinese. Source: Internet World Stats, http://www.internetworldstats.com/stats.htm*

That said, even if you have transformed your website into Arabic, Chinese, French, German, or Japanese versions, you may not get a lot of the traffic you want unless you have optimized your content with the right set of keywords, the terms and phrases searchers in those places actually use to look for what you have. Even search engines, including Google, have their own versions for different countries, and many searchers use search terms in their national language. Optimizing your website for a country foreign to you can be a tricky job because you need to be aware of specific foreign language keywords used there to search. Your keyword research is the most important element for reaching searchers in foreign languages.

The first thing you need to be able to do is move around through foreign languages. Translators who are expert in specific languages can be employed later to clean up any text edits, but you must make sure they refrain from changing the keyword-focused content integral to your multilingual search engine optimization (SEO) efforts.

To find foreign language keywords, you could start with Google Trends and the Google Keyword Tool for research. As you can see in Figure 2.2, Google Language Tools (www.google.com/language_tools) translates keywords in a foreign language and searches them for you, translating the results back to your language.

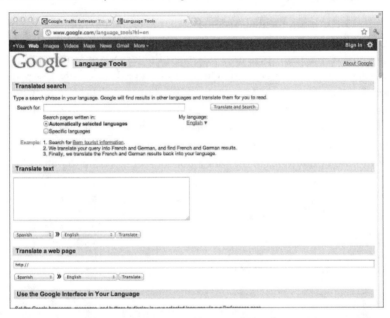

Figure 2.2   *Google Language Tools searches in another language.*

To understand keyword cost and click rates, you can run keywords through Google Translate, but keep in mind that doing so is not likely to bring forward slang or phrases in common use. For example, in German, the direct translation for "cell phone" is "mobiltelefon," but far more Germans call it a "handy." In Brazil, "Telemóvel" has a small fraction of the searches than the term "Celular"

"Your main challenge in entering any foreign market will be keyword selection with attention to local idiom and culture."

does, which you'll note, though adapted from the U.S. term "cellular," is spelled differently.

Although Google Translate is useful for deciphering instructions and navigating content on some non-English websites, it is *not* a good choice for translating keywords, text for your ads, or content for your landing pages. For these critical communications to your potential customers, you are best finding a native speaker who is familiar with local custom and manner of speech. Your main challenge in entering any foreign market is keyword selection with attention to local idiom and culture. Even in other English-speaking countries, word use and idioms vary. You need correct keyword usage to optimize for organic search results as well as paid search advertising. Here, we discuss the basics common to all multilingual keyword research. We cover keyword research specifics for each country in the coming chapters. When you do your multilingual keyword research, keep in mind the overall issues discussed next.

Language Coverage: Universal Versus Local Penetration

It is important to define the language for which keyword research will be conducted and its targeting purpose. The targeting purpose implies whether the language to be used will be universal, localized, or regional:

- **Universal Version**—A *universal version* is more suitable for internationalization purposes. For instance, if you are developing a website in Chinese, the purpose may be to target all Chinese-speaking communities—in China, Hong Kong, Macau, Singapore, Indonesia, Taiwan, and Malaysia. Instead of using dialects that are typical to any particular country or region, you should focus on developing standard content that will be understood in all these countries without colloquialisms, idiomatic expressions, or any connotation used by a local, regional, or specific ethnic subgroup.

- **Localized Version**—A *localized version* is important when the website content is targeted for the customers of a specific country such as Singapore. For this purpose, you need to include idioms, cultural aspects, and idiosyncrasies of the particular groups of a target audience.

- **Regionalized Version**—A *regionalized version* further applies to geographical areas. Even though there are differences in terminology and applicability among a group of nearby countries (such as Malaysia and Singapore), they are somewhat homogeneous compared to countries that are farther away from each other (such as Hong Kong and Singapore). For example, Chinese is a rich language; whereas the English word "shopping cart" is written as 購物車 in Simplified Chinese, it is written as 購物車 in Traditional Chinese. Which word you choose to use on your site will depend on its penetration in your intended market.

Human Talent

When you understand the coverage of the language in your target market, you need to look for the appropriate human talent to help you with the research. Software and machines still cannot replace humans. Using online dictionaries, translators, encyclopedias, and keyword research tools with no human intervention is a big risk to the entire project. One mistranslation or wrongly identified keyword and your website may be impossible to find even if your potential customers are trying hard to reach you!

Tools such as Wordtracker, Keyword Discovery, Compete, Quantcast, Hitwise, Google Analytics, and AdWords can help you to a certain extent, but human intervention is very important for a multilingual keyword research. The sociological, contextual, and intrinsic aspects of a language all count when your goal is to attract maximum traffic on your website. You can start by using a keyword research tool to develop a list of useful and popular keywords for a seed list. However, what matters most is the connotation and context of the keywords' uses. Work with the speakers of your intended language who are familiar with the dialects in the geographical area for which you are developing the website. Even better, find such native speakers who also have experience in keyword research.

Employing the right human talent is integral to the success of your multilingual keyword research. Although translators may be familiar with the standard terminology, they may lack a good understanding of the context in which the terms apply. For example, in the English language, terms such as "bonds trader" and "bondsman" may confuse people. "Bonds trader" is a word for someone who deals in bonds in financial markets. In contrast, "bondsman" is conventionally used in the U.S. criminal justice system to refer to an agent who pays bail guaranteeing the accused will appear for trial.

Finding such people is admittedly not easy. Finding an experienced search engine marketer is tough while demand exceeds supply, and the difficulty is amplified as you look in an unfamiliar country. Some of the places we have found multilingual employees is in visiting scholar programs at our local universities, and visitors to our local trade and professional organizations. Also, we network in our travels. It is helpful to look at who is writing articles and blogs on international SEO, or on SEO in your targeted countries, to observe who the leading local SEOs are. Many countries now have conferences on digital marketing, and search engine marketing, and often we meet future associates at these events. Even if you can't get to the events in person, you can learn a lot from reading about the speakers on the event websites.

As you interview and select candidates for employees, contractors, or local providers, it is critical to get good references, and ask for case studies and sample client work. Be sure to ask what successful results their efforts produced for their clients. Another note—a really good multi-lingual SEO agency will have a team to second guess the agency's work in a language, which provides a reality check. Be wary of translation services that claim to know search engine marketing, and be sure to ask to see the results of the efforts for clients. Knowing what to ask and more importantly, what the answers should be are more reasons you need to be an experienced search engine marketer before expanding globally.

Keyword Research Tools

Selection of keyword research tools for multilingual keyword research is more challenging than keyword research in English. To begin with, there are not many tools that help you perform keyword research in other languages. Many of the keyword research tools used today are not even UTF 8 ready—the UCS Transformation Format system that represents any character in the Unicode standard. If you are performing a keyword research in Simplified Chinese to rank your website in the Chinese search engine Baidu, and the keyword research tool does not have UTF 8, all you get to see is gibberish instead of Simplified Chinese words.

Keyword research can become further complicated when generic tools are used for finding search volume estimates for a specific keyword in a specific country. This research becomes even harder for low-volume search keywords. Google Trends, for instance, is a tool that gives good results for high-volume searches, even for specific countries, but tends to ignore low-volume search keywords. Look for Поисковая оптимизация сайта (Russian for "search engine optimization") in Google Trends, and you will see what we mean.

Certain keyword research tools, such as Keyword Discovery, provide information from different countries for localization purposes. Often, though, such tools provide relevant estimates for high-volume searches but not enough for low-volume ones to be useful. When using the Google Keyword Tool or Traffic Estimator, be sure to install the target language packs for your operating system.

After you define a list of keywords for your target country and have them vetted by someone familiar with the target language and search marketing, the rest of the keyword research process is much the same one you already know, as an experienced SEO—expand your keyword list based on search terms you find in your analytics reports, test new ones, and revise your keyword list as you find the best-performing ones.

In multilingual keyword research, you need to fine-tune the keywords you find for use in your web content. In any language, it is important to use the keywords in the right form without twisting the entire meaning of the words. Google ranks websites in other languages by the quality of content, just like websites with English content. Of course natural language words may appear in text regardless of SEO goals, but forcefully inserted keywords that are not relevant on a web page—better known as "keyword stuffing"—deteriorate the quality of your entire website and affect its visibility.

As you attract new users who were hitherto becoming confused or abandoning your standard English website, you can better observe the intent of your customers by tracking their behavior on your site. This further helps you to refine and optimize your website for them. In addition, well-done multilingual keyword research can help in optimizing your social media content, as you share links to relevant content on your local language website from platforms such as Twitter, Facebook, and Google+.

Cultural Localization

Apart from performing multilingual keyword research, you also should augment geographically based non-English websites with good design, images, color schemes, hosting, and accessibility features. Ensure that no form of content is offensive to any ethnic group. Also, be sensitive to localized usability, such as calendars that read right to left for Arabic countries. We cover individual characteristics of other countries online in the following country-specific chapters.

Analyze Your Competition in Search Results

Next, run a few searches using the keywords you have identified to observe what websites turn up in the results. They might or might not belong to companies already on your competitive radar. The point for search engine marketing is that space at the top of search results is limited, so any listing above you is your competition, and you need to develop tactics to overtake it. Analyzing the competition, again, is Search Marketing 101, but it is too often overlooked. This is best done before you start, rather than after, as is often the case in our experience.

After you identify your competition for search results, map their search marketing performance, both organic and in pay-per-click (PPC) advertising. A number of great tools can help you gauge other companies' performance online, among them

Compete.com, Majestic SEO, and SEOmoz. You can even use Google Translate to navigate sites in different languages.

Tips for Multilingual Keyword Research and Competitive Analysis

- Set your goals for your multilingual website, select the KPIs to measure your progress, and establish their baseline before you change anything.

- Start your multilingual keyword research defining the language goals and deciding the version of language—universal, regional, or local.

- Employ human translators who have a good understanding of your niche or products and services and who know the market for which you want to localize your keyword list.

- Use keyword research tools and translations to build your seed list of keywords; then have a native speaker review and localize your keywords to conform them to local connotation and context.

- Use your keyword list to run searches to identify what competing listings are taking the space you want at the top of search result pages. Google Translate can help you find your way around sites in different languages.

Using Google Around the Globe

In terms of media, global search marketing is divided into two worlds. In most countries, Google has achieved world dominance and is the leading online media by far, while in Japan and Taiwan, Yahoo! is popular, although search results for Yahoo! Japan are provided by Google. In three countries—China, Russia, and South Korea—local favorites have claimed the market. Aside from those countries which we will cover in the chapters on each, for most of your search marketing overseas you will be working with familiar platforms and, indeed, from within your current AdWords accounts. Sounds easy, right? Not so fast.

Familiar tools and technology are the least of what you need to attract future customers in foreign markets. You need to know how to speak to them in their own language and, equally as important, understand what appeals to them. Good marketing practice means you need to consider what appeals to your target customers if you want your advertising to be effective, and there are significant differences among customers in different cultures, some obvious and some more nuanced. Landing pages, too, need to speak to potential customers in their own languages, and if you are selling products online, even your shopping cart and the methods of payment you offer need to be familiar to each culture.

The following chapters provide information to help you build a more accurate picture of specific countries, how search marketing operates in them, and how people go about their business every day. If you can think like a marketer in that country, you are more likely to be successful in doing business in that neck of the woods. This is an important takeaway for anyone who reads this book: If your search marketing effort takes into account the complexities and the different "shades" of a culture, you are more likely to be successful there. In later chapters, we discuss China, Russia, and South Korea, where local favorites reign, taking a look at how the biggest—Yandex, Baidu, and Naver—work on their own turf. Here, though, let's look at Google.

How to Show Google Where You Want to Be Seen

Working with many multinational campaigns, we have observed much confusion in Google's results pages in other countries—for example, Spanish-language results from Spain showing up on searches in South America. In our opinion, where there is confusion, that is your opportunity to rise above the competition by providing greater clarity to identify your intended audience for your content. Seize the chance to get ahead by taking advantage of every indicator for Google.

The following sections describe the signals Google uses to determine where to display any website in its results and how much that website is of interest to searchers there.

Country-Code Top-Level Domain —ccTLD

In general, a country-code top-level domain (ccTLD) or directory inspires confidence that you are a trustworthy entity with which to do business. Is this not the first step to a solid customer relationship? It serves as the same source of credibility in your site's relationship with Google. In search engine marketing, your URL—your website's address—is the first piece of code on your site that Google's algorithm scans. If that URL says .es for Spain or .ar for Argentina or .mx for Mexico, Google has a clear indication as to the country where your intended viewers live. When you set up your website, it's a good idea to register country-specific domains for all the countries where you think you may do business, to prepare for the time when you do and to prevent your competition from registering them.

It is certainly true that registering all these domains might not be practical, in which case setting up directory extensions on .com/—for example, www.yourdomain.com/es or /ar or /mx—is a fully workable alternative, as long as you map it to your target country in your Google Webmaster Tools account. Read on for instructions on how to do this at the end of this section. This way, you can make sure your intended audience is clear. It's important to note that you might have more difficulty attracting links from your target country to a subdirectory, and in our experience, linking these to your .com domain tends to send traffic to the .com, not your country-specific content. Note that the directory extension you use should point to a specific country. Google treats regional extensions .eu and .asia as generic, not country specific.

You can also set up subdomains, such as mx.yourdomain.com for Mexico. As with directory extensions, a subdomain may not be as successful in attracting and benefitting from good links. If you use subdomains for your different country-focused sites, you need to add each subdomain to your Webmaster Tools account and verify it individually. This step is not necessary if you are using subdirectory folders for your countries. They are verified under your core domain automatically.

If you have a general or international top-level domain, Google relies on several other signals. These same signals also can be helpful in gaining better rankings, especially if your competition has not provided as many clear signals as you have. This also is true for country-specific domains.

The Language of Your Website's Content

The language of your content is a key indicator to Google as to the country your website is targeting. For example, German-language content on the www.your-domain.com/de page reinforces for Google that it is intended for searchers in Germany. Of course, many of the major languages of the world, such as Spanish, French, Arabic, and English, are spoken in multiple countries. This is why choosing a country-specific top-level domain is so important.

Location Information on the Website

If your content includes an address in the country you are targeting, that address helps Google recognize the content as relevant to that country. This, of course, presumes you have a physical location in that country, something that is not always available or practical.

Inbound Links from Sites in the Country You Are Targeting

It is no secret that Google relies heavily on inbound links to determine the popularity of a website and where to rank it in results. When you set up a version of your site in another country, make sure to use links to that site from websites in that country and use a specific domain from that country. Doing so helps Google determine where your content should be seen.

Google Places

Where Google Places is available (which is not everywhere as of this writing), including any relevant location information about your website provides a signal to Google that you want to do business there.

Hosting

The place where your website is hosted is a very low-level signal to Google. That said, hosting your site near your target market may increase the speed of delivery of your pages to your potential customers' browsers. It may also be an additional signal if you are marketing a nonspecific domain such as .com or .net in a foreign language.

Some countries, such as Australia, require you to have a license or even a local business presence to host your site there, making it complicated and even expensive to do so.

The People's Republic of China is the one country where actually hosting your site in the country is a must because the Chinese authorities have been known to block sites not hosted there. If your content is hosted in the United States, for example, it may never be seen in mainland China. This has been referred to as the "Great Firewall of China."

Geo-Location

Google recommends that if your site is on an international or generic domain and is not hosted in the country where you would like it to be seen, you should use Webmaster Tools to tell Google which country should be associated with your site. You can find a current list of "geo-targetable" domains in the Google Webmaster Tools forum at www.google.com/support/webmasters/bin/answer.py?answer=1347922.

As mentioned earlier, it is very important to provide this information if you are using directories for each country instead of ccTLDs. However, if you intend to reach a number of people in different countries who speak the same language—for example, Spanish—it is better not to restrict the location where your site will be shown. Remember, if you do set the location in Webmaster Tools, Google shows your site in that country only.

To set your location in Google Webmaster Tools, first add each country-specific directory or subdomain as an individual website. Then geo-target it by following these steps:

1. On the Webmaster Tools home page, click the desired site.

2. Choose Site Configuration, then select Settings.

3. Select Geographic Target and choose your preferred option.

Note

Want to make sure that you don't associate your site with any specific country or region? Simple—choose Geographic Target and select Unlisted.

Pay-Per-Click with Google AdWords Around the World

With Google's dominant hold on market share, the tools and interfaces you already know—AdWords, Google Analytics, and Google Webmaster Tools—should help you successfully implement a PPC campaign. In the few countries where market shares for Google and Yahoo! are small, you can use your AdWords account to target searchers there also, but your results will be less successful if you ignore the local favorites where they are the leaders.

Starting a PPC campaign in Google-dominated markets is fairly straightforward using your AdWords account. Creating separate AdWords campaigns for different countries is best because you can track, expand, and refine your keywords and ads in each language individually. If you are targeting multiple languages, create a separate campaign for each language and optimize it accordingly, as recommended by Google AdWords Help. Note that Google does not translate your ads for you.

Google provides location targeting to combine with language targeting to reach expatriates in their own language—for example, English speakers who live in Spain. In this case, set your country targeting to Spain and your language targeting to English. When Google detects an English speaker on Google.es, your ad can be shown. Google recommends creating a separate campaign for each language and country pair.

By setting up a separate campaign for each main location such as a country and selecting the relevant language for each campaign, you make it easier to manage your account and track each region's return on investment (ROI). It also means that you can create very customized and targeted campaigns by tailoring your keywords and ad text to each individual market.

Google further recommends making your keyword list and ad text for each ad group in the same language to ensure ads appear in the same language as the keyword entered. For example, when a searcher enters a keyword in Japanese, the ads appear in Japanese.

You also need to work around differences in time zones because Google sets your ad schedules based on the time zone where you set up your account, not the time zone of the country you are targeting with your campaign. If you want your ads to show during business hours in a different time zone, for example, you need to calculate the time difference when you set the time you want your ads to show.

For most countries, the text ad length limits are the same standard ones you know already—25 characters for your title, and 35 characters each for your two lines of ad text and display URL. However, Google allows longer ad text for selected countries in Asia and Eastern Europe. For China, Hong Kong, Japan, Taiwan, and South Korea, Google allows you to put 15 characters in your title, 19 in your two lines of ad text, and approximately 17 in your destination URL, to accommodate these "double-byte" languages that take up two spaces in coding for each letter. For Russia, Belarus, and Ukraine, Google increased the limits to 30 characters in your title, and 38 characters each in your two lines of ad text.

Google provides detailed information on its AdWords Help Forum, where you can ask a question or enter your topic and browse others' questions and answers. Go to www.google.com/support/forum and click on AdWords.

SEO for Organic Results in Google

To optimize organic results for Google, first make sure Google knows where to show your site. Refer to the checklist earlier in this chapter of signals Google uses to determine location and see which you need to improve to increase the clarity of the directions your are providing Google.

As with SEO in your own language, attention to the basics pays off. Just as you would do when working in your own country, when working outside your home country and language, be sure to build your site with algorithm-friendly architecture, load it with relevant content, and attract inbound links from authoritative sites. Now let's look at the particular spin that search marketing overseas puts on the tactics you know.

Crawler-Friendly Website Architecture

Successful SEO starts with search-friendly architecture on your site, and this is equally as true for your foreign language sites as your home site. In our experience, a review of your technical architecture often reveals many quick fixes that can improve your global search engine results rapidly. Of course, you know you can't rank well and receive traffic that converts if your site is not in Google's index, and this is just as important for websites targeting other countries than your home. Here are the most common places to look for easily fixed issues:

- **Missing, incomplete, or broken XML site maps**—Be sure to make full use of this powerful and often-overlooked tool to get your content indexed.

- **Duplicate content, especially when a single language is replicated across a number of pages targeting different countries**—If you are using content in the same language across a number of specific country sites, be sure to map each site to its intended country in your Google WebMaster Tools account, and obtain high-quality links from each country to its targeted content to point the way to your intended users.

- **Multiple duplicate page titles**—As with your home language site, unique page titles that accurately describe the content specific to each page help spiders find, index, and rank your content, as well as attract clicks from traffic looking for it.

- **Content Management Systems (CMS) that overwrite your SEO changes**—Many CMS systems automatically rewrite all the fields on a page when you update part of it. A few are more flexible, and if you are shopping for a new CMS, look for one that takes making SEO changes into account. If you are stuck with a system that is not as flexible, be sure to build workarounds into your process for maintaining your SEO elements such as unique page titles and descriptions.

- **Page templates that default to English content where no local language content is available**—You should avoid this shortcut for building country-specific pages if possible because it causes confusion in targeted country detection, and much of your content will be devalued by duplicate content filters. Moreover, providing only English content to foreign language readers certainly falls short of speaking your customers' language and reduces your marketing effectiveness.

Attracting Good Links

As you already know, obtaining inbound links from high-quality websites is an effective way to improve your visibility in search engines, Google in particular. For your offshore domains, the most effective links are ones from high-quality sites in the individual countries you are targeting. Your site in France should have links from sites in France with an .fr domain, whereas your sites in Argentina should have links from sites in Argentina with an .ar domain, and so forth.

Links from sites in the same country as your site serve as endorsements for Google that the site's content has value for searchers there. For years, in-bound links have been valued as heavily as on-page SEO factors in ranking results. Quality matters more than quantity; a few links from highly authoritative sites count far more than hundreds of links from lesser ones.

> "Y our site in France should have links from sites in France with an .fr domain, whereas your sites in Argentina should have links from sites in Argentina with an .ar domain."

On a site in a language used in more than one country, such as German or Spanish, using inbound links is a good way to avoid tripping duplicate content filters by providing clarifying endorsements from the intended country. A German-language page with links to it from sites on .de domains or the /de directory is more likely to rank well and be seen in Google results in Germany than in Austria, even if the language is the same.

Without such links, Google determines where to show the results based on the top URL, language, and Google Webmaster Tools mapping. However, if the language is the same on both German and Austrian sites, a significant indicator is no longer clear to Google, and although GWT mapping may help you avoid one or the other being filtered out of the index as a duplicate, your ranking and visibility will be much better with the added indicator of such links.

In our experience, not many multilingual sites take advantage of the power of high-quality country-specific inbound links, which spells opportunity for sites that do. You can find potential linking sources by searching Dmoz listings for your target country and reviewing the sites in it (see Figure 2.3). Dmoz has 1.9 million listings in 46 languages, besides English, from Afrikaans to Ukrainian, including the countries profiled in this book. You can find a complete list at www.dmoz.org/World.

Figure 2.3   *The Open Directory project (www.dmoz.org) has country-specific listings in many categories, such as this listing for animation sites in the Netherlands. Note that it also is further cross-referenced to other languages for the same category.*

You can also find possible links partners on Google by performing a wildcard (*) search for "web directory site*" using your target country extension to search. You need to filter out Google results by specifying "-Google" in your query. To search for sites in Argentina, your query would be "www.web directory site:*.com.ar – Google" and would produce results like the ones shown in Figure 2.4.

Figure 2.4   *Here's how a wildcard search for directory sites in Argentina would look.*

Use Google Translate to find your way around results when you are not familiar with the language, but be sure to have someone who is familiar with the language check over the findings.

Optimizing for Universal Search Results Pages

Google displays many forms of content on its results pages in almost all countries worldwide, including video and images, so do not overlook optimizing those important elements on your site. Keep in mind that optimizing for YouTube has different techniques from optimizing for Google or Bing. There are several good books on how to optimize videos for better visibility on YouTube. We've listed a few of our favorites in Appendix A, "SEO/SEM Resources."

In the United States, optimizing images and videos is still often overlooked as an effective way to get content into search engine results pages, and we find this is also true in other countries, as you can see in Figure 2.5. This oversight gives you many opportunities to increase visibility for more of your content and outpace your competitors.

Figure 2.5 *As this sample search results page from Google Egypt shows, images and maps gain greater visibility above the fold.*

Analytics

Google Web Analytics provides the insights you need and is free of charge from Google.

An alternative is Yahoo! Web Analytics; it also is free and often a good second guesser to Google, with the added advantage of more in-depth demographics. If you are using paid tools, such as Webtrends or Omniture, they support languages around the globe.

Tips for Global Search Marketing in Google

- Make as clear as possible to Google where you want your site to show in search results by engaging as many signals as practical.

- When your site is in a popular language such as French or Spanish, be sure to map it to your intended country with Google Webmaster Tools.

- Attract inbound links from authoritative sites in the country where you want your site to rank well.

- Take advantage of Google universal search results by optimizing your images, videos, news, and maps, as well as your website content.

- Make sure your website architecture can be crawled by search engines and it retains the optimization you want, particularly if you are using a CMS to generate new pages.

3

China, Hong Kong, and Taiwan

Throughout the past 5,000 years, China has been one of the leading civilizations of the world. However, in the nineteenth and twentieth centuries, the heavily populated country—which has a land mass that is slightly smaller than the continental United States—was preoccupied with famines, military defeats, foreign occupation, natural disasters, and civil unrest leading to the establishment of the People's Republic of China (PRC) in 1949, and separating Taiwan as an independent country. In 1999, Hong Kong reverted to China's dominion when the British lease on it expired, creating a third major Chinese market. Although Hong Kong is part of the PRC, it is allowed to interact with the rest of the world in a somewhat less restricted way, especially when it comes to Internet censorship, which is a fact of life on the mainland.

Although China, Hong Kong, and Taiwan are all Chinese in language and heritage, for the purposes of search marketing, each of the three markets is quite unique from the others and needs to be approached differently. Besides differing political systems, the most obvious reason is that in the PRC, the local search engine, Baidu, is far and away the favorite. Neither Google nor Facebook has much reach in the PRC. In Hong Kong and Taiwan, Google and Yahoo! Hong Kong share the search market. Facebook also has much further reach. These are facts that you need to know if you plan to market your business online in either Hong Kong or Taiwan. The PRC is generally referred to as China, and in this chapter, we profile its online scenario separately and introduce you to Baidu, China's popular search engine that serves up results to more the half the searchers in Asia.

In Chapter 2, "Common Territory: Search Marketing Without Borders," you can find tactics for gaining visibility in Google, and these methods also work with Yahoo!. Later in this chapter, you find additional profiles on Hong Kong and Taiwan online to give you insight into the cultures and opportunities in each country.

To get the whole picture, let's consider where the market in China ranks among her Chinese and Asia-Pacific neighbors and why we think it's so important. As you can see in Table 3.1, China's online population is larger than half that of Asia. However, the proportion of China's online population is only little more than half that of more mature online markets in Japan, Taiwan, and South Korea. This looks like a lot of potential to us, and the best time for gaining a toehold in it is surely while China's online community is on the rise.

Table 3.1 Top 10 Asia-Pacific Online Populations

Country	Online Population	Penetration	Share of Asia Online
China	485,000,000	36.3%	53%
Japan	99,000,000	78.4%	10.6%
Indonesia	39,600,000	16.1%	4.2%
South Korea	39,440,000	80.9%	4.2%
Vietnam	29,268,606	32.3%	3.1%
Philippines	29,700,000	29.25%	3.2%
Thailand	18,310,000	27.4%	2.0%
Malaysia	16,902,600	58.8%	1.8%
Taiwan	16,147,000	70%	1.7%
Hong Kong	4,878,713	68.5%	0.5%

Profile of China Online

> "...there are 332 million urban Chinese Internet users—more than all the people living in the U.S."

The year 2000 marked a new beginning for China. By then, economic development had quadrupled since 1978 and living standards had improved dramatically. China became one of the fastest-growing economies in the world and by 2011 comprised more than half the online population of Asia and nearing a quarter of those in the world. To put it another way, about one of every five persons around the world who went online in 2011 did so from China.

To be sure, the China Internet Network Information Center (CNNIC) which provides these stats, counts *everyone* who goes online, even if only once or twice in the past year. Further, 35 percent of those online in China in 2010 were 10–19 years old, and 30 percent of all those online were students. The real potential of China's online market will evolve as these youngsters fluent in Internet use mature. Even if we discount the youngsters, currently there are 315 million other people who go online in China. Moreover, currently the urban population online in China represents more than 70 percent of those online throughout the whole of China. That means there are 332 million urban Chinese Internet users—more than all the people living in the U.S.

Chinese is the second most-used language online, after English, and is spoken by about one-fifth of the world's population in seven countries. Although Mandarin, or "Modern Standard Chinese" is spoken in China, in 1950 the PRC adopted a streamlined form known as "Simplified Chinese" for written use to improve literacy rates on the mainland. Besides that, the Chinese spoken in China comes in literally hundreds of dialects—all with their differences, some major and some minor. This applies to both spoken and written versions of these dialects. As if the diversity of languages, size, and population did not make China complicated enough, consider how different the Chinese search ecosystem is. The reason has to do partly with Baidu's monopoly, which is aided by Chinese government restrictions on foreign sites and partly because of social and cultural factors.

By the end of 2010, 34.3 percent of the 1,336,718,015 people in China accessed the Internet, which is up from 384 million in 2009.[1] By June 2011, Internet World Stats pegged the number of people online in China at 485 million, which is 36.3 percent of all the people there. The number of people online was projected to grow to more than 50 percent of the total population by 2015, and more than 70 percent would use their mobile phones as well as PCs to go online. This number is up sharply from only 22 million online in the year 2000. By 2011, China was the largest online population in the world; only India threatened the Middle Kingdom's hold on the top spot.

---

1. Source: China Internet Network Information Center website (cnnic.net.cn)

Although population online does not necessarily mean customers online, increasing comfort online and a growing middle class indicate a lot of potential ecommerce. It has been said that China will be a great market, though through 2010 most online commerce was business-to-business (B2B) and not business-to-consumer (B2C). Western marketers have needed to be part of a very large or very niche enterprise to succeed in China. Because of the complexities of doing business online in China, it has been largely untapped by U.S. marketers and underserved. With increasing interest in American products among China's growing middle class, China has the potential to be a huge market online.

Indeed, Forrester Research and Internet Retailer projected China's 2011 retail sales would be $48.8 billion US or 317.36 billion RMB (Chinese Renmibi, also referred to as "CNY"—the new currency launched by the PRC in 2009, for which the "yuan" serves as the basic unit). Forrester Research and Internet Retailer also projected that these numbers would triple in the next four years. The Asia Digital Marketing Association (ADMA) noted that China is outpacing Japan's lead in Asian ecommerce. In September 2011, with a development that signaled expected growth in online consumer activity, Taobao Mall (a subsidiary of China's huge ecommerce group, Alibaba) invited 38 smaller online retailers to join its retail platform. Rivals 360buy.com and Beijing Jingdong Century Trading were said at the time to have also amassed healthy war chests to move into the consumer market.

That said, online marketing in China was still very much under development, with slow-growing adoption. Online ad spending was projected to grow substantially between 2010 and 2013, as the projections in millions of U.S. dollars in Table 3.2 show. Indeed, the gap with Japan's more developed market is closing.

Table 3.2   Asia-Pacific Online Ad Spending ($ Millions US)

	2010	2011	2012	2013
Japan	8,279	8,903	9,785	10,666
China	4,702	5,972	7,674	9,708
South Korea	1,205	1,326	1,459	1,604
Taiwan	259	301	322	348
Hong Kong	183	211	228	239

Source: ADMA Yearbook 2011

Of the total online spending, search marketing in China alone was projected to grow 50 percent per year from 2011 to 2015 from its 2010 value of 11 billion RMB ($1.7 billion US).[2]

---

2. Source: eMarketer

What interests Chinese users online? According to the China Internet Network Information Center (CNNIC), in 2010:

- Online music—82.5 percent
- Online news—78.5 percent
- Search engines—76.3 percent

 Note

In general, search queries used by Chinese searchers showed the same searcher intent categories as their fellow searchers worldwide, including transactional, informational, navigational, and application searches.

- Instant messaging—72.4 percent
- Online games—70.5 percent
- Video—63.5 percent

Email, blogging, and social networking were used by little more than half of all Chinese online. China Daily reported that there were 100 million microbloggers in China in 2010 and that group would increase to 253 million by 2013. "Weibo" means microblogging in Chinese, and is owned by Sina and the Chinese version of Twitter. Most of the categories CNNIC reported on in 2010 had changed little from the year before, save for online payment and banking, which grew 48.2 percent and 45.8 percent, respectively. Online payment system Alipay reported more than 460,000 merchants and 550 million registered users. Daily transaction volume was $378 million US, or 2.5 billion RMB in 8.5 million transactions a day.

Although online shopping was done by only about a third of China's population in 2010, those who did shop online totaled 142 million online buyers. That number grew 48.6 percent from the prior year.[3] Ernst & Young noted increasing Chinese purchasing power driven by youth with greater discretionary spending. The most popular shopping categories were clothes and shoes, accounting for more than three-quarters of online purchases. Clothes and shoes were followed by books and gifts. The fifth most popular online purchase was beer.

 Note

It is important to note that one factor retarding widespread growth of ecommerce in China is that most Chinese shoppers don't have credit cards and are highly suspicious of using them for online payment. Just under a third of online shoppers there use debit cards, which work like online bank transfers. However, these accounts often carry daily limits of 300 RMB (about $44 U.S.). More Chinese people prefer to pay cash or check on delivery, which can be complicated for ecommerce transactions.

---

3. Source: China Internet Network Information Center (CNNIC)

The CNNIC's 2010 study further named China as one of the emerging markets where mobile subscription volume exceeded broadband, Internet, and television, a conclusion that signaled a huge potential market for mobile entertainment.

Marketing to mobile devices, as well as on them, is a big topic that justifies a separate book. Having said that, search marketers would do well to keep in mind the huge number of Chinese people who access the Internet with their mobile devices. According to Reuters, in 2011, there were 841.9 million mobile phone subscribers in China, which is more than in any other country. The mobile market in China is remarkably young,

> "...in 2011, there were 841.9 million mobile phone subscribers in China, which is more than in any other country."

with more than 70 percent between the ages of 10–29. Of the Chinese mobile phone subscribers, McKinsey reports that 230 million accessed the Internet from their phones. In late 2011, eMarketer forecast that by 2015 half those using mobile in the world would live in the Asia-Pacific because of the rapid adoption of mobile phones in emerging markets such as China, as well as leaders such as Japan. In fact, by 2014, eMarketer expected the number of Japanese mobile phone subscribers to be 1.3 billion—the entire population in 2011. Of these, 957 million would go online from their phones.

Not many homes in China have landlines for their phones or Internet. For many people in China, the mobile Web is the only one they use. When they go online, they don't sit down to a desktop PC because they have everything they need to access the Internet in the palm of their hands. According to Nielsen, mobile Internet has become more popular in China than in the United States, with 38 percent of subscribers in China accessing the Web from their mobile phones, compared to 27 percent in the U.S.

By June of 2011, 43 percent of city dwellers in China were accessing the Web via mobile phones. These numbers mean China is catching up to Japan, which is currently number one in this category. The United States is well behind at 22 percent. That same year, the largest provider, China Mobile (60 percent market share), reduced subscription rates 15 percent.

Although people in China who cannot afford a computer can nevertheless access the Web on their mobile phones to see your content, there are a few things to keep in mind to make sure they can actually view your site:

- Most of the mobile devices in China are web-enabled "feature" phones, not sophisticated "smart" phones, with small screens and limited browsing capability. This means your mobile content needs to be small in scale—in file size and screen size.

- Most mobile users in China are limited by prepaid and pricey data plans and therefore are resistant to scroll or even spend any more time than necessary on a mobile site. Consequently, you should make sure your content is succinct and put your most important message where it will be seen first.

- Smart phones make up only a small share of mobile devices in China; to attract more mobile users, set up your website to detect them and redirect them to a mobile-specific site you have created that has localized SEO, such as putting the menus at the bottom of the pages, rather than at the top.

- For mobile marketing anywhere, you will do better with separate campaigns as well as landing pages.

Search Media in China

By far, the largest search engine in China in early 2011 was Baidu, at more than 66 percent, as shown in Table 3.3. Google.cn had less than half that. Other local sites included Sougo, which was created by the biggest news site in China, and Soso, the most popular online chatting site in China.

Table 3.3   Search Engine Market Share—China

Search Engine	Percentage of the Search Market
Baidu.cn	66.4%
Google.cn	30.2%
Yahoo.cn	1.5%
Bing.cn	1.4%
Others	0.4%

Source: StatCounter: June 2011

Baidu is shown in Figure 3.1.

Figure 3.1   *Baidu is the most popular search engine in China.*

In February 2011, China Mobile and the government-owned Xinhua News Agency launched search engine Panguso.com. Note the international domain .com rather than the local .cn for China.

After withdrawing from China and moving to Hong Kong in 2010, Google developed a strategy to grow ad revenue from Chinese exporters eager to reach international markets, where Google is the dominant search media. Google achieved this by getting small- and medium-sized Chinese businesses to advertise on its platform. Although the impact for international marketers targeting China is small, they could expect to see more competition on Google results pages outside China from Chinese marketers.

Common Mistakes

Do not jump into the Chinese search market unprepared. Among the mistakes foreign marketers make when marketing via search media in China is to ignore the differences between Baidu and other mainstream search engines worldwide. Foreign marketers also tend to give up too soon when campaign tactics and communication issues become difficult.

According to Baidu, incomplete localization—only simple translation of content and pricing—is the most serious problem that foreign marketers face when they attempt to optimize for Chinese customers. There are 56 different ethnic cultures in China, and they use hundreds of dialects, with huge differences in spelling and nuance. For most campaigns, your best bet is to stick with Simplified Chinese to communicate with the broadest market there. That said, even Baidu notes "Chinese culture has some identity-forming meanings that affect user behavior strongly, namely in color, number, symbol, language, and so on." This is especially true with language and Chinese characters. For example, there are at least 38 ways of saying

"I" in Chinese. Because of these complications, it's best to have a native speaker help you make sure you are communicating as clearly as possible in the way that is likely to attract the attention you seek.

Another common mistake is to launch campaigns from outside China without local partners, support, or at least some connection to the market. Understanding China's culture and languages is vital for the success of your online visibility there. Even though help is available from Baidu International Support, if you do not have Chinese language capabilities, you should partner with agencies that have worked in China before and understand the market. This is ever so important when you are launching your first campaign and have no experience with this complex market. The best way to find those who do have experience is to look online for people sharing their experiences with regard to search marketing in China. We have listed a few we know of in Appendix A, "SEO/SEM Resources."

Pay-Per-Click (PPC) Advertising

There are only two options for pay-per-click (PPC) in China:

- The native search engine Baidu, which, according to comScore, is the world's second largest search engine (see Figure 3.2)
- Google

Figure 3.2   *Baidu shows its PPC results in a similar way as Google.*

With Google results likely blocked by the "Great Firewall of China," reaching Chinese searchers is far more effective on Baidu. Plan on either using both Baidu and Google or at least Baidu.

Getting PPC advertising up and running in Baidu has become easier over the past few years, but you still need a good understanding of Chinese. It's best that your team or search marketing agency has the ability to read and input Chinese. When you have that capability in place, setting up a direct account should be relatively easy. You set up your account on Baidu's advertiser website at https://cas.baidu.com/. If you can't interact in Chinese, you can work with Baidu directly through its international support site at http://is.baidu.com/paidsearch.html (see Figure 3.3).

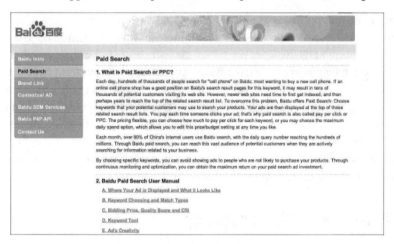

Figure 3.3   *If you are not able to interact in Chinese, you can use Baidu's international support site.*

Success in PPC on Baidu depends on remaining aware of several unique factors:

- Of course, your site should be written in Chinese, but when you do so, remember each Chinese character takes two spaces, which means you have to be economical with your message and call to action.

- In Chinese, the words around your key phrase provide context that may alter its meaning. With this issue, your native speaker will be very useful to help you make sure your meaning is clear.

- Baidu ranks paid ads with a method similar to Quality Score on Google AdWords. Take similar care to make sure your text and landing page optimization are relevant to your key phrases as you do with AdWords.

Organic Visibility

As with PPC, your choices for organic visibility are Baidu and Google. Until 2009, Baidu results showed largely paid listings, at least on the first few pages. This changed when Baidu launched its Phoenix Nest professional platform, which moved paid results to the right side of the page, with a few at the top, as was a common layout with other search engines. This allowed many more organic listings to rise to the top and also meant that sites less accessible to Baidu's crawler, such as those coded in Flash animation, encountered the same visibility issues as on other search engines.

The organic ranking factors are similar for both. According to Baidu, more than 90 percent of China's Internet users use Baidu to search each month, with the daily query volume in the hundreds of millions. Using both Baidu organic and paid search, you can reach this vast audience of potential customers. To rank well in China, do the following:

- **Write your content in Chinese.** Simplified Chinese is the principal *written* language of mainland China. It is important that you not only have your text in that language but also guide Baidu in the right direction by using the correct language tags, such as <META http-equiv="Content-Language" content="zh-CN">.

 Note

Double-byte character sets take up two spaces for each character in computer memory, and therefore, web coding as well. This means that you will need twice as much space in your code for the keywords. What's more, unlike English and other languages based on the Latin alphabet, Chinese has no spaces between words. This is a big problem for keyword-driven Western search engines because they must parse the meaning of Chinese words without seeing where they begin or end, and so often fall back on known combinations of Chinese characters in their database. For new combinations, they are dependent on surrounding words to clarify the meaning. If you happen to be using new terms, for example, a new product category, and you can't find your content using the keywords on a Chinese search engine, try contacting the engine's help team and ask them to include your search phrase in their database.

- **Place important content high on pages.** Baidu's algorithm ranks content that is higher up on a page as more important (as do most search engines). However, Baidu puts additional weight on content that is within the first 120,000 characters—fewer, and therefore higher up than on all the other major search engines. Keep in mind, too, the double-byte Chinese letter forms take up two characters each.

- **Increase keyword density.** Baidu favors keyword density. Although Google might be okay with 3 to 7 percent, Baidu wants more. Baidu also seems to allocate large-scale websites more weight during ranking, if all else is equal, unlike Google, which looks more at content and whether or not it is original.

- **Limit Flash animation.** Whereas Google has developed the ability to read Flash animation files, Baidu has not. In an interesting twist of outcome, as Baidu moved paid advertising out of the main search results on the left of the page in favor of algorithmic, many large enterprise Flash-laden websites could no longer guarantee themselves top spots by simply outbidding all the others.

- **Consider hosting your site in China.** In China, online visibility can depend on local hosting, unlike other countries, where it's way down the list of factors. Though you can host a Chinese ccTLD (country-code top-level domain; that is, .cn) anywhere, local hosting is more important in China than in most other countries mainly because poor connections can slow delivery, and being closer can speed things up. Even more likely is getting stalled by government firewalls. Chinese authorities have created "The Great Firewall of China," often blocking entire servers if they host sites they seek to ban. This has happened with popular hosts outside China—for example, Google and Yahoo! Host your site on such a server, and it may never be seen in China. At all.

 Note

Many companies offer web hosting in China. To find a reliable one, you will need to do a bit of sleuthing to identify the ones other international companies use. One way to do this is to look up the WHOIS records for such companies to find the IP addresses of the servers they are using in China. By then searching on the IP address, you should be able to identify the web hosting companies they use.

- **Obtain local links that Baidu values.** As with Google and Bing, inbound links from authoritative websites in the country you are targeting help Baidu recognize the relevance of your content to searchers there. However, whereas Google still ranks each site using Page Rank (PR) value, Baidu pays more attention to reciprocal links from large portals and government sites. Focus your linking efforts on the latter for better position on Baidu.

- **Use Baidu's XML site map protocol.** Recently, Baidu introduced sitemaps to help marketers gain visibility. Unlike Google, Baidu relies on getting pages through robots.txt documents. By creating an XML file of your Chinese language pages and listing it on your Robots file using the sitemap syntax, you make it much easier for Baidu to identify the pages focusing on China. Not so far in the past, however, there was a big blur between organic and PPC results on Baidu. For some of the most competitive commercial phrases, as many as the first 5 to 10 pages of results were all paid. Because of this, you might still see marketing firms attempt to charge you by the click rather than the hour for work in China, but this is changing fast as Baidu is making more and clearer distinction between paid and organic.

- **Learn to use Baidu's vertical categories.** Universal search as you know it—the incorporation of vertical search categories into general search results—is far less developed on Baidu than on Google and Bing, so what works for them does not do you much good in China. Baidu has its own vertical categories matrix; for example, Baidu Knows (Wiki) and Baidu

Youa (ecommerce), which means you need to be aware of opportunities to create content to appeal specifically to those instead of the more familiar news, image, and video categories on Google and Bing. Note that all search engines continue development and refinement of their algorithms, which can alter the effectives of your tactics. With Baidu, as with all the others, you need to study your target media, test methods, and track what works. If you don't speak Chinese, try using Google Translate to navigate around Baidu's search results pages to see what is going on.

Analytics

Foreign marketers frequently adapt Google Web Analytics or other web analytics tools to track search campaigns in China. However, Google Analytics and other web analytics tools face challenges of reasonable data accuracy and real-time support, and even customization in China. Though Baidu Statistics is no real substitute for Google Analytics, it is your best bet. Baidu Statistics is far from maturity but is the best option when tracking Baidu PPC.

Because Google moved its servers out of mainland China in April 2010, data transmission is at best lost to slower response time, and can be blocked completely as well. These are risks also for any analytics provider that is not hosted there.

Press Releases

For press releases, there are several options. The most effective we have found is Marketwire, which accepts your press release in English and then translates and distributes it. Your press release is distributed both direct to media and via Google and Baidu.

When you are sending press releases to a Chinese market, the key to success is understanding your target and which language they are likely to use. Where are you sending it, and what part of China is your focus? For Hong Kong and even Shanghai on the mainland, you could do well writing your press release in English. Distributing throughout greater China sends your release to key general, business, and consumer newspapers; magazines; newswires; broadcasts; and websites in mainland China, Hong Kong, and Taiwan, which means a press release written in Chinese would be more effective.

Which language you use—or even whether you make a case for doing a press release in both English and Chinese—depends on what language is preferred where your target audience is. Where English is predominant, use English. Where Chinese is preferred, use Chinese. If you want to reach multiple areas, you may find it effective to write two releases, one in each language. The language you use also provides an indicator for search engines about where your content is relevant, especially on Google, as we discussed in Chapter 2. This can be helpful if you are also expecting your press releases to provide valuable links back to your site.

If you need a vendor, Marketwire includes translations into Simplified and Traditional Chinese, as well as distribution via Asia Release, ISTIC, and Xinhua Infolink, regional news agency partners in China. Other companies that provide similar services are Presswire, China Newswire, and Xinwengao.com (both owned by Vocus). ("Xinwengao" means "press release" in Chinese.) China Newswire is shown in Figure 3.4.

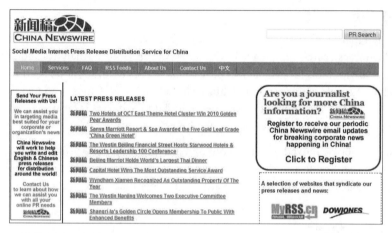

Figure 3.4 *Like Marketwire, China Newswire can help U.S.-based marketers translate press releases.*

Tips for Search Marketing in China

- When you research your key phrases, keep in mind that each Chinese character takes up two spaces, and their meaning is often nuanced by the surrounding words.

- Learn your way around Baidu because not all the techniques that work well with Google work the same way with Baidu.

- Host your Chinese site in China.

- Consider your audience when choosing which language to use for press releases.

- Make your site feature-phone friendly. (If you dropped in here to grab the tips, go back and read the whole chapter!)

Profile of Hong Kong Online

Although Hong Kong has a tiny number of people online compared to the China of which it is a part, its Internet usage (68.8 percent) is twice the penetration of its governing entity. Indeed, you could say the Internet market in Hong Kong more closely resembles those in Japan and South Korea than its compatriots to the north.

Well educated (35 percent have university educations), employed full time (69 percent), and evenly divided between men and women, the 4.87 million Hong Kong Internet visitors of 2011 enjoyed speedy and ubiquitous access from home and work. Of the households with Internet access, 80 percent used broadband to go online, and at least 9,000 public WiFi hotspots spattered the country of little more than 400 square miles, about the size of San Antonio, Texas.

> "Hong Kong also has the highest use of mobile phones in the world, at 185 percent penetration in July 2010—meaning people there had more than one device or subscription."

In Hong Kong, people were online an average of 25.9 hours in December 2010, and they watched more video than any of their Asia-Pacific neighbors, averaging 127 videos each in January 2011, a total of 476 million videos altogether, and 99 percent of them on YouTube.

At the same time, they averaged 125.1 searches each. Searching is the top online activity in Hong Kong, reaching 85 percent of those online. This was above the global average of 109.5 searches at the same time.

After searching, Hong Kong's next favorite activities were social networking, multimedia, news, email, and photo sharing. Online visitors shopped online far less than those in Japan or China, or indeed the world average. However, in 2011, 4 in 10 people online in Hong Kong said they planned to purchase from a retail website (largely travel or clothing and gifts).

Hong Kong Internet visitors frequent online banking more than anyone else in Asia-Pacific, with 35.5 percent of those online doing so in 2011, visiting most often HSBC, the Bank of China Hong Kong, and Standard Chartered.

Hong Kong also has the highest use of mobile phones in the world, at 185 percent penetration in July 2010—meaning people there had more than one device or subscription. About a third were using 3G or 3.5G service, consuming 214MB per person per month, a near twenty-fold increase in just two years. Moreover, smartphone penetration at 48 percent is nearly twice the global rate. Mobile payments are making their way in, too, and were used by 18 percent of purchases in 2010. SMS messages have been extremely popular, especially among the under-24-year-old age bracket. More than 66.8 million 2011 New Year's wishes were exchanged by SMS in Hong Kong. Nearly a third of mobile users in Hong Kong said they would not mind receiving ads on their mobile if they delivered incentives and benefits.

Search Media in Hong Kong

Google's share of the searcher market in Hong Kong was almost 63% percent in August 2011 (see Table 3.4). Yahoo! had nearly a third of the audience share. Baidu's share was far below 1 percent. More than half the people there, 52.5 percent, used Facebook.

Table 3.4 Search Engine Market Share—Hong Kong

Search Engine	Percentage of the Search Market
Google	66.62%
Yahoo!	31.37%
Bing	1.52%
Baidu	0.22%
Ask	0.14%
AOL	0.04%
Others	0.09%

Source: RealTimeStats.com: August 2011

Tips for Search Marketing in Hong Kong

- Yahoo! Hong Kong and Google are the top search media in Hong Kong, so adjust your search marketing efforts to those, as discussed in Chapter 2.

- Take advantage of Hong Kong Internet users' enthusiasm for online banking, videos, mobile, and photos as an opportunity to make your content rise above your competitors'.

- Ditto social media: Use its popularity in Hong Kong to gain visibility for your site there.

- Google increased text ad limits for Adwords in Chinese targeting Hong Kong to 15 double-byte characters for your title, and 19 each for your ad description lines.

Profile of Taiwan Online

Taiwan, also known as the Republic of China or Nationalist China, is very different from its Communist neighbor. Among 16.22 million online in 2010, more than half were 41–60 years old, and the penetration rate for individuals is 70.9 percent, with 80.7 percent of households online, 81.3 percent of them accessing with broadband. Women outnumbered men online, 55.8 percent to 44.2 percent.

Taiwanese web users averaged nearly three hours online per day, and favorite activities were checking news (80 percent), comparison shopping for consumer goods (61 percent), getting directions via maps (54 percent), and getting health information (49 percent). Though as many as 90 percent of Taiwanese online in July 2010 watched videos, they spent less time than either their neighbors or the rest of the world—only 7.2 percent of their time. Don't ask them for personal information. More than half quit sites that asked them to input personal data to access information.

Ecommerce is strong in Taiwan, in 2010 generating $127.5 billion NT ($4.24 billion US). Nearly 6 out of 10 Internet users shopped online, with women dominating the spending, 61 percent to 53 percent. The group age of 21–30 was the most enthusiastic; 80 percent of this age online said they like to shop on the Internet.

Payment methods are different from the West. About 45 percent preferred using money transfers by banks and post offices, whereas only 40 percent liked using credit cards, perhaps because research showed they spent 10 times as much when they used credit cards at that time. About a third chose cash on delivery; and a quarter, payment at convenience stores.

Among 27.5 million mobile subscribers in late 2010, nearly 70 percent had mobile Internet access, but only about half were using it.

Search Media in Taiwan

As in Hong Kong, Yahoo! Taiwan and Google more or less evenly divide the top spots for market share (see Table 3.5). In January 2011, Yahoo! had almost 14 million unique visitors to Google's nearly 11 million. Facebook had 9.2 million, and Baidu didn't even get on the top-10 radar, according to comScore.

Table 3.5 Search Engine Market Share—Taiwan

Search Engine	Percentage of the Search Market
Google	50.47%
Yahoo!	48.34%
Bing	0.93%
Baidu	0.13%
Ask	0.06%
Others	0.07%

Source: *RealTimeStats.com: August 2011*

The Sina Weibo microblogging site had half a million members in 2011. More than a third browse political or social commentary but fewer than 5 percent offer their own comments.

Tips for Search Marketing in Taiwan

- Yahoo! and Google are the media to target in Taiwan. Baidu has very little presence.

- Offer a variety of alternatives to credit cards for payment methods on your site because Taiwanese have many ways to pay cash and often prefer to do so.

- Avoid requiring too many private details in this market because those who live in it don't like giving up private details—unless there is something in it for them.

- Google increased text ad limits for Adwords in Chinese targeting Taiwan to 15 double-byte characters for your title, and 19 each for your ad description lines.

4

Japan

Japan is the world's second largest economy by nominal GDP (gross domestic product that has not been adjusted for inflation). In fact, Japan ranks second worldwide to the United States, meaning that the average person living in Japan enjoys very high living standards. According to the International Telecommunications Union (ITU), the number of Japanese Internet users grew from around 48 million in 2000 to just shy of 100 million in March 2011, making Japan the fourth largest online market in the world. More than 78 percent of Japan's 126.8 million inhabitants were online by then, which is nearly three times the world average. Japanese is the fourth most used language on the Internet after English, Chinese, and Spanish. This is testament to the size of the Internet market on this island nation that is slightly smaller than the state of California.

Japan has long been a forerunner in technology, embracing life online and on mobile long before other regions of the world and advancing it further faster. Consumers there have been able to pay by mobile phone much the way Americans use debit cards since 2005—and not just online, but also at vending machines, gas stations and shops. Social networking began there in 1999 and has grown to become an integral part of life on PCs and mobile devices. Online purchasing in Japan, once the biggest ecommerce market anywhere, is valued at 6.7 trillion Japanese yen, and generates $30 billion US in sales of products and services. That sum is separate from digital downloads and travel, which are large categories in themselves.

Profile of Japan Online

Japanese online users are relatively well divided evenly between women and men, at 46.1 percent women to 53.9 percent men, but there is a slight age difference. Among Japanese women, 68 percent online are between 35 and 39 years old, whereas for men the similarly largest group online is between 45 and 49. Both groups skew older than other countries in Asia as well as other regions of the world. This has many implications for marketers, including more developed tastes and spending ability.

Altogether, the Japanese people averaged 17.1 hours online per month in December 2010. They watch more online videos than any of their Asia-Pacific neighbors—an average of 158.3 videos in May 2010. In fact, they spend nearly twice the regional average time on entertainment—16.2 percent for Japan versus the average of 9.3 percent for the Asia-Pacific region. However, the Japanese spend very little of their online time gaming, despite the popularity of social gaming sites Gree and Gomage. Nearly 30 percent reported they prefer to get news online, with 24 percent saying they do not read a printed newspaper at all, instead turning to online news sites.

Close to 90 percent have access to search engines and directories, averaging 126.2 monthly searches per searcher, topping the regional average of 109.5 monthly searches per searcher. Nearly half of the searches done in Japan are done via Google. As you can see in Table 4.1, researching purchases was the most popular activity in 2010, followed by keeping up with news and information. The next most popular activity was researching how to do things, followed by a need to fill up spare time and researching for work.

Table 4.1   Top Five Activities Online in Japan

Reasons to Go Online	Share
Perform shopping research	51.1%
Locate news and information	39.3%
Research how to do things	37.4%
Fill up spare time	27%
Research for work	26.9%

Source: Asia Digital Marketing Association 2011 Yearbook

The Japanese people have long been avid users of social networks. In 2011, 39.1 percent of Japanese users said they use social networks to stay up to date with friends, and 10.5 percent said social networks were the place they meet new people. Although local favorites Mixi and Gree have long dominated the market there, Facebook attracted more than 4 million Japanese by July 2011. Interestingly, Facebook use in Japan is more formal, in some ways resembling business networking on LinkedIn elsewhere. This may be due to Japan's cultural heritage of valuing privacy. Facebook requires members to use their real names and faces, whereas on Japanese social networks people frequently create alternate identities. In response to Facebook's advancement on its turf and increasing cultural comfort online, local favorite Mixi added the capability to display real names in 2011. Still, Japanese users spent only 4.4 percent of their time engaging on social networks in 2011, which was significantly less the 13.9 percent spent by other Asia-Pacific countries.[1]

Of those online in Japan, 46 percent access the Internet using both computers and mobile phones. The Japanese mobile search market is the most developed on the planet. And it's growing. Fast. According to the Mobile Computing Promotion Consortium of Japan, mobile customers there snapped up smartphones in 2010 at a blistering 55 percent growth. Because Internet-enabled WAP (Wide Area Protocol) phones have been available in Japan since the 1990s, mobile web surfing there is the second most popular activity after reading e-mail.

About 7 percent of Japanese Internet users made purchases from their mobile phones in 2010, which exceeds the percentage of U.S. and European users who have made purchases with their mobile phones (5.5 percent and 4 percent, respectively). This number shouldn't be surprising because, as we've already discussed, Japan leads the rest of the world in mobile use.

---

1. Source: Asia Digital Marketing Association 2011 Yearbook

Although the number of Japanese users who have made purchases with their mobile phones might appear small, 7 percent of the total Japanese population is a sizable number of people. Forward-thinking marketers would do well to consider a mobile campaign in Japan, and include creating a mobile application for their product or service. A whopping 42.3 percent of Japanese people used apps in June 2010, a larger proportion than in the reportedly app-happy United States, where barely more than 31 percent did so, and in Europe where under 25 percent used them.

Furthermore, spending for advertising on mobile use in 2010 was 120.1 billion yen, up 16.5 percent from 2009, according to Dentsu. The largest portion was for advertising on mobile social network sites; mobile search advertising alone was 28.5 billion yen, up 27.2 percent in a year.

Mobile marketing requires different tactics and methods from marketing aimed at personal computer shoppers, and is beyond the scope of this book. There are good resources for more information on mobile marketing; see Appendix A, "SEO/SEM Resources."

Payment by mobile has been available in Japan for five years, and as of 2010 had been used by 20 percent of mobile subscribers. Online, 10 percent—9.8 million people—used their mobile wallets to make a purchase in December 2010.

Japanese online shoppers are like most others in the world: They mostly search for information about a product they want to buy, often returning to the same sites several times while conducting that research. But unlike in many other countries in the world, in Japan, searchers often return to make their purchase online instead of purchasing offline. This is true for both B2C (Business-to-Customer) and B2B (Business-to-Business) online shoppers, and implies that smart marketers use many channels for advertising and use analytics to look deeper than the last click to properly attribute return on investment (ROI).

Search Media in Japan

According to comScore, in 2009 there were 6.8 billion searches each month in Japan. Yahoo! had 3.5 billion, just over 51 percent of the market, compared to Google's 2.6 billion. NetMarketShare reported Google taking the lead in 2010 with a 47.59 percent share and Yahoo! trailing with only 45.9 percent. When Yahoo! Japan switched from displaying Yahoo! search results to those of Google in 2011, Google looked likely to have close to 95 percent market share in Japan (see Table 4.2).

Table 4.2   Search Engine Market Share—Japan

Search Engine	Percentage of the Search Market
Google.jp	72.1%
Yahoo.jp	25.3%
Bing.jp	2.1%
Baidu.jp	0.1%

Source: Statcounter Stand: June 2011

The fact that Google became the search engine used by Yahoo! Japan and then by local portal Rakuten has been one of the more remarkable developments in Japan. Until 2011, Yahoo! Japan was the leading search engine in Japan, while popular Rakuten used results from Infoseek. At that time, Japan was one of a few countries in the world where Google's market share was not dominant. That all changed in January 2011 when Yahoo! Japan began to display Google results instead of results from Yahoo.com, making Google the dominant search engine in Japan (see Figure 4.1). In mid-2011, Rakuten followed, adopting Google search results and giving Google nearly the entire market (see Figure 4.2). A few small players exist, but none have significant share of the search market: Microsoft Bing, South Korea's Naver, and China's Baidu.

Figure 4.1   *Google began supplying Yahoo! Japan with its search results as of January 2011.*

Figure 4.2 *Rakuten, with 2.3 percent market share, around 150 million searches per month, also switched to displaying Google results in mid-2011.*

According to Yahoo! Japan, the main reason for the switch to Google was that the Microsoft search technology soon to be used by Yahoo! worldwide was not robust enough for handling Japanese language search complexities. Two-thirds of Yahoo! Japan was owned by mobile provider Softbank; therefore, it had the autonomy to make such a change away from its long-time partner. The reason Rakuten gave for its change was to increase the speed of results by incorporating Google rather than working with its previous provider.

In addition to PC-based search media, each mobile provider in Japan uses a specific search engine:

- NTT DoCoMo—Google
- KDDI—Google
- Softbank—Yahoo!

Given the switch to Google made on the nonmobile side, it was anticipated that Softbank's mobile network would eventually switch to carrying Google results, thereby granting Google near total dominance in the mobile search market share, too.

This near-total switch to Google eased search marketing efforts in Japan, in that marketers then had to consider only one media platform, instead of three as before. However, even with this switch you may need to observe different guidelines and procedures between Google and Yahoo! Japan, as we discuss in the "Pay-Per-Click" section later in this chapter.

Most Common Mistakes

It is crucial that you do your homework before attempting to market to the Japanese. The marketing strategy that works in your home market isn't necessarily going to work in Japan. For example, for a long time, many companies used

Google AdWords only, ignoring the better half of the market share owned by Yahoo! Japan. Now that Yahoo! Japan has switched to Google results, this strategy may be less of a problem. However, you still need to set up your accounts for Yahoo! and Google separately because you will be running campaigns targeting different audiences between the two sites. This illustrates a common global search marketing error—repeating efforts across multiple markets instead of treating each one individually.

Also, many companies, including some so-called global agencies, merely translate English keywords to Japanese for their PPC and SEO campaigns. This shortcut risks mistakes that will be detrimental to building trust—a key element of Japanese culture. It is far better to have a native speaker review the translations and then have your work vetted by an SEM expert who is also familiar with both the language and search engine marketing methods.

Though each region of Japan has its own dialect, all Japanese people learn standard Tokyo Japanese at school. This means there should be no communication breakdown because of variations in the dialects in Japan as you might see in China and Russia. That said, there are four different character sets: kanji, hiragana, katakana, and romaji. Further complicating matters is that searchers might mix keywords from more than one character set. Also, a searcher's location might affect what character set he or she uses—much in the same way various regions of the United States use words and phrases (colloquialisms) that are particular to that region. Without native-speaker knowledge, you can easily get into trouble translating keywords in Japan.

Last, for those living in the West, the Japanese sensibility might seem extreme, however it's wise to keep in mind even the smallest gesture can carry great meaning. Success in Japan is based on understanding the nuances of the culture and utilizing the language to support those.

Pay-Per-Click

With Yahoo! Japan's shift over to Google search, PPC in Japan will become less complex. Not only do you have to deal with just one tool, but also you can manage your campaigns through Google's PPC management tool. Keep in mind that you still need a separate account for each site and that Yahoo!'s policy against trademark infringement, for example, may not become the same as Google's policy.

In December 2010, Google announced changes to the AdWords ad format allowing marketers to use more characters in their ad titles and descriptions. This policy is very helpful for those advertising through Google AdWords in Japan because Japanese keywords are often longer than their English-language counterparts, and Japanese writing takes up two spaces of online code for each character, making it a double-byte language. The increased number of allowable characters means more effective PPC ads.

Table 4.3 shows how the longer ad limits compare for double-byte characters.

Table 4.3   Google's Longer AdWords Ad Format

	Standard Settings	Longer Text Ad
Title	25 letters/12 characters	30 letters/15 characters
Ad copy line one	35 letters/17 characters	38 letters/19 characters
Ad copy line two	35 letters/17 characters	38 letters/19 characters
Display URL	35 letters/17 characters	35 letters/17 characters

Landing pages are as important in Japan as they are in any other market, but what sets the Japanese aside from searchers in the Western part of the world is a tolerance and even appreciation for pages that would be considered "noisy" or "busy" in the West (see Figure 4.3). Pages chock-full of information and places to click might actually help convert more Japanese customers, especially when the words are written in kanji characters, each of which represents a different meaning. Japanese users may prefer a different color scheme for the website. It is best to test to find out the design that works well for the Japanese audience.

Figure 4.3   *This Japanese HP landing page (on the left), successful in Japan, might be considered noisy by Westerners; the image on the right is a comparable image found in the United States.*

Organic Search

In general, because Google has the most market share and also powers results for Yahoo! Japan and local Rakuten, focus your optimization on the methods for Google, as discussed in Chapter 2, "Common Territory: Search Marketing Without Borders," including using your Google Webmaster Tools account to map your site to Japan, and obtaining inbound links from authoritative sites within Japan. The main challenge will be in your keyword research, as discussed previously, and then making sure you use the Japanese character set that is most likely to be used for queries by the searchers you hope to attract.

Note

> As discussed earlier in this chapter, there are four Japanese character sets
> in use in Japan: kanji, hiragana, katakana, and romaji.

Many Japanese companies have chosen to use international domains such as
.com or .net instead of .jp, something you should keep in mind when researching
Japanese sites from which you want to request links. For example, in Figure 4.4, the
site golf-goods.net turned up sixth in a search for "golf equipment" (in Japanese
characters), despite the site's having an international domain ending in .net. The
reason is that the language used on the site indicated to Google that the site was
relevant to the Japanese search, even if the top-level domain did not.

Figure 4.4 *Japanese site golf-goods.net comes up on the top 10 list when searching for
"golf equipment" on Google.*

The Japanese watch more videos online than almost anyone else. Therefore, don't
neglect to optimize your images and videos for universal search results. The reason
is that Japanese searchers are more likely to click on images and videos when they
search. Note that Yahoo! uses its own results for the vertical searches and blends
them in the organic search results. This means you also need to attend to optimizing images and video for Yahoo!.

Analytics

Both Google Analytics and Yahoo! Web Analytics (see Figure 4.5) seem to handle
the Japanese language quite well. Among major vendors, both Webtrends and
Omniture provide service.

Figure 4.5   Yahoo! Web Analytics showing results of a search made using Japanese in Japan.

Until 2011, the main analytics challenge in Japan was tracking two major search engines. Now that Google is the dominant search engine in Japan, monitoring PPC campaigns using Google Web Analytics is a familiar and convenient choice, as much as using Google AdWords.

Public Relations

As in North America, public relations is a well-developed profession in Japan. However, although the Internet has made the world a smaller place, there are still differences in culture and language between the West and East. Although the Japanese are very aware of Western habits—and indeed often greet you with a handshake as well as a bow—it is important for good relationships to remember that Japan is a high-context culture. Even the smallest gesture carries great meaning. This can often carry over to the perception of written material and needs to be taken into account when you are drafting press releases as well as web content.

We highly recommend that when you write a press release in Japanese for the Japanese market you have it translated by a native speaker; written in a Japanese press release format; and then have it reviewed by somebody who knows the language, culture, and search engine optimization. This way, you can ensure the tone of voice is correctly nuanced so that it gets maximum visibility online.

Distributing press releases in Japan is straightforward using one of the several major service providers. Marketwire includes free translations as part of its service and has a good partner in Japan: Japan Corporate News. Others worth looking at are the eNewsPr network and NewsCertain.

Search Marketing Tips for Japan

- For keyword research, keep in mind the Japanese language has four character sets, and searchers often use more than one set in a single keyword phrase.

- Google provides results for Yahoo! Japan and Rakuten, as well as its own searchers, so optimize using best practices for Google.

- Even though Google AdWords serves results to Yahoo! Japan, giving you wide coverage in this market, you need to set up separate accounts for Google and Yahoo! Japan, and rules for trademarks and other legalities may differ between the two.

- The Japanese watch more videos than anyone else in the region, so be sure to include videos in your marketing plans and optimize them.

- Your landing pages can be a lot busier than you may be accustomed to in the West.

5

Russia

The Russian online market is full of opportunity, and this has not gone unnoticed. Look at the expansion of principal search engine Yandex, which operates in Russia, Belarus, Ukraine, and Kazakhstan. Now, Yandex is making a global push in the United States, the United Kingdom, and other major markets around the world, with an English-language version of the search engine. Meanwhile, Russian searchers using Yandex can search for sites written in Latin character-based languages, as well as their native Russian.

Russia's size is the most obvious difference from its European and Asian neighbors. This Eurasian land mass covers nearly 6.5 million square miles (17m sq km), with a climate ranging from Arctic in the north to the generally temperate south. The country spans nine time zones, more than any other on the planet.

According to the U.S. Census Bureau, Russia was estimated to be home to about 139 million people in 2010. According to the International Telecommunication Union, less than half (43 percent or just under 60 million) use the Internet. Total Internet usage is up from around 2 percent in the year 2000. This is relatively low penetration compared to other Internet populations, and was not enough to put Russia on Internet World Stats' 2010 list of the top 58 countries with more than 50 percent of their inhabitants using the Internet. That said, Russia's growth toward the end of the decade is what makes the Russian online market exciting.

Profile of Russia Online

After years of relatively slow adoption rates, there were more than twice as many Russians online in 2010 as in 2007, passing the UK to make it the second largest population online in Europe. Though fewer than half of all Russians are online and most of them live in Moscow and St. Petersburg, Russia is well on its way to becoming an Internet mega market. Internet World Stats show the country now is the seventh largest Internet market in the world, trailing only Germany, Brazil, India, Japan, the United States, and China. At the current rate of growth, Russia has the potential to be a top-five worldwide Internet market within the next three to five years, and could become the biggest in Europe.

Internet penetration and usage in Russia varies a lot between locations. Moscow has 70.8 percent Internet penetration. However, in the northeast part of Russia, Internet penetration drops to 48 percent. In the south part of Russia, Internet penetration drops to only 30 percent. As in most countries, the 18–24-year-olds have the heaviest concentration of users with 73 percent overall. As you can see in Figure 5.1, more than 9 out of 10 Muscovites (inhabitants or natives of Muscovy or Moscow) between the ages of 18 and 34 are online. Folks 55 and older trail a long way back with only 7 percent of them online overall and only 20 percent in Moscow.

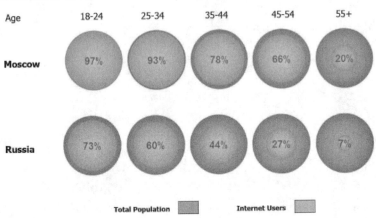

Figure 5.1 *Internet usage in Moscow dwarfs the usage in the rest of Russia. Source: Yandex and TNS.*

In Russia, ecommerce is probably three or fours years behind western markets. After 60 years of Soviet government–controlled availability of both goods and disposable income to spend on said goods, Russian consumers have some catching up to do. Based on Russia's enthusiasm for world markets and western lifestyle, we expect this will change rapidly.

"Because modern Russians are new to consumer credit, ecommerce is fairly new to them."

Because modern Russians are new to consumer credit, ecommerce is fairly new to them. Though ecommerce is still a fairly small opportunity, compared to more established markets in the West, it has been growing fast. In January 2011, com-Score reported that Russia experienced the highest growth in online retail penetration in Europe, posting gains of 15.8 percentage points. This rate of growth was matched only by Ireland in the same period (see Table 5.1). The Russian online retail market grew nearly twice as fast as that of Europe as a whole.

Table 5.1   Online Retail Penetration Growth

	January 1, 2010	January 1, 2011	Point Change
Europe	66.00%	74.50%	8.5
Ireland	64.90%	80.70%	15.8
Russian Federation	43.10%	59%	15.8
France	76.40%	87.00%	10.5
Austria	61.30%	71.40%	10.1
Germany	73.10%	82.10%	9.0

Source: comScore Media Metrix, Reach of Retail Sites in European Countries January 2010 vs. January 2011, Age 15+, Home and Work Locations

Like many cultures new to online shopping, Russians who are using ecommerce generally use the Web to find information on products and then make their purchase transactions offline. This makes attribution of sales sometime difficult to pinpoint.

Search Media in Russia

Russia is one of the few countries worldwide where Google is not the dominant search media. Yandex (short for "Yet ANother inDEX") is Russia's largest search engine with 61 percent market share in traffic in November 2011, according to LiveInternet.ru. At that time, Google had more than 25 percent, Mail.ru (an email service provider) had 7.1 percent, Rambler had 1.6 percent, and Bing had less than 1 percent (see Table 5.2). The remainder were half a percent or less each.

Table 5.2   Search Engine Market Share—Russia

Search Engine	Percentage of Search Market
Yandex	61.0%
Google	25.5%
Mail.ru	7.1%
Rambler	1.6%
Bing	0.8%

Source: StatCounter, June 2011

Like other major search media, Yandex is a full-service portal, providing many online services (including email, real-time search, GIS mapping, comparison shopping for banks and finance, real estate search, a jobs site, and even an online payment method) to Russians and Russian speakers in Ukraine, Kazakhstan, and Belarus.

Yandex is the largest internet company in Russia by revenue and generated more than $400 million in 2010, which is said to be a growth from the previous year of more than 40 percent. As you can see in Table 5.3, Yandex clocked 91 percent growth in 2009, nearly double the previous year to rank seventh worldwide. Yandex then rose to sixth by early 2011 according to comScore, just behind Facebook and ahead of eBay.

Table 5.3   Top 10 Search Properties by Searches Conducted (Searches in Millions)

	September 2010	September 2011	Percent Change
Worldwide	145,145	171,005	18%
Google Sites	95,658	118,550	25%
Baidu.com Inc.	10,411	11,322	9%
Yahoo! Sites	10,325	10,905	6%
Microsoft Sites	4,597	4,682	6%
Yandex Sites	2,590	3,049	18%
NHN Corporation	2,568	2,858	11%
Facebook.com	3,043	2,827	−7%
eBay	2,278	2,669	17%
Alibaba.com Corp.	1,224	1,516	24%

Source: comScore qSearch, Total Worldwide, Age 15+, Home and Work Locations, September 2011

In 2010, Yandex generated 64 percent of all search traffic in Russia. The Yandex home page attracted a monthly average of 21.5 million users. In the summer of 2010, Yandex reported processing about 100 million search queries daily—25.9 million of those by searchers in Moscow. According to comScore research published in late 2010, Yandex attracted a monthly audience of more than 53 million users from all over the world. By March 2011, Yandex reported 38.3 million unique visitors.

Yandex dominance and growth are a result of their 20 years of development specifically for the RuNet, which are Russian-language Internet users who numbered well more than 40 million in 2011, including those in Belarus, Ukraine, and Kazakhstan.

Yandex is the leading online destination in Russia with 10.8 billion page views per month and 2.8 billion search results pages reported in Yandex logs in April and May 2010. Besides being the largest search engine in Russia, Yandex is clearly becoming a global player. Yandex bet on global growth when it opened a U.S. office in the Boston area. From that office, Yandex expects to attract U.S. online commerce to serve searchers in Russia. Online, Yandex expanded Yandex.com to allow its searchers to query for sites in other Latin character sets, principally English. Furthermore, Yandex.ru offers searchers the opportunity to apply a global filter to see results in their own countries, such as Ukraine. All of this points to ambitions beyond the Russia borders for homegrown Yandex.

Yandex.com allows searchers to find sites in their own languages (see Figure 5.2) and looks quite different from Yandex.ru (see Figure 5.3).

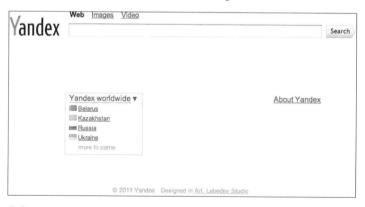

Figure 5.2   *Yandex.com allows searchers to find sites in their own languages.*

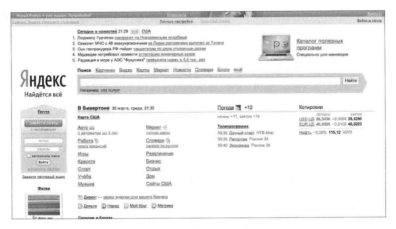

Figure 5.3   *The Russian version of Yandex—Yandex.ru.*

Local competitor Rambler.ru is shown in Figure 5.4. Rambler has only 2 percent of the Russian searcher market, far behind Russian favorite Yandex and even Google.ru itself.

Figure 5.4   *Rambler.ru is a popular email provider, but trails Yandex and Google in share of searches.*

Most Common Mistakes

Yandex reports many foreign advertisers come to Yandex "thinking Google" in that they try to apply their Google campaign strategies to advertising on Yandex. These foreign advertisers are not taking into account local specifics and the structural elements of the Russian language. If you merely translate an English-language campaign using an automatic translator, you may find that only a dozen out of thousands of keywords you choose can be used effectively in the advertising campaign.

Another mistake we have often encountered is advertisers using English when marketing to Russians. Only about five percent of Russians actually speak English, so using only English keywords can prove a futile tactic for online search marketing campaigns. Russians search largely in Russian, as you would expect.

Further, Yandex favors the Russian language in ranking sites on Yandex. ru because Russians who speak foreign

> "Only about five percent of Russians actually speak English, so using only English keywords can prove a futile tactic...."

languages prefer their native first language. Also, Russian is the official language in Belarus, Kazakhstan, and Kyrgyzstan; and the unofficial but widely spoken language in Ukraine, Latvia, and Estonia; and to a lesser extent, the other countries that were once part of the USSR.

Although you will find differences in culture in different regions in Russia, we see a bigger issue of making sure that marketers understand Russia as a whole. To be successful, marketers must recognize the importance of Moscow and St. Petersburg as major civic, cultural, and financial centers and understand how they get special treatment because of their prominence. For example, searchers in those two cities are more likely to get accurate geo-location results because the Internet service providers (ISPs) have more accurate data for these two cities than they have for other parts of Russia. You are more likely to hit the nail and not your thumb geo-targeting to those main cities.

Russian Language Issues

Regional differences also produce variations in the language, both spoken and searched, which means search queries will likely be phrased differently in different regions. Those speaking Russian in Moscow may do so somewhat differently from those in St. Petersburg, or those in St. Petersburg from those in other regions, and so on. You will want to research regional vernacular, idiom, and even spelling among your target regions of Russia.

A simple example is what Russians call the entry to an apartment house. In Moscow, it would be подъезд, an entrance to an apartment house, literally a "carriage drive," a holdover from the 19th century; people from St. Petersburg are more likely to call it a парадное, "main entrance to an apartment house." In St. Petersburg, there is also "черный ход," meaning the back entrance, which are more common there than in Moscow. Similarly, Muscovites call bread a "буханка," more like brick-bread than a loaf, whereas their kin from St. Petersburg would say "булка хлеба," meaning "bun of bread," but a bun itself there would be "булка" alone. Sometimes even Russians find this confusing.

Another example is the word "download" (as shown in Figure 5.5). Although a marketer might be tempted to use the word "загрузить (zagruzit)" in Russian, which translates to "load," the word "скачать (skachat)" is used more often to indicate the action of downloading.

Keyword	Competition	Global Monthly Searches ⑦	Local Monthly Searches ⑦	Local Search Trends
☆ загрузить	🔍	165,000	90,500	▃▁▃▁▃▁▃▁▃▁▃▁
☆ скачать	🔍	618,000,000	45,500,000	▇▇▃▃▃▃▁▁▃▃▃▁

Figure 5.5   *The words "загрузить (zagruzit)" and "скачать (skachat)" both relate to the English word "download." As you can see, "скачать" has a far larger search volume.*

And just to make things more complex, Russian use six grammatical cases, to the two known to English speakers, and Russians do not use articles of speech such as "the."

Pay-Per-Click

Yandex services pay-per-click (PPC) advertisers on Yandex Direct, which will look quite familiar if you have advertised using Google AdWords or Microsoft adCenter. To find your keywords, you can check estimated search volume for any keywords/ phrases in any region using Yandex Wordstat (see Figure 5.6). It provides keyword suggestions together with monthly search volumes.

Figure 5.6   *In Yandex Direct, you can place pay-per-click ads in Yandex search results pages. (See http://direct.yandex.com.)*

Like Google, Yandex offers several types of placements and several types of targeting, as well as exact match and phrase match. The variety of placements offered includes Yandex Search, partner search sites such as Bing.ru, Yandex advertising network, and catalog and market pages (see Figure 5.7). You will find a lot of detailed information at the Yandex Direct Help site (see http://help.yandex.com/direct).

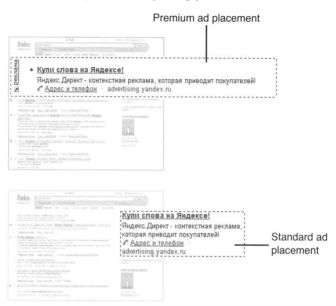

Figure 5.7   *Yandex pay-per-click advertising provides premium placements and standard ones.*

The Yandex targeting options are very much the same as Google's, but because of the market size, in our experience using both search engines, Yandex tends to result in more accurate targeting. Targeting via contextual ads triggered by keywords is available. Also available is geographic targeting, which can be as specific as by city level, thematic targeting by keyword, targeting the time of day for displaying an ad ("day-parting"), or behavioral targeting based on Yandex registration information.

For PPC advertising on Rambler, you have to go through Google. Google automatically targets Rambler unless you specifically tell it not to do so. Also, you can target just Rambler via the Google.ru AdWords interface, but our experience as of this writing has been that Rambler reaches a negligible part of the market. Google AdWords allows longer text ads when you target Russia, Belarus, and Ukraine (see Chapter 2, "Common Territory: Search Marketing Without Borders").

Yandex also provides a contextual advertising service similar to Google AdSense. According to a February 2011 study by comScore, Yandex had the biggest advertising network on the Russian market with an audience reach of 87.6 percent. Yandex says participation of the sites in its advertising network helps expand audience reach and increases the number of impressions and clicks it provides to advertisers.

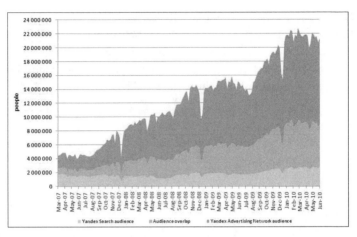

Figure 5.8 *Yandex Advertising Network (YAN) is a group of high-quality websites that display ads served by Yandex Direct, similar to Google AdSense. Source: Yandex.*

Organic Search

Yandex rates websites with a system called a "citation index," which ranges from 0 to 150,000 to indicate how trusted a site is. This system is similar to Google's "Page Rank." The higher a website's citation index, the more authority it has (see Figure 5.8).

In 2010, Yandex reached outside its native Russian language and started indexing websites written in Latin alphabet–based languages as well as those written in the Russian Cyrillic character set. At that time Yandex indexed more than 4 billion pages in languages based on the Latin alphabet, accounting for about 15 percent of all searches on Yandex; the majority of these pages were in English. Still, Yandex search prioritizes Russian-language websites before Latin-alphabet sites, unless the global search filter option is used. Yandex also offers its searchers the ability to translate from English, French, German, Italian, and Spanish.

> "Yandex search prioritizes Russian-language websites before Latin-alphabet sites..."

For those users who want international results, Yandex offers a global search filter. You cannot enable the global search filter in Yandex.ru, but you can use Yandex.com.

It is all about the needs of our audience, says Yandex. Ukrainian users, for example, are expecting to get more Ukrainian results, whereas Russian users expect Russian results. Even those Russians who do speak foreign languages often prefer their first, native language. Hence, Yandex's general formula will prioritize Russian sites. Moreover, Yandex gives priority first and foremost to pages that offer answers to the most popular user queries in Russian.

Organic ranking in Yandex heavily favors good-quality, information-rich content. Despite the expansion into other languages, it is important to keep in mind the emphasis Yandex puts on the Russian language to satisfy its native speaker searchers. If you want to reach Russians via Yandex, you are best off writing your content in Russian and also using a Russian country code top-level domain or ccTLD (.RU) in Cyrillic characters. Doing so will ensure Yandex recognizes your site as relevant to its customers. Getting a Russian domain isn't hard at all. The registration procedure is transparent and simple. Almost any registrar allows registration of .ru and .рф domains online. All you need is your ID.

Like Google, Yandex has its Webmaster tools, which are a handy set of tools that can help you get your site indexed, connect to Yandex's API, and assist with keyword research (see Figure 5.9). Good places to start are http://wordstat.yandex.ru/?cmd=words and http://adstat.rambler.ru/wrds/. Yandex Webmaster tools is a great place to look for the most current information on how to gain visibility in their index.

Figure 5.9   *Yandex Webmaster tools in English can be found at webmaster.yandex.com.*

Links play a role in ranking in Yandex organic results. Key factors are the language and the Citation Index of the link source site. You may also see the Citation Index referred to as the Quotation Index, named so by a blogger. It's similar to Google PageRank in that the higher the number, the better; but Yandex ranking is much more granular, scoring sites from 0 to 150,000. Many of the factors that improve your score are similar to Google PageRank, such as the quality and relevance of your inbound links. Reportedly, Google PageRank will have no effect on your Yandex Citation Index.

A good place to start link building in Russia is the Yandex Catalog, a link directory for Yandex searchers (see Figure 5.10). It is similar to the Yahoo! Directory you have most likely used to gain authoritative links for your English-language sites. As with Yahoo! and DMOZ, submissions to the Yandex directory are reviewed by choosy editors, and there is a long list of rather specific requirements on the Catalog section of the site. Experienced Yandex marketers report that the real value of a Yandex Catalog is the authoritative and relevant link it provides to your site, which should help improve your ranking on Yandex.

 Note

Figure 5.10 shows a website that has been translated by Google Translate. Note the bar at the top of the page that shows what language the page has been translated to and from.

Figure 5.10   *The Yandex Catalog is a directory of links to sites reviewed by human editors. This image has been translated from Russian.*

You can submit your site free and wait for review, but if you pay a fee of 12,500 Russian rubles (approximately $400 to $450 US), your site will be reviewed within three days of receipt of payment, according to Yandex.

Two other directories for getting links are

- **Mail.ru**—http://list.mail.ru
- **Rambler**—http://top100.rambler.ru/top100

Mail.ru's "Katalogue" is the giant email service provider's directory of news, entertainment, and information in Russian. Rambler's directory has many categories, including regional sections for the largest cities in Russia and Ukraine.

 Note

> At the time of this writing, the directories discussed here and instructions for submitting to them are available only in Russian. You can use Google translate to make your way through the sites.

Analytics

Yandex provides its own analytics solution called Metrika (http://metrika.yandex.ru/). Metrika tracks all the normal traffic and referral data and also integrates its conversion functionality into the Yandex PPC platform. Yandex is also integrating recently acquired WebVisor to provide behavioral analysis into Metrika.

In our experience, Google and Yahoo! Analytics have shown fairly accurate results when it comes to tracking PPC and organic visitors from Russia, but neither integrates with Yandex results for tracking. That means using Google Analytics alone would miss traffic from the far more dominant search engine for Russian speakers. If your company runs large PPC campaigns in Russia, it's a good idea to run the Yandex tool parallel to Google or Yahoo! so that you can compare the results for a complete picture of your performance. As of this writing, Kenshoo and SEOMoz were the only tools in which you could track Yandex. This was expected to change before long as major vendors catch on to the opportunity in the Russian market.

One of the possible advantages for software companies is that neither Yandex nor Rambler seems to filter out searches for illegal or politically incorrect words that Google does filter out. This capability can be useful for such companies when they want to want to see whether some searches related to their services are in fact looking to open them illegally, such as through hacking.

Public Relations

Because of the language barrier, getting online visibility in Russia via press releases is not as easy as in most of the other markets we discuss in this book. Because so few Russians are completely fluent in English, the key to success is writing your press releases in Russian. Also, because Yandex prioritizes content in Russian, you will want to write your press releases in Russian. Look for online press release services that include translations and distribution to major consumer, business, and trade presses.

Your best bet are services such as sovanet. eu that specialize in online copywriting and public relations for the Russian market. Other services worth looking at are ivan-pr.com, Marketwire, and Presswire,

"...getting online visibility in Russia via press releases is not as easy as in most of the other markets..."

which all translate press releases as part of their services. Journalists might search Yandex news, but they also might use alerts, so it's best to reach out to them directly using the wire services.

The images in Figure 5.11 and Figure 5.12 illustrate ways your press release can be incorporated into Yandex results pages, in doing so passing before the eyes of journalists searching. Yandex inserts a news crawl on its results page (Figure 5.11) as well as displays press releases (Figure 5.12).

Figure 5.11   *Yandex News results crawls like those on Google.*

For link-building purposes, this approach might prove to be little more complicated than when targeting Western markets. Having said that, directly engaging stakeholders such as journalists by sending them press releases via the wire services can lead to links from news sites with a very good Yandex Citation Index score, pushing your site up the rankings.

Figure 5.12   *Results from a Yandex news search.*

Search Marketing Tips for Russia

- Russians search mainly in their own language, so you are best off targeting Russian keywords and providing Russian landing pages.

- Moscow and St. Petersburg are by far the biggest markets, and geo-targeting those will be more accurate because Internet Service Providers (ISPs) have more sophisticated and reliable infrastructure there than in other smaller rural markets.

- Yandex is Russia's primary search and information retrieval portal. Although Yandex crawls English, French, German, and Italian, it favors Russian-language sites and ads.

- Use Yandex Webmaster Tools—available in English—to find a lot of information about getting Yandex to index your site, list it in the Yandex Catalog, and perform other services.

- Similarly, http://help.yandex.com/direct has a lot of useful information on PPC advertising and is in English.

- Though it's a distant second in search engine usage, it should not be forgotten that Google.ru has gone from close to zero in 2005 to more than 20 percent market share in 2010.

6

United Kingdom

The United Kingdom holds big potential for using the Internet for marketing because the Internet culture is well integrated, there is high penetration of broadband, and UK users are very "mobile" savvy. The United Kingdom ranks eighth in the world for Internet use. In 2011, more than 82 percent of the UK's population used the Internet, and almost 48 percent also used Facebook. The United Kingdom seems to be Europe's most opportune market to communicate via those two media. The 82 percent is to close to 51.5 million people, a huge growth from the 15.4 million users in 2000.

That said, if you are tempted to market in the United Kingdom because you believe a common language and some shared history with the United States make the United Kingdom easy to enter, think again. The United Kingdom is fiercely competitive in all sectors of Internet marketing, especially search. The country is home to many leading global search engine marketing firms, indeed some of the pioneers of the industry. Many leading firms from other countries, in particular the United States, have had offices in the United Kingdom for years. You would be well advised to enter the UK market with your complete arsenal of sophisticated information and tools; you also should pay close attention to the fine distinctions between the U.S. and UK languages and cultures to appeal successfully to British people online.

Profile of the United Kingdom Online

Brits have been online for a long time; they are web savvy and active Internet users, with a larger proportion of their population engaged each month than in the United States. According to the UK Office for National Statistics, 60 percent of British adults accessed the Internet every day in 2010 (see Figure 6.1). This amounts to more than 30 million people.

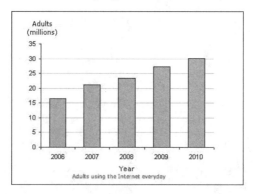

Figure 6.1   *Sixty percent of British adults access the Internet every day.*[1]

In 2010, the number of people in the United Kingdom who had never accessed the Internet in their lives decreased to 9.2 million, comprising 97 percent of those 65 and older, compared with just 1 percent of those aged 16 to 24. Whereas 97 percent of adults educated to degree level had accessed the Internet, only 45 percent without a degree had. Your online market in the United Kingdom is clearly younger, well educated, distributed beyond urban limits to towns and countryside, and quite possibly has money to spend.

And your UK audience is well connected. The United Kingdom has an excellent broadband infrastructure, with high-speed DSL reaching more than 5 million households in early 2011 and cable reaching more than half of all households. Of the 19.2 million households in the United Kingdom with an Internet connection, representing 73 percent of all households, the region with the highest level of access is London, at 83 percent; the lowest is in the Northeast at 59 percent, still well more than half.

> "The United Kingdom is the world's most active ecommerce market, with revenues of GBP 100 billion..."

---

1. Graphic courtesy of the UK Office for National Statistics.

The United Kingdom is the world's most active ecommerce market, with revenues of GBP 100 billion, a share that is projected to grow 10 percent annually. A growing significance in the UK economy, online exports contribute 2.8 GBP for every 1 GBP in imports, whereas offline exports bring in less than imports, 90p for every 1 GBP.

Among European countries, the United Kingdom is a leader in reaching potential customers online. In 2010, 31 million UK adults, or 62 percent of all adults, bought online in the previous year. According to a January 2011 comScore study, 89.4 percent of UK's Internet users had some contact with retail sites, and while there, they spent some 84.1 minutes browsing (see Table 6.1). Within the retail category, the subcategory with the highest market penetration was comparison shopping; the next, apparel; and the third, consumer electronics. The most popular products bought online were clothes and sporting goods, bought by 52 percent of UK Internet shoppers.

Table 6.1   Reach of Retail Sites in European Countries

Percent Reach of Internet Users

	Jan 2010	Jan 2011	Point Change	Average Minutes per Visitor
Europe	66.0%	74.5%	8.5	52.4
United Kingdom	83.2%	89.4%	6.3	84.1
France	76.4%	87.0%	10.5	83.2
Germany	73.1%	82.1%	9.0	63.8
Ireland	64.9%	80.7%	15.8	35.7
Netherlands	75.3%	80.2%	4.9	50.2
Spain	68.4%	76.7%	8.3	39.7
Denmark	68.2%	75.1%	7.0	40.6
Sweden	73.8%	73.6%	−0.2%	43.7
Norway	66.7%	73.4%	6.7	38.0
Belgium	71.7%	73.3%	1.6	29.7
Switzerland	70.3%	73.2%	2.9	34.5
Poland	N/A	72.4%	N/A	20.4
Austria	61.3%	71.4%	10.1	34.1
Turkey	68.0%	69.8%	1.9	73.0

Italy	67.4%	69.5%	2.1	21.4
Finland	63.8%	66.5%	2.7	29.8
Portugal	60.2%	65.9%	5.7	23.9
Russian Federation	43.1%	59.0%	15.8	33.7

Source: comScore, Home and Work, Ages 15 and Up, January 2010 vs. January 2011

As you can see in Table 6.2, Amazon led the way in the United Kingdom, with close to 19 million unique visitors. Home Retail Group came second, Apple.com Worldwide Sites was third, Tesco supermarket chain was fourth, and Play.com sites were fifth.

Table 6.2   Top Retail Properties in the United Kingdom

Site	Total Unique Visitors (000)	Percent Reach	Average Minutes per Visitor
Amazon Sites	18,876	48.8%	21.2
Home Retail Group	9,981	25.8%	18.8
Apple.com Worldwide Sites	8,933	23.1%	9.6
Tesco Stores	6,932	17.9%	16.9
Play.com Stores	4,714	12.2%	7.8

Source: comScore, Home and Work, Ages 15 and Up, January 2011

Online grocery shopping is more popular in the United Kingdom than anywhere else in the world (see Figure 6.2). eMarketer estimated more than 68 percent of web users ages 14 and older would buy online at least once per month in 2011. Eurostat reported that 16 percent of Brits bought food and groceries in 2010 versus 7 percent in Germany and 5 percent in France. By way of comparison, fewer than 1 percent of Internet users in the United States reported buying most of their groceries online, according to a January 2011 survey done by the SupermarketGuru and National Grocers Association.

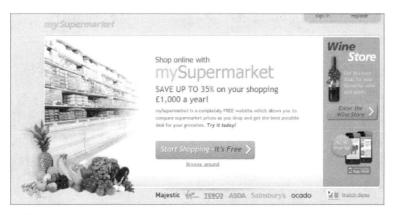

Figure 6.2   *Price comparison websites such as mySupermarket have helped UK shoppers make decisions on where and how to buy groceries online.*

UK online payment methods are much like the United States. Debit and credit cards are used most, with online prepaid funds, also known as "wallets" and prepaid cards being the next most common form of online payment. PayPal has 23 million members in the United Kingdom.

Search Media in the United Kingdom

As you can see in Table 6.3, Google has been by far the most dominant search engine and the most visited site in the United Kingdom. YouTube ranks eighth. Between Google.co.uk and google.com, more than 91 percent of UK searches were on Google in June 2011 (see Table 6.4). In January 2011, Nielsen/UKOM research tabbed 35 million unique UK visitors for Google every month.

Table 6.3   Most Popular Search Engines by Share of UK Searches

Rank	Search Engines	Share of Searches March 2011	Share of Searches February 2011	Monthly Change	Share of Searches March 2010	Yearly Change
1	Google Sites	90.02%	90.68	−0.66%	90.63%	−0.61%
2	Microsoft Sites	4.39%	4.11%	0.28%	2.96%	1.43%
3	Yahoo! Sites	3.53%	3.33%	0.21%	4.06%	−0.52%
4	Ask Sites	1.49%	1.44%	0.06%	1.70%	−0.21%
5	Other	0.56%	0.44%	0.12%	0.66%	−0.09%

Source: Experian Hitwise

Table 6.4 Search Engine Market Share—United Kingdom

Search Engine	Percentage of the Search Market
Google.co.uk	91.5%
Bing.co.uk	3.0%
Yahoo.co.uk	2.5%
Ask.co.uk	1.4%
Others	1.6%

Source: Experian Hitwise, June 2011.

Bing and Yahoo! together claimed another 7 percent of share in 2011, though creeping up slowly. Indeed, Bing grew most rapidly up to March 2011, though only nipping at the heels of big dog Google. Still, although single-digit percentages may not seem like much, the sheer volume of Internet use in the United Kingdom made the increase a tidy uptick for Bing.

Search media in the United Kingdom is advanced and sophisticated; you would be wise to note both Google and Bing roll out updates quickly there after the United States and before the rest of Europe.

Social media should not be ignored when it comes to marketing to the United Kingdom. According to a Nielsen study done in May 2010, social media usage was up by 159 percent in the United Kingdom and accounted for almost 23 percent of time spent online. In 2010, 43 percent of UK Internet visitors posted messages to social network sites or blogs. Though skewing young, with 75 percent of 16- to 24-year-olds online posting messages and 50 percent uploading content, social media also appeals to older folks in the United Kingdom. Of those 45–54, 31 percent have posted messages and 28 percent uploaded content, according to Experian Hitwise.

With close to 30 million Facebook members, the United Kingdom is the world's third largest Facebook population in absolute numbers of members, and third fastest growing in the 12 months leading up to May 2011, topped only by the United States and Indonesia. In March 2011, Facebook claimed more than 56 percent of all social networking in the United Kingdom (see Table 6.5). That said, YouTube remains enormously popular, chipping away at Facebook's lead, and creeping up over 19 percent of social network visits that year.

Table 6.5   Most Popular Social Networks by UK Internet Visits

Rank	Social Network	Share of Search Clicks March 2011	Share of Search Clicks February 2011	Monthly Change	Share of Search Clicks March 2010	Yearly Change
1	Facebook	56.42%	57.64%	−1.22%	52.26%	4.16%
2	YouTube	19.06%	18.32%	0.74%	16.85%	2.21%
3	Twitter	2.63%	2.40%	0.23%	2.10%	0.53%
4	Yahoo! Answers	1.98%	1.86%	0.12%	2.27%	0.29%
5	Gumtree	1.47%	1.39%	0.08%	1.01%	0.46%
6	LinkedIn	0.66%	0.63%	0.03%	0.39%	0.26%
7	Tumblr	0.53%	0.49%	0.04%	0.12%	0.41%
8	MySpace	0.51%	0.54%	−0.03%	1.42%	0.91%
9	Moshi Monsters	0.49%	0.44%	0.05%	0.31%	0.18%
10	Club Penguin	0.40%	0.49%	−0.09%	0.67%	−0.27%

Source: Experian Hitwise

Most Common Mistakes

The most common mistake made by marketers is thinking that English words are used in the same way, regardless of whether spoken by an American or a British person. Though not as much of a major hurdle as is marketing in a foreign language, it is important to take note of how different words are used, such as "aeroplane" and "airplane" and, more commonly, the slang for mother—"mum(my)" in the United Kingdom and "mom(my)" in the United States. Nike sells "football boots" in the United Kingdom, not "soccer cleats," as in the United States.

As you can see in Figures 6.3 and 6.4, the term you choose can make a big difference in your reach.

Figure 6.3   *When searching for "airplane" on Google UK, we get totally different results than when we search for "aeroplane," as shown in Figure 6.4*

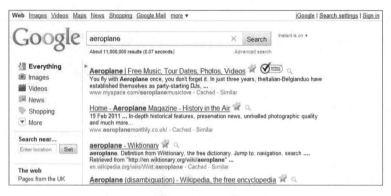

Figure 6.4   *Searching for "aeroplane" on Google UK.*

You should also go the distance and localize the copy on the page. Brits are not likely to get offended when they see content in U.S. English being pushed to them. However, they are likely to ignore U.S. English content because it just does not register. Although it's widely understood that there are differences in spellings, with the odd "u" inserted in words such as "harbour" and "favour," what is more telling is words that may have completely different uses and meanings. For example, "pavement" is the British term for what in U.S. English is called

"Ireland should be treated as Irish, not British, if you want to get a good response from the more than three million Internet visitors there."

a "sidewalk," whereas in the United States, the pavement is the place where cars and trucks belong. If you don't use the term they know, you risk failing to engage your British audience or confusing them.

Another mistake is to treat the Republic of Ireland as part of the United Kingdom. Other than Northern Ireland, the Emerald Isle is its own independent country— and proud of it, too. Ireland should be treated as Irish, not British, if you want to get a good response from the more than three million Internet visitors there.

Pay-Per-Click

Pay-per-click (PPC) is widely used and well developed in the United Kingdom, both by Brits targeting Brits and foreigners targeting those living in the United Kingdom. Find and use keywords in UK English for best results. The dangers of using non-UK English words in PPC are, first, there are fewer searches for them, and second, ads using words that are foreign to the searcher are likely to be ignored. This lowers your click-through rates and dampens your success. In the United Kingdom, searchers look for "holidays" and "lifts," whereas their U.S. cousins seek "vacations" and "elevators" (see Figures 6.5 and 6.6).

Keyword	Competition	al Monthly Searches ⑦	Local Monthly Searches ⑦
☆ lift		5,000,000	550,000
☆ elevator		1,220,000	60,500

Figure 6.5   *Good examples of UK/U.S. English differences are "lift" (UK) and "elevator" (U.S.).*

Keyword	Competition	Global Monthly Searches ⑦	Local Monthly Searches ⑦
☆ holiday		24,900,000	9,140,000
☆ vacation		9,140,000	246,000

Figure 6.6   *Other good examples of the same language but different words between the United Kingdom and United States are "holiday" (UK) and "vacation" (U.S.).*

So, when we target the United Kingdom for travel to Iceland, we use "Holiday in Iceland"; but for the United States, "Vacation in Iceland," with a surprisingly big difference between the click-through volume and impact of those ads.

PPC in the United Kingdom is very competitive, and keywords and messages tend to be generic. According to UK Online Measurement (UKOM) in its "Information for Media Owners" in March 2010, only 5 percent of all advertising money spent online went to advertising with a branding objective.

Nielsen's 2010 clickstream research for Google on the UK finance sector in finance found 32 percent of those who researched savings accounts online and 43 percent of those who applied for accounts used generic terms, while a quarter of retail apparel searches were generic terms. Because those searching with a brand name in their searches are likely to stick with that brand, generic search phrases become even more important and more competitive to win over searchers.

Apart from the need to take care with your keyword research to make sure you target UK English words and phrases, you'll find nearly everything else about targeting PPC advertising to the United Kingdom quite similar to doing so in the United States. You can geo-target UK regions and cities in your Google AdWords and Bing accounts.

Google AdWords Quality Score has been active in the UK market for nearly as long as in the United States. Make sure you follow all the best practices for relevant ads and landing pages for your campaigns there as you would in the United States.

Organic Search

When you optimize your web pages for organic search results, the language is important; this is well known. Even though British English uses many words differently from U.S. English, you might get away with sticking to U.S. English because Google tends to show results based on the searcher's location and correct spelling of words for that location; and it shows relevant results based on user behavior there.

However, counting on Google alone to do the work is not the most effective way to move forward in the UK online market. As we said previously, search engine marketing in the United Kingdom is very competitive, with many experts using sophisticated and well-developed tactics. If you want to penetrate the UK market, you need to make use of every play in the SEO book.

> "If you want to penetrate the UK market, you need to make use of every play in the SEO book."

Use a UK top-level domain (country-code top-level domain) on your site targeting British customers—for example, www.*yourdomainname*.co.uk or www.*yourdomainname*.org.uk.

Develop links from sites with UK ccTLDs. You can find them by searching within Google and inserting **web directory site:*.co.uk**, as shown in Figure 6.7.

Figure 6.7   *If you search for web directory site:*.co.uk *on Google, you might find some good web directories that allow you to link them to your site.*

You can also choose Advanced Search and click the Dates, Usage, Rights, Region and More link to limit results to the United Kingdom.

Be sure to include optimizing your images, videos, and local news in your organic strategy, just as you would in the United States. Both Google and Bing search results pages display all these in universal or blended results.

In early 2011, Google refined its algorithm in a massive update codenamed "Panda" to bring forward unique content that was determined by Google to be valuable to its searchers, while reducing visibility for lesser ones that were made up of replicated content and cluttered with clickable ads to make money for their owners. Shortly afterward, Google rolled out the Panda update in the United Kingdom, the first country outside the United States where they did this. This is another good illustration of how sophisticated search engine marketing is in the United Kingdom. You would be wise to make sure you are up to date on Google's latest updates and techniques for dealing with them. You can be sure your UK competitors will be. The best place to learn is in the online publications listed in Appendix A, "SEO/SEM Resources."

Analytics

Using analytics is the United Kingdom is very much the same as in the United States. You can choose from a wide selection of familiar analytics tools discussed in Chapter 2, "Common Territory: Search Marketing Without Borders," to measure your search marketing progress. Google Web Analytics is the most popular free analytics tool, while WebTrends and Onmiture are among the top paid tools.

Online PR

The United Kingdom as a PR market is very mature, and many great PR agencies in London have strong online PR capabilities. If you want to handle your online press releases yourself, you can use services such as Marketwire and eNewsPR for both online-only and direct-to-media distributions.

Besides providing more visibility in search engine results pages (SERPs), online PR agencies in the United Kingdom help you gain better visibility among journalists. According to Nordic eMarketing research, in 2008 and 2009, British journalists used the Internet heavily when researching their topics. In the same study, Nordic eMarketing found that British journalists stayed within Google UK when searching, as was the case in more than 80 percent of researched incidents.

Search Marketing Tips for the United Kingdom

- The United Kingdom is a very competitive market in which you need to leverage all SEO tactics, such as using a UK top-level domain and acquiring links from authoritative UK domains.

- Keywords in U.S. spelling may not register with Brits online, and many similar words have different meanings.

- The analytics tools you already use, such as Google Analytics and Yahoo! Web Analytics, Webtrends, and Omniture, all work well in the United Kingdom.

- UK journalists use Google News widely for their research. Use ePR to place your news in front of them.

- Google generally rolls out advances and algorithm changes in the United Kingdom shortly after rolling them out in the United States, so stay current with its updates.

7

Germany

Germany is one of the most mature online markets in Europe. According to the International Telecommunications Union (ITU), nearly 80 percent of the 82.2 million people living in Germany were Internet users in March 2011. That is just over 65 million, up from 24 million in the year 2000. Altogether, Germany is the largest economy in Europe and the fourth largest in the world after the United States, Japan, and China. Germans online made up the largest group, nearly 20 percent, of all EU population online, more than the United Kingdom and France. At 13.5 percent of all in the larger group known as Europe, Germany has more people online than Russia or the United Kingdom, according to June 2011 Internet World Stats. That all equates to a lot of online opportunity for marketers.

Keep in mind that Germany is not a single culture as such. There are key differences between regions, although these may play a minimal role if your specific campaign is a general topic, such as business software or laptop computers. Germany is a diverse federation of 16 states—each with its own government and "Ministerpräsident" ("prime minister" in English). Each state has its own constitution, which is in line with the Basic Constitutional Law of the Federal Republic of Germany. State "Land" governments are further divided into administrative districts. Cultural differences abound among the land districts, including language, use of words, and use of different words to say the same thing.

German is spoken by 95 percent of the country's inhabitants, and in other countries nearby. In Austria, 89 percent of the people speak German. In Switzerland, 65 percent speak German. German is also spoken by the majority of the populations of Luxembourg and Liechtenstein. Last, German is spoken in East Belgium, South Tyrol in Italy, and the Alsace in France. German ranks sixth among the languages used most online, and is spoken by 3.6 percent of the world online, more than Arabic, French, Russian, or Korean—a fact that underscores the size of the German market online.

Profile of Germany Online

The German online market is well developed, with Germans leading Europe in many categories in 2010, including ecommerce and video watching. Their online audience is distributed fairly evenly across all age groups and between men and women. Time spent online varied between a low of 18 hours per week for the 55-plus users to a high of 25 hours for the youngest age group. Top categories online were local search and entertainment (50 percent in October 2010), information on computers and electronics (45 percent), and travel (33 percent).

In terms of culture, Germans are very thorough and careful, and this is equally so when they go online. According to a study done by Forrester, Germans are very cautious on websites. They pay particular attention to Internet privacy policies and local payment methods, for which they prefer direct debit rather than incurring debt by using credit cards online. Make sure that your "About Us" page reflects security and trust. The information there plays a major role in how Germans

"Germans value quality highly; you will have better results if you focus your content on the quality of your product or service, rather than how economical it is."

evaluate your site, according to research done by Nordic eMarketing and another study by Visual Revenue. Visual Revenue found that although merely 1 percent of ecommerce sites' total traffic, on average, visits the "About Us" page, 23 percent of the revenue, on average, was from customers who had visited the "About Us" page before they bought. When Nordic eMarketing did similar research, it found that German-speaking visitors were close to three times more likely to use the "About Us" page to weigh whether they wanted to do business on the site.

Germans value quality highly; you will have better results if you focus your content on the quality of your product or service, rather than how economical it is. Indeed, Germans often equate cheap with shoddy, so be careful pitching low prices. Germans also prefer to have as much information as possible, to bolster confidence in the quality of your products or services. To make a positive impression, you need to make sure that your content is of the highest quality. Don't publish translations without doubly scrutinizing them. Get a native to translate and then get another native with knowledge of search engine optimization (SEO) to review the translation.

Along with the rest of the European Union (EU), Germany has adopted stricter Internet-related laws than the United States. In particular, the E-Commerce Directive (2000/31/EC) imposes specific requirements on direct marketing. You would be well advised to look into these laws and seek professional opinions from someone familiar with the laws protecting privacy, for example. Indeed, although search is widely used, German authorities have tried to stop Google from collecting information through Google Analytics and, for that matter, any analytics tools from collecting data, period. According to the German online news site Zeit, German authorities stated in 2009 that what Google was doing to collect data about its users was illegal, mainly because of privacy issues. The issued continued to be negotiated and, in 2011, resulted in Google recommending website owners disclose use of Google Analytics, which we explain in more detail later in this chapter.

Effective marketing in Germany requires establishing trust most of all, and more so than in other countries. Make your site look as German as possible, with a German domain and content in the German language, even though many Germans— especially those online—are very capable of doing business in English. They will trust your site more if you return the favor by doing business in German and also underscore your reliability by being transparent about contact information. Provide local addresses and telephone numbers if possible.

In 2010, Germans conducted 4 billion searches per month, of which 37 percent were one-word queries; 32 percent, two words; and 25 percent, three to four words long. This is quite a bit lower than U.S. averages for long-tail search phrases, so your keyword research for Germany will need to be enlarged to include many variations of long-tail queries compounded into single words.

Search is the dominant category online; according to the Internet Advertising Bureau (IAB), around 47 percent of the total ad spend online went to search. Despite the overall decline of 9.3 percent in the German advertising market during the world economic crisis of 2008–2009, online ad spend increased by 5.2 percent, according to the IAB, and rose again in 2010 as the German economy got back on track. Germany's total media spending in 2011 will hit a new high, according to PricewaterhouseCoopers, achieving between $22.6 billion and $26.3 billion, according to eMarketer.

According to the Internet Advertising Bureau Europe, in 2011 Google held the biggest online advertising reach, reaching 90.8 percent of Germans through its sites and partners. Microsoft was next with 64.6 percent, and Facebook around 55 percent. Locally, there was ProSieben/Sat1 sites with 47.8 percent reach and Deutsche Telekom with 47.1 percent.

Search Media in Germany

As you can see in Table 7.1, Google holds 94 percent of the German market, according to Webtrekk. By way of competitors, only Bing and local site T-online can claim more than 1 percent of the market.

Table 7.1   Search Engine Market Share: Germany

Search Engine	Percentage of the Search Market
Google.de	93.9%
Bing.de	1.7%
T-online.de	1.3%
Yahoo.de	0.9%
Others	2.3%

Source: Webtrekk Stand: March 2011

The other major players count for 1 percent or less. Moreover, both T-online and Web.de are powered by Google, giving the global search giant a total market share close to 96 percent. For better or worse, this means Google should have your undivided focus when targeting Germany.

Most Common Mistakes

English-speaking businesses tend to "force" English into their German campaigns by using simple translations and overlooking in-country vernacular when they target non-English markets. This can lead to seriously missed opportunities. For example, Germans more often use "PC" or "Computer" instead of their own term "Rechner," which can be a PC or a mainframe. If you look at the Google Keyword Tool, the word "Rechner" has 7.5 million searches per month, the term "Computer" has 9.1 million searches per month, and the term "PC" has 11.1 million searches.

Another example of a missed opportunity is the search phrase "mobile telephone" versus "mobile." The direct translation of "mobile telephone" is "Mobiltelefon," and Google returns a lot of results for this word (see Figure 7.1). However, in reality, the most commonly used word in Germany is "Handy"—a term not to be confused with its English meaning "convenient," though you could say that describes a mobile phone precisely. Figure 7.2 shows that even if you use Google's Translator tool, you won't learn that "Handy" is the most commonly used word to describe a mobile telephone.

Figure 7.1   *Google results for "Mobiltelefone" search.*

Figure 7.2   *If you ask Google to translate "mobile telephone" to German, you get "Mobiltelefon," not "Handy," even though more people search for the word "Handy."*

When launching an advertising campaign in Germany using the German language, you would do well to seek help from an agency that understands the language and culture. This should maximize the impact of your campaign and make it easier for you to manage it yourself within your organization. There are keyword research tools that can be used also for the German market; these are tools such as SEMRush and KeywordSpy, both tools that give good insights. We cannot recommend using Google Translate for languages like German that have fairly complex grammar. It is all right for navigating foreign language sites but should never be the tool that shapes your final results. The first problem any automated translation has with German is the way words are defined by compounding them with descriptive phrases, making longer words that auto translators are unable to parse to determine meaning. The other problem is more general, concerning local idiom.

Take a look at this example of a headline taken from *USA Today:*

> "Kansas City stunned San Diego in overtime, moving the Chiefs into an improbable tie atop the AFC West with the Chargers and Raiders."

Google Translate returns this:

> "Kansas City betäubt San Diego in Überstunden, zog die Chiefs in einer unwahrscheinlichen tie Spitze der AFC West mit den Chargers und Raiders."

"Betäubt" in German can mean "stunned," but is not translated correctly for this context. The word "Überstunden" means overtime, but only in the sense of working overtime and would not be used for sports. Finally, "tie" is an English word and is not used in German. The bottom line is that the German sentence is not correct in word usage or grammar.

Pay-Per-Click

Because Google has the largest reach of any search engine in Germany by far, managing your pay-per-click campaign is fairly straightforward following the guideline for AdWords we outlined in Chapter 2, "Common Territory: Search Marketing Without Borders." It really is as simple as this: Google tools in Germany work the same as in other countries where Google is dominant. The real difference to pay attention to is understanding how the market is different, as described in the profile earlier in this chapter.

Also, it's important for you to understand that the competition in paid search is fierce in Germany, because there are many experienced and talented search marketers already there. Do not underestimate your search engine marketing competition in this market.

When you do keyword research for Germany, keep two factors in mind: German word composition is different from English; for example, "car insurance" (two words) is "Autoversicherung" (one longer word) and "women's boots" are "Damenstiefel," but people in Germany also use "Stiefel Damen" or "Damen Stiefel." This means your keywords may be very different in length and in some cases may be one word, not two, and in some cases also hyphenated. Other difficulties are that this may increase the value of long-tail keywords and make it more difficult to work within the limits of Google AdWords text lines and title tags for your organic listings.

Consider cell phones again. Figure 7.3 shows the dominance of the term "Handy" over "Mobiltelephon."

Keyword	Competition	Global Monthly Searches	Local Monthly Searches	Local Search Trends
handy		6,120,000	5,000,000	
mobiltelefon		246,000	74,000	
mobile phone		7,480,000	60,500	
mobile phone manager		9,900	2,400	
mobile phone i98		390	320	
outdoor mobile phone		480	46	
handy ohne vertrag		301,000	246,000	
samsung handy		301,000	246,000	

Figure 7.3   *The Google Keyword Tool shows clearly that the word "Handy" draws many more local searches (meaning within Germany) than do the direct translation and also the English.*

Cultural differences unique to Germans need to be taken seriously when it comes to online marketing, certainly in respect to their language. They are exacting and not easy to please, especially in ecommerce.

> "They [Germans] are exacting and not easy to please, especially in ecommerce."

Fundamental errors in PPC ads or description tags and page titles are likely to throw them off. You would also do well to provide clear, prominent, and specifically reassuring privacy standards.

Organic Search

As with PPC, Google is the only significant player in Germany. If you know how to optimize for Google U.S., you know how to optimize for Google.de (Google Germany). But knowing how to do something and actually doing it are two separate things. To be successful, you need skilled translators and search engine optimizers who know and understand Germany and the use of the German language. Germany has many highly sophisticated and experienced search marketers, so as in the United Kingdom, you need to use all the tactics in your arsenal to succeed. Use every tactic available to you: optimize your images and video for local search results and press releases for new results.

For local search results in Google, you can rely on the help of Google Webmaster Tools to geo-locate your site or a geo-targeted part of it. However, link building and search engine optimizing need to go hand in hand. Start by letting Google know what sections of the site target Germany and Google's German results. Then seek to get links from .de sites with content in German. That and good unique content in German on your own site should get you a long way when it comes to organic visibility in Germany. One tip for linking in Germany is to be prepared to pay for links you exchange with other webmasters. Most German website owners value their sites and expect to see tangible reward for that value.

Analytics

As mentioned previously, Zeit Online reported in 2009 that German federal and state government officials are convinced that Google Analytics is against the law in Germany and that it should be forbidden. The case they built is around German laws forbidding the exporting of data.

Even so, Google is not likely to be thrown out of the country; thus, Google Analytics (GA) remains the main player for analytics. You might also want to look at Yahoo! Analytics, also free, which comes with an option to integrate with Google PPC. A local tool worth mentioning is WebTrekk (see Figure 7.4).

Figure 7.4 *The WebTrekk English home page.*

Most of the other big-name tools such as Omniture, Unica, and Webtrends also work well in Germany. Using analytics when focusing on the German market is not that different from focusing on your own, but is likely to have at least one difference—that is, how much German users value security and privacy. It is recommended that you set yourself Key Performance Indicators (KPIs) based on that knowledge, especially if you are running an ecommerce site. This includes using some kind of a revenue participation metric for content optimization insight, such as looking at how the "About Us" page touches revenue and where potential users are dropping off in the buying stages.

In early 2011, a German government report surfaced about how Google records IP addresses to collect user data for analytics. This report indicated that fines might be levied on companies that use Google Analytics to collect data on German users. Late in the fall of 2011, Google suggested on its German site that website owners clearly state in their privacy policy that they were using Google Analytics and offer users the possibility of disabling it. Google Germany also recommended enabling an IP mask function to instruct Google Analytics not to save the full IP addresses of individual visitors. It would be a good idea to follow up on this as things advance to see whether you need to continue following these recommendations.

Public Relations

Online public relations in Germany is not as evolved as in the United States, but there are loads of options that can be really helpful for media relations and search marketing via press releases. There are several good vendors that should be able to help you in both cases. Marketwire works well for direct-to-media distribution, but for search visibility, it is not our favorite. In Germany, we prefer channels such as OpenPr.de, Presseanzeiger.de, prcenter.de, and firmenpresse.de. There are also the eNewsPR and NewsCertain networks.

To maximize the effectiveness of your online press releases, write all the copy in German and send it through .de channels or at least channels focusing on Europe. You might want to look at channels like OpenPR.de that normally gets good pick-up both on Google Web and Google News. We highly recommend you have a native speaker translate your copy and then also have it read over by a second reader to make sure that obvious words and phrases are not left out.

Search Marketing Tips for Germany

- Be as German as possible on your website to win the trust of German users. Use the German top-level domain and write your content in German. Beef up your "About Us" and privacy pages.

- Allow for longer key phrases in German for your tags and text ads, and plan to use many more one-word long-tail variations than you would in English.

- Unleash all your top tactics for the German search market because your competition there is expertly skilled at SEO and PPC.

- Focus on the quality of your products rather than low prices to impress German online shoppers.

- Budget funds to pay for reciprocal links exchanges with German webmasters. However, don't confuse this practice with mass buying of links from large networks.

8

South Korea

South Korea is a top-10 trader in world markets and the home of household brands such as Samsung, LG, and Hyundai. The South Korean economy in 2011 was the third largest in Asia and the thirteenth largest in the world. By 2012, a majority of Korean Internet users will have access to 1 Gbps services, which is 10 times faster than they had in 2010.

South Korea is officially known as the Republic of Korea. It was an independent kingdom under Chinese control for most of the past millennium. However, after World War II, Korea split in two, with the Republic in the southern half and a communist government in the North. Since then, South Korea has quickly achieved robust economic growth per capita. In 2011, per capita economic growth was roughly 14 times larger than that of North Korea.

Profile of South Korea Online

According to a June 2010 International Telecommunications Union (ITU) report, South Korea has some 48.6 million Internet users, which represents 81.1 percent of the population. This makes South Korea the eleventh largest Internet population in the world. The Korean language ranks tenth among languages used on the Web. Nearly equal numbers of men and women are online, and virtually 100 percent of all Koreans under the age of 30 are online, including students, professionals, managers, and office workers. It seems only housewives and production workers go online less often.

All of this makes the country worth noticing, with a fast-growing market in which Internet usage is widespread and widely mobile. But if ever there were a country for which you must have local help, South Korea is it. For one thing, the search media in South Korea favor Korean content and offer little help in English for international advertisers. Moreover, although South Koreans have integrated the Web into their daily lives in many ways, their expectations of what their searching should do for them is quite a bit more complex than simply producing a choice of links to click through. They appear to want their searches to solve their problems for them. (It has been interesting to observe Western giants Google and Bing moving toward the same practice by introducing universal, blended, or integrated search results worldwide.)

A big advantage for South Korea is having the fastest Internet connections in the world, averaging 14.6 Mbps in 2011, and the most DSL connections. ADSL is standard, and VDSL (very high bit rate digital subscriber lines, up to 52 Mbps downstream and 16 Mbps upstream) is gaining momentum. More than 90 percent of homes there have high-speed Internet connections. The Korean government is committed to upgrading the network to allow for convergence of Internet, television, and telecommunications, and it is behind the plans to bump the connection of every household in South Korea to 1 Gbps by 2012.

In South Korea, Internet subscriptions are among the cheapest in the world. Most apartments and houses can get a 100 Mbps Internet connection for KRW33000 (about $30 US) per month.

Besides widespread and inexpensive connectivity, another reason for this high activity in a relatively small population may be the Korean passion for online games, which for some could be called obsessive. The *Digital Economic Daily* (dt. co.kr) estimated two million web visitors in South Korea could be described as addicts because they spend most of their nonwork time online. That's close to 8.5 percent of all the Internet users in the country.

More than 75 percent of Koreans have mobile phones, and the country has the fastest-growing mobile penetration rate in the Asia-Pacific region. South Koreans are also widely adopting smartphones as their way of connecting online; the number of smartphones was expected to reach 20 million in 2011. According to Google's AdMob, mobile traffic from South Korea grew faster than any other country in Asia in 2010, with 97 percent of it coming from smartphones in December 2010, a rise of 75 percent from the year before. A contributing factor was the launch of Google's Android mobile operating system to power LG and Samsung devices, causing a surge of from 3 percent to 60 percent of Korean mobile subscribers in the 10 months leading up to January 2011.

Groupon, Twitter, and Facebook have taken advantage of the mobile opportunity in South Korea, all launching Korean-language sites in 2010.

> "South Koreans are mighty bloggers... nearly 40 percent of web users there have written their own blogs, second only to the Chinese."

In its annual survey, ad agency Cheil Worldwide observed 2010 was a good year for media in South Korea because it produced increased spending across all media. Traditional print and broadcast gained the least, with ad spending on newspapers and radio spending trailing at below-2008 levels.

South Korean banking is a further indicator of the extent to which South Koreans have integrated their lives online. The *eCommerce Journal* noted in April 2010 that online and mobile services were offered by every bank, and major credit card and wireless companies were developing an array of virtual currencies. Indeed, by 2010, e payments by smartphones were in wide use, in addition to the more conventional credit cards.

South Koreans are mighty bloggers. As you can see in Figure 8.1, nearly 40 percent of web users there have written their own blogs, second only to the Chinese. Some of the most popular are produced on platforms provided by Naver, Daum, and Yahoo! Korea, as well as Egloos, Blogin, Tistory, and Textcube.

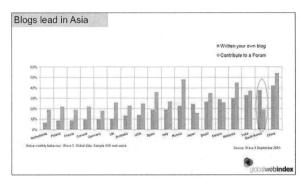

Figure 8.1 *South Koreans are second only to the Chinese in their love for writing their own blogs. Source: GlobalWebIndex*

Search Media in South Korea

As you can see in Table 8.1, South Korea's busy online market is one of a handful of markets on the planet in which Google has a smaller market share.

Table 8.1 Search Engine Market Share—South Korea

Search Engine	Percentage of the Search Market
Naver.com	55.4%
Google.co.kr	35.2%
Daum.net	4.8%
Yahoo.com.kr	2.8%
Others	1.7%

Source: StatCounter: June 2011

Local search engine Naver led with a 62 percent share in 2010, according to KoreanClick (see Figure 8.2). Daum was number two at 21 percent in 2010, having built a loyal following by providing free email. In third place at 10 percent was newcomer Nate, launched in 2009 by the wildly popular Korean social network Cyworld. Together, these South Korean search engines hold more than 90 percent of the market, and Google and Yahoo! Korea have less than 10 percent...combined. That said, Yahoo! Korea provides limited paid search results for Naver and Nate, and Google does so for Daum.

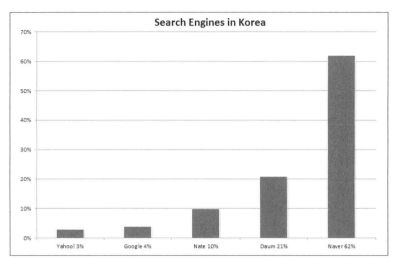

Figure 8.2 *Local search engine Naver had a commanding share of the search market in 2010, whereas Google was barely a player at all. Source: SearchEngineWatch, May 2010*

Results pages on Popular South Korean search engine Naver and Daum look like portals or intranets. Instead of the organic links on the left and sponsored links on the top and along the right side that are familiar to Westerners, these sites aggregate a lot of different kinds of content on their pages (see Figure 8.3). They mix paid content with blogs, news and academic articles, real-time results, shopping comparisons, and a great deal of user-generated content (UGC). South Korean searchers reportedly trust user-generated content more than they trust links to sites they find while searching.

Figure 8.3 *Naver is the most popular search engine in South Korea.*

Naver and Daum search engine results pages (SERPs) are too long to reproduce entirely here, but if you want to see just how extensive they are, go to Naver.com or Daum.net and search on a brand such as LG or Samsung or Hyundai (see Figure 8.4). If you use the Google Chrome browser with Google Translate installed, you are able to see many, many links on the page as you scroll. Lightyears away from the Western conventional 10 blue links, one such search on Daum produced 37 links, many of them paid; 10 videos and as many images; one box for real-time results; and a continuously updated box of most popular searches.

Figure 8.4   *South Korea search engine Daum's results page, above the fold. Most of these results are paid.*

You might say this is universal search on steroids. Still, it tells us a lot about the amount and type of information Korean searchers expect to find. Another search for the LG Xnote laptop turned up 19 paid links before any other results, going well below the fold (see Figure 8.5).

Figure 8.5   *On the Naver search results page, note all the top listings are paid ads.*

Often organic results are way down the page, well below the fold, leaving the top spots to as many as 15 or 20 paid links. This is how South Korean web visitors expect to see content, and it is what they find useful. They are not dismayed by the number of paid links. You could say the separation of editorial and advertising so central to Western publishing simply is not a factor in South Korea. In fact, both Naver and Daum appear to favor pushing traffic to other properties in their networks or paid listings, and this is what their searchers expect.

As for social networks, South Korea leads the Asia-Pacific region in social media use by far, with 30 percent of Koreans online reporting they belong to some kind of a social media network, and 60 percent of twentysomethings reporting a purchase of products or services using social media, according to the Korea Chamber of Commerce and Industry. Further, according to the Samsung Economics Research Institute study in March 2011, 67 percent of Korean CEOs believe social networking will revolutionize corporate communication, and such channels were the most popular for communicating with employees and customers. Among South Koreans online, 40 percent say they use corporate blogs and 20 percent share videos.

Top South Korean social network Cyworld had more than 25 million members in 2010. Facebook was far behind with just under 4 million. South Korea's second largest search engine, Daum partnered with Twitter in 2011 to allow Koreans to log on and micro-blog from inside the portal. Accordingly, South Koreans use Twitter at a rate twice the global average, and Korean is the seventh language Twitter supports.

Though Google's YouTube is the most popular video sharing site in South Korea, there are others, including Naver Video, which is the biggest native channel used by South Koreans.

Table 8.2 shows some of South Korea's most popular social networks.

Table 8.2   Top South Korean Social Networking Sites

Social Network	Owner	Uses
Cyworld	Nate	Personal home page
Facebook	Facebook, Inc.	Place for friends to connect
Twitter	Twitter, Inc.	Microblogging
me2DAY	Naver	Microblogging
Nate Connect	Nate	Place for SMS friends to connect
Yozm	Daum	Connected game play

Social Network	Owner	Uses
sfoon	Nurien	One screen for Twitter, me2DAY, Flickr, YouTube
itgling	Mediare	Socializing by web use
Daum Agora	Daum	Email, messaging, forums, shopping, and news
DC Inside	Kim Yusik	Forum
NateOn	Nate	Instant messaging
KakaoTalk	KAKAO	iPhones and Android messages
YouTube	Google	Video sharing
Naver Video	Naver	Video sharing

Most Common Mistakes

The most serious mistake marketers make when targeting South Korea is to use conventional Western search marketing strategies for optimization and pay-per-click. Even website pages with relevant content and links are as few as a mere handful on Naver results pages, tucked in among 40 or 50 paid listings and links to user-generated content. Paid visibility is not so easy to achieve either, because access for businesses located outside South Korea is limited to one or two listings on a results page. A much more productive strategy requires leveraging all opportunities to viralize content.

Another mistake is to focus on Google, a relatively small player in South Korea. Although you can geo-target this market from inside your AdWords account, keep in mind Google and Yahoo! *together* hold less than one-tenth of the market while Naver, Daum, and Nate claim the rest.

A third likely mistake is to consider South Korea to be similar to China or Japan. South Korea is a unique and lively Internet market with its own preferences and rules of play.

"The most serious mistake marketers make when targeting South Korea is to use conventional Western search marketing strategies for optimization and pay-per-click."

Pay-Per-Click

The only really effective way to penetrate pay-per-click (PPC) advertising in South Korea is via Yahoo! Korea's Overture because it partners with both Naver and Nate and also shows ads on Yahoo! Korea, Paran, MSN, HanaFos, and DreamWiz. Even at that, opportunities for foreign sites to advertise on Naver and Daum are limited to one or two listings from Yahoo! Korea, among as many as 50 on a typical results page. To place more PPC ads, your business must have a location in South Korea.

Even using Yahoo! Korea, you need someone who speaks Korean, as Figure 8.6, translated by Google, shows.

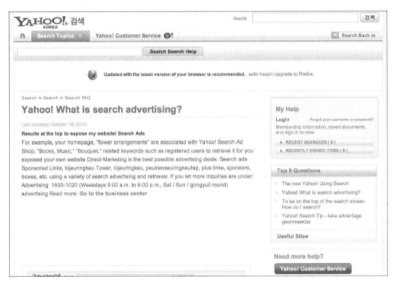

Figure 8.6   *Probably the most useful thing on this translation of the Yahoo! Korea Search Advertising information page is the Customer Service button.*

Although Google AdWords' share in Korea is very small, Google provides access to Daum, Empas, and Enur through its display network, which might make AdWords useful to you. Naver's own PPC service is called Click Choice. Advertisements bought through Click Choice show only on Naver. Similar to Naver, Daum has its own services, called Clix, whose ads are shown only on their results pages, followed by Google's sponsored links.

Advertisers on Naver can buy several listings on a single results page. Paid results run straight down the main section of the page with all the other links, not at the side as on Google and Bing. Naver has several levels of PPC: Sponsored links, Power links, Plus links, and business links, and offers fixed-rate pricing for text ads as well as pay-per-click. You will also find Naver Kin, similar to Yahoo! Answers, and directories from Naver's own database.

If you want to market through Naver's Power links, see http://searchad.naver.com/. This site is your best shot of getting help although you need to read and understand Korean to manage your campaign (see Figure 8.7). You will see that Naver's page for marketers does not provide much help for those who do not read Korean. Google Translate doesn't help decipher the pages much, possibly because of the content embedded as images. You will definitely be better off with assistance from a native speaker.

Figure 8.7   *The PPC page on Naver is not much help if you don't speak Korean.*

Organic Search

Although all the largest search engines in South Korea display results from sites written and hosted outside Korea, Naver rankings are heavily influenced by local language and links from Korean sites, and hosting in Korea can also help. You are better off translating your site to Korean and using a Korean top-level domain, such as co.kr or or.kr.

Because Naver and Daum search results pages have so many links—so few of which are directly from websites—you need to consider a very different strategy, with a much greater engagement in social media, images, news articles and blogs, and other user-generated content. Koreans value and trust UGC highly. If you want

"If you want any visibility in front of Korean searchers, you better have a process for encouraging posts and Tweets."

any visibility in front of Korean searchers, you better have a process for encouraging posts and Tweets. Although this kind of holistic approach to search marketing would be a best practice anywhere, the need for it is much more pronounced in South Korea because of the structure of search results pages there.

Analytics

Because of Google's small market share, Google Analytics results are not likely to give you the accurate figures you might be accustomed to seeing in the United States or other countries where Google is popular and data from it can be reliably compared across categories and markets. A local analytics vendor would be a better bet for a complete picture of your performance there.

In South Korea, the three largest local vendors are BizSpring.co.kr, Amazingsoft.com, and Nethru.co.uk. All three are more popular in South Korea than Google Analytics and although Webtrends has an office in South Korea, it is smaller compared to the three local players. You are best off using one of the local companies and getting help from someone who speaks Korean.

Online PR

Online press releases are an important tool to socialize your news in South Korea, which can then in turn become an effective way to bring it to the attention of searchers there via their user-generated content. Both PR Newswire and Business Wire translate and distribute press releases there. In addition, there are 600 public relations agencies in South Korea, reported by *PRWeek* in August 2010, including the major worldwide firms Edelman, Webber Shandwick, Ogilvy, and Prain.

Tips for Search Marketing In Korea

- Local search engines, especially Naver and Daum, are much more popular than Google and Yahoo!, but have up to 50 results on a single page, including only a handful of links directly to websites and only one or two links available to non-Korean advertisers.

- To place PPC listings, use Yahoo! Korea to get the one or two links shown on Naver and Daum.

- For organic visibility in Naver and Daum results, go for quantity of content on all channels, and use blogs, UGC, local and real-time, such as Twitter posts, for organic visibility.

- Use locally sourced analytics for a complete view of your performance in South Korea's search media.

9

India

In India, 100 million of its 1.2 billion people are online. It is the second most populous nation in the world and the third-largest Internet population. What makes India remarkable is that its share of the world's Internet use was the same as Japan in 2011, 4.7 percent, but only a fraction of Japan's online penetration. In India, merely 8.4 percent of all people are online, compared to 78 percent in Japan. Surely, the sheer size of this potential market in India is notable for search marketers.

Profile of India Online

Among the BRIC countries (Brazil, Russia, India, and China—a loosely grouped collection of countries whose economies are growing at a similarly rapid rate), India was second only to China in population online in 2011. According to comScore, India's average hours spent online were just over half the world average, which was about the same as China. At the same time, Russia and Brazil were at or over the world average, along with established EU markets such as Germany and France. In fact, in most of the Asia-Pacific region, average hours per user were much higher than India or China, but the size of their Internet populations skewed the regional average.

Even with less than 10 percent of the total population online, the market has been growing by more than 20 percent each year. According to Internet World Stats (IWS), the number of people online in India has increased 1,900 percent since 2000 and more than doubled between 2007 and 2010, and was projected to double again by 2015, according to 2011 research by investment bank Caris & Co. That India's Internet market growth met and exceeded expectations is evident in observing a February 2009 eMarketer projection that Internet use there would reach 73.3 million, just over 6 percent of the people. In fact, this number proved to be far less than the actual penetration reported by IWS updates when December 2010 rolled around. Even the Indian consumer watchdog group CUTS agreed that the online market there could become the largest in the world. CUTS has issued a statement calling for an investigation into Google's monopoly, calling it a public risk.

According to McKinsey & Co., 20 percent of urban citizens were online in 2010, but only 7 percent throughout the entire country. Many observers speculate that growth beyond urban centers was critical to India realizing its potential online, and would be accomplished only with more widely available broadband and perhaps adoption of local languages online. At the close of 2010, only 20 million Indians had broadband access, according to estatsindia.com. Shared access volume in India was almost as large as access from home and work in 2011. India's shared access volume is similar to that of Brazil, but very much unlike that of China, where shared access via Internet cafes and such places was much less than from work and home.

In 2010, comScore found that 76 percent of those online were 34 or younger, and only 30 percent were women. However, women are going online in increasing numbers, nearly doubling their presence between 2009 and 2010. In 2011, 65 percent of India's population of 1.2 billion was under 35. Of those online, there was a 2-to-1 men-to-women ratio (these stats vary greatly from the worldwide and regional distribution). Gartner Group surmised in 2011 that the large youth market online is a significant factor in the size and potential of India's market. Many of these young people were born into the age of computers and mobile telephones and take this technology for granted.

In 2010, there were 601 million mobile subscribers in India, which was 54 percent of the population. This number of mobile subscribers far exceeds the Internet and Mobile Association of India (IAMAI) prediction that mobile use would reach 460 million by the end of 2011, after 15 percent growth quarter by quarter since early 2009. More than 76 percent of the active mobile telephone users lived in major metropolitan areas then, as did 70 percent of the mobile Internet users. Although fewer than 1 percent of the population went online on a mobile device in 2011, many industry observers predicted rapid growth on the mobile platform. eMarketer anticipated mobile growing to 853 million subscriptions by 2014, while Gartner Group projected even more, reaching 993 million by 2014, from a pro-jected 660 million subscribers in 2010. India is the fastest-growing mobile market in the world and is the second-largest mobile phone market after China.

In 2010, 76 percent of those online in India used PCs to get there. McKinsey pro-jected that by 2015 the number of PC users would shrink to 21 percent and the proportion of mobile-only web access would grow to more than twice that. At the same time, said McKinsey, the proportion of users accessing the web on *both* PC and mobile would grow to be more than twice the number of those using PC alone. With the cost of handsets and plans going down, and availability of mobile networks up, such as a buildout of 3G networks during 2011 and 2012, McKinsey predicted that India's Web users would increase five times over by 2015, and three out of four would go online on a mobile device, a potential of 340 million mobile Web visitors.

In 2011, venture capitalists in India eagerly noted that if 51 million people online in the United Kingdom—a market of more than 10 times the online penetration in India—supported a $100 billion ecommerce market, the opportunity existed to grow a huge market in their home country. Indeed, the IAMAI suggested the ecommerce market in India would reach $10 billion by the end of 2011, even though penetration still would be shy of 10 percent. Flipkart, India's home grown competitor to Amazon.com, was said to have closed in on a $1 billion US valuation in 2011 after just four years of operation, fueled with $150 million from General Atlantic.

More than 70 percent of urban Indians spent about $1 per month in 2011 to get digital content offline, such as television, DVDs, and CDs. Often they received this content on their mobile phones via offline channels such as shops that specialize in streaming digital content to mobile. This market was estimated to have reached $4 billion by 2011. McKinsey projected in 2011 that total digital content consumption would double to $9.5 billion, creating a $20 billion market in related support. This support market would be twice the anticipated growth rate of digital consumption in China. Indeed, Indians' eagerness for digital content is illustrated in a popular story circulating about groups of rural mobile subscribers who don't have televi-sions using their mobile phones to listen to only the audio portion of shows and movies. It sounds a bit like the early days of radio, when families would gather around the wireless to hear broadcasts.

According to a 2011 comScore report, online entertainment proved a popular category in 2011, with 30 million Indians spending more than 9.1 billion minutes watching 1.7 billion online videos. Close behind were news and sports content. Seventy-two percent of the online population watched an average of five hours of video content, which is an average of 58 videos. Google's YouTube represented 44.5 percent of all videos viewed, dwarfing viewing on Facebook, Metacafe, Yahoo!, and DailyMotion. Network 18 and Rediff—both India-based sites—were among the top 10 sites viewed (see Figure 9.1). In 2011, both Google's YouTube and Yahoo! launched functionality to stream Bollywood movies online.

> "Indians' eagerness for digital content is illustrated in a popular story circulating about groups of rural mobile subscribers who don't have televisions using their mobile phones to listen to only the audio portion of shows and movies."

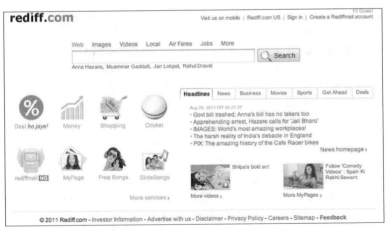

Figure 9.1   *Rediff was a popular online entertainment site in India in 2011.*

India's reach with its entertainment sites matched fellow BRIC country Russia and fell second only to Brazil. Music, movies, news, and humor were as popular or more popular in India than they are in any other country worldwide. However,

Indians spent less time on average online than those in other countries. Time online is expected to increase in India as broadband access increases.

Although worldwide growth was flat nearly everywhere else, India's online retail growth was 14 percent, with about half of all Indians visiting a retail site in March 2011. Computer software was the most popular category, with twice the reach of other Asia-Pacific countries and a third more than the worldwide average. Consumer electronics and computer hardware were next, each about level with the regional average but less than worldwide. Comparison shopping was the only other sector in India with more than 10 percent reach in 2011 (and half the worldwide average at that). According to Google data, 65 percent of Indians use the Internet to research cars and motorbikes before purchasing, with purchase inquiries making up 49 percent of all car-related queries in 2011. The auto vertical saw 100 percent growth in 2009 and 84 percent growth in 2010. Not surprisingly, giant online retailer Amazon.com announced plans to launch a site for India in early 2012.

One in 10 people online in India visited coupon sites. Snapdeal led the pack with 1.5 million users in July 2011, funded by $40 million in U.S. venture capital. DealsandYou and Mydala.com followed with 1 million users each. Snapdeal was just 17 months old in March 2011 and one of the single largest private investments into an Indian Internet company. U.S.-based global giant Groupon entered the market when it purchased India's SoSasta.

Travel sites were the most popular retail vertical in India among all the BRIC countries, growing 32 percent to 18.5 million visitors from April 2010 to April 2011. The category was more popular in India than the worldwide average and nearly twice the average for the Asia-Pacific region (APAC). Among travel sites, Indian Railways, Yatra Online, Makemytrip.com, and Cleartrip.com (all Indian companies) enjoyed greater reach and time spent on their sites than global brands Expedia and Travelocity. Other India-launched travel sites, Indiarailinfo.com and MustSeeIndia.com, drew traffic, underscoring opportunities in the travel sector.

Visits to business and finance sites surged to 45 percent in 2010. Fully half of India's online population looked to sites for online banking, trading, and financial news, which is an indication of growing purchasing power in an expanding middle class, as well as the country itself. In 2011, comScore described India as a vibrant global financial center.

Visits to education sites in India were above average, compared with actual declines in the region and worldwide. Forty-one percent of online Indians visited an education-related site in March 2011. This traffic was equal to visits in Brazil but far ahead of China and even the Russian federation. Similarly, websites about jobs and career development–related services draw 40 percent of the web population in India—higher than similar sites in the EU and North America and more than twice those of the other BRIC countries. Reach for these sites in India grew

8 percent year over year to March 2011, while it declined worldwide (down 8 percent) and for the region (down 14 percent).

Sports enthusiasm in India has been fueled by cricket. Forty percent of Indian users visited cricket sites in 2011, while cricket sites in general have grown by 38 percent. Cricket's popularity in India is much higher than in any other country worldwide. Sites devoted to the game of cricket made half the top 10 most popular sites in both reach and average minutes per user in March 2011, no doubt boosted by the Cricket World Cup taking place that month.

Personals such as dating sites formed another popular category, attracting more visits in India than nearly anywhere else, except for Russia. The year up to March 2011 saw a 7 percent increase, compared to 15 percent decline in the Asia-Pacific region and 8 percent decline worldwide.

Local Indian news sites garnered significant traffic from Indians living outside their home country, some more from outside India than in it. Worldwide, Indian ex-pats consistently contributed greatly to visits to India travel and information sites. For example, the *Times of India* (see Figure 9.2) had almost twice as many visits from outside India. Its home page, when accessed in the United States, displays ads for American cars and car rental agencies. Travel vendors may find a successful market among Indians who live elsewhere and want to keep in touch with and often visit home.

Figure 9.2 *The Times of India, accessed from the United States, displays American advertisements.*

Lastly, apart from the popularity of website verticals, the most popular online activity by far in India continued to be browser-based email. Despite that category declining almost everywhere else in 2011, 78 percent of people online in India in March of that year used email. This number tracked with the widespread use of shared Internet access in India and could be expected to decline there as broadband and mobile penetration increase, providing more readily available individual web access.

Search Media in India

Search engines and directories in India had 84.9 percent reach in 2010, according to comScore APAC, with 79.2 average searches per searcher. To put this in perspective, consider that reach in the Asia-Pacific region varied from a low of 67.3 percent in China to 92.5 percent in South Korea. India was third from the last, though grouped with the majority of Asia-Pacific countries with reach in the 82 to 89 percent range in 2010. In terms of average searches per searcher, only China and Vietnam spent less time searching, and many in the region were half again more. At just under 80 average searches per searcher, India was well below the worldwide average of 109.5. By 2011, search media use in India grew to 129 searches per searcher, an increase of 63 percent.

As you can see in Table 9.1, Google has by far the most searches and unique users in India, being used by close to 98 percent of those online there. Table 9.2 shows India's most popular search media.

Table 9.1   Search Engine Market Share—India

Search Engine	Percentage of the Search Market
Google.co.in	97.9%
Yahoo.com.in	1.1%
Bing.in	0.7%
Others	0.3%

Source: Statcounter Stand: June 2011

Table 9.2   India's Most Popular Search Media

Media	Searches (Millions)	Search Visits (Millions)	Visits per Searchers	Results Pages per Searcher
Total Internet	4,427	1066	25.7	129.2
Google Sites	4,010	999	24.4	116.5
Facebook	155	69	4.1	15.0
Ask Network	78	37	2.9	7.8
Yahoo! Sites	76	33	3.2	9.7

Source: comScore India August 2011

Research firm ViziSense put the Google share even higher, reporting that Google attracted 56.3 million visitors in India in March 2011, making it the country's most popular website.

Though Yahoo! is hardly much of a force by market share, it added India to the 16 other countries worldwide in which organic search results were powered by Bing in the Microsoft Yahoo Search Alliance.

More than 8 of 10 of all Internet users (84 percent) in India use social networking sites. These users spend 21 percent of all their time online at social media sites. Facebook overtook Google's Orkut as the most popular media in July 2010, even though Orkut grew 16 percent from the year before. A distant third was BharatStudent.com with 4.4 million members. As you can see in Table 9.3, Facebook use in India rose to more than 20 million by July 2011, up from 7.4 million year over year.

Table 9.3   Top Social Networking Sites in India (Searches in the Millions)

	July 2009	July 2010	% Change
Total Internet Audience	35,028	39,562	13%
Social Networking	23,255	33,158	43%
Facebook	7,472	20,873	179%
Orkut	17,069	19,871	16%
BharatStudent.com	4,292	4,432	3%
Yahoo! Pulse	N/A	3,507	N/A

	July 2009	July 2010	% Change
Twitter	984	3,341	239%
LinkedIn	N/A	3,267	N/A
Zedge.net	1,767	3,206	81%
Ibibo.com	1,562	2,960	89%
Yahoo! Buzz	542	1,807	233%
Shtyle.fm	407	1,550	281%

July 2009 vs. July 2010 Ages 15 and Up Home and Work
Source: comScore Media Matrix

Until 2011, the increase in social networking seemed consistent with widespread projections that India was poised to increase online activity rapidly. According to 2009 comScore data, India's share of all unique visitors to social networks worldwide was just 3 percent, compared to the U.S. share of 17 percent. In 2010, social networking grew to reach nearly 72 percent of Indians online and occupied 14.4 percent of their total online time. Although still a small percentage of world use, India's growth in unique visitors to social networks by 2010 was 43 percent, more than France, Japan, the United Kingdom, and the United States. The average Indian user spent less time online than the average user in the Philippines, Indonesia, or Malaysia, but more than South Korea, Vietnam, Japan, and China.

When Google+ was launched in June 2011, India became the second-largest audience in the world, rising to 2.8 million in three weeks, behind first-place U.S. with 5.3 million, and far ahead of third-place UK with 866,677. Although the United States accounted for 27 percent of the new social network use, India accounted for more than 19 percent worldwide, and more than the United Kingdom, Germany, Brazil, or Turkey, indicating more evidence of an Internet market poised for rapid adoption.

Although online advertising spending in 2010 was only 3.4 percent of India's total ad spending, this was a 20 percent increase from the year before. The IAMAI projected display ad spending would grow 28 percent by 2011 to more than $20 million US. The IAMAI also predicted that text ad and search spending would increase by $10 million US. Banking and finance looked to be the leading categories, and travel a close second. The fast-moving consumer goods (FMCG) category, always a big spender on television advertising, was projected to grow 30 percent from 2010 to 2011, with online display ads for the category expected to grow 50 percent.

Common Mistakes

There are two main issues to consider in search marketing in India. The first is that only slightly more than 8 percent of the population is online, so mass appeal is difficult to achieve. You will have better results targeting popular verticals in the market there.

The second is that although Hindi is spoken by 30 percent of the people, it is only one among 24 official languages each spoken by a million or more people native to India. What's more, the people who speak one of these languages very likely cannot understand those who speak the others. Despite this diversity—or perhaps because of it—English is the language used on nearly all the computers. Most searching is done in English, even on local search engines, and English is the preferred medium for browsing the Internet.[1]

> "...only slightly more than 8 percent of the population is online, so mass appeal is difficult to achieve. You will have better results targeting popular verticals in the market there."

Even the few regional websites that have a strong local presence use English commands. Some comments on local blogs suggest that this near-exclusive use of English is the reason Internet use is so low throughout the country. On the other hand, regional and local ads are the fastest-growing form of advertising online, and some writers point to a desperate need for local language content—ebanking and health information, for example. Nevertheless, online customers in India in 2011 were pretty much limited to those who speak English.

Pay-Per-Click

Because Google is by far the dominant search media, your AdWords account is your best place for PPC advertising focused on India. This is also true if you are targeting Indians living in other countries. In fact, because you will be using English to reach Indians, it is important to geo-target your campaigns, whether you are looking for responses from Indian customers in Mumbai, India or Manchester, United Kingdom. As we discussed in Chapter 2, "Common Territory: Search Marketing Without Borders," you will be better able to track, evaluate, and refine

---

1. *Source: comScore India*

your keywords by setting up separate campaigns—in this case, for the different locations, even though all your ads for Indians will be in English. Within your Google AdWords account you will be able to target the location where your desired audience is located. For example, if you are advertising travel deals to Indian expatriates who want to visit home in Delhi, do your homework to find out where most are living. Then set your AdWords campaigns to show ads in those locations.

Organic Search

Similarly, you are able to use all your Google best practices to optimize your sites for organic rankings in Google India. Because the language you will be using is English, be sure to indicate clearly your intention to provide content for the Indian market by using a country-specific top-level domain (.in) or by placing your content for India in a country-specific directory of your .com domain and by indicating India in your webmaster tools account. Don't neglect optimizing content for YouTube, both for Google universal results and also to capitalize on the Indian enthusiasm for videos.

Attracting inbound links from India-based sites, preferably with domains ending with .in., is as important here as anywhere else. However, in our experience, finding high-quality sites based in India to link to you has proved surprisingly more difficult than we anticipated. It's best to plan on extra time for researching to find good links.

Analytics

You will be able to use familiar Analytics tools in India, especially Google Web Analytics, because Google is the search engine used most. Google Analytics is your best choice among the free tools. Yahoo! Web Analytics would be another good choice. If you are looking for a paid tool, both Omniture, and Webtrends provide tracking for India. Whatever tool you use, you'll be tracking referrals and user behavior in English, because that is the language used online most there.

Online PR

English is the language predominantly used for new releases. When you write your press releases for online PR, be sure to use local references in your content—for example, "Suzuki 600 motorbike Mumbai"—to clearly indicate to Google your intended audience.

Tips for Search Marketing in India

- To reach the fewer than 1 in 10 people online in India, target popular verticals such as personals, sports (especially cricket), education, careers, banking and finance, and technology and software.
- Keep in mind the Indian online market is two-thirds young, urban men when selecting your categories and messaging.
- Reach Indians living outside their home country by advertising on India online news and entertainment media.
- Use video to reach Indians online.
- Remember that Google is the dominant search media, for both organic and PPC, and searching is done in English throughout India.
- Allow extra time for research to find high-quality link partners in India.
- Use social networks to reach Indians; Facebook and Orkut are favorites there.

10

Nordic Countries

Scandinavia consists of three countries: Denmark, Norway, and Sweden. Finland and Iceland are sometimes mentioned in that group, but they are more correctly placed in the Nordics or the Nordic countries, which include the Faroe Islands and Greenland, which are both governed by Denmark.

The Nordic countries are among the most connected in the world, with 85 to 92 percent of the population online (see Table 10.1). This connectivity underlines the massive opportunity these countries offer for search engine marketing (SEM). In this summary, we focus on Denmark, Finland, Norway, and Sweden—countries with a combined online population of around 22 million users.

Table 10.1   Online Reach in Scandinavia by Share of Population

	Population	Online	Online Reach	World Rank 2011
Denmark	5,529,888	4,750,500	85.9%	6th
Finland	5,259,250	4,480,900	85.2%	7th
Norway	4,691,849	4,431,100	94.4%	2nd
Sweden	9,088,728	8,397,900	92.4%	4th
Europe Average	816,426,346	476,278,755	58.3%	3rd region
World Average	6,930,055,154	2,110,765,810	30.5%	N/A

Source: Internet World Stats—Europe, updated June 30, 2011 (www.internetworldstats.com/stats4.htm#europe)

According to the Interactive Advertising Bureau's (IAB) AdEx 2010 report, "European Online Advertising Expenditure," the Nordic nations are fast-emerging markets. Though relatively small, the audience is quite web savvy. Even better, this audience has money to spend. Scandinavians achieve a high level of education, and English is widely spoken throughout the region. You might be able to do business well enough using just English, but keep in mind that many words—for example, "laptop"—can be said in several different ways in each country.

The languages spoken in Scandinavia are properly called the Scandinavian languages. Though closely related, with the exception of Finnish, all Scandinavian countries have unique and different individual languages, and each has its own culture and diversity. Further, most of the Nordic countries have several dialects within its language, and some also have several languages. For example, a version of Finnish is spoken in Northern Norway, where you can also find Nynorsk and Norsk (Bokmål). Finnish is also spoken in parts of Sweden, and Saami is spoken in northern Norway and Sweden.

Although all the countries have their own languages and cultures, they are indeed very similar. Your opportunities for successful search engine marketing in the region are good as long as you mind the differences and remember that despite some strong English influences, the local languages play a major role when it comes to marketing in these countries.

Profile of Denmark Online

According to the International Telecommunications Union (ITU), the leading United Nations agency for information and communication technology issues, 85.9 percent (4.75 million) of all Danes used the Internet in June 2011. Of those online, 43.4 percent had broadband subscriptions in 2010, which represents 37 percent of the entire population.

In May 2011, they numbered 3.6 million unique visitors, spending an average of 21.7 hours online viewing an average of 2,256 pages per visitor.[1] In December 2010, Google claimed the lion's share of reach, at 95.5 percent, and 3.3 million unique visitors. However, Facebook averaged more page views per visitor—1,174 compared to Google's 985. The average Facebook users also spent almost 50 percent more time online than did their Google counterparts. Moreover, Facebook had 2.7 million users in 2011, Twitter had 270,000 in 2010, and LinkedIn received 2 million visits per month from 510,000 users.

> "Danes are heavy mobile Internet users. In fact, there are more mobile phones than people in Scandinavian countries."

Although demographics were spread fairly evenly among men and women, as well as across all age groups, the 15–24-year-olds spent more than a third more time online than those older than 55. According to eMarketer, growth of this country's homogeneous population will level off after 2015. Although active online, Danes prefer their traditional media, especially the older population groups. Reach of radio, television, and print was 94 to 99 percent in 2010, greater than online, according to eMarketer. Most of the difference was among Danes age 55 and older, who made up two-fifths of newspaper readers. This can only mean less readership as an aging population dwindles.

One quarter, equivalent to $677 million US, of the money spent by advertisers in Denmark is spent online. Also, 39 percent of all online advertising expenditures are for search engine optimization (SEO), which is a higher proportion than in U.S. search marketing. ZenithOptimedia projected in 2010 that web spending would overtake newspapers in 2012 and become the largest ad spending channel.

Danes are heavy mobile Internet users. In fact, there are more mobile phones than people in Scandinavian countries. According to eMarketer, penetration of mobile phones is expected to rise to 150 percent by 2015. More than 97 percent of all Danes had 3G coverage in 2009. In 2010, half of all mobile phone sales were

---

1. Source: comScore MediaMetrix

smartphones, and more than half of that number was iPhones. This heavy reliance on smartphone technology points to a great opportunity for mobile marketing with either mobile browser–friendly sites or mobile apps.

Search Media in Denmark

As you can see in Table 10.2, Google had 97.5 percent of the market in Denmark as of mid-2011. A study published by business.dk in July 2009 gave Google 78 percent of the market, meaning that Google's share has increased dramatically in a short period of time. Bing and Yahoo! have little market share in Denmark.

Table 10.2 Search Engine Market Share—Denmark

Search Engine	Percentage of the Search Market
Google.dk	97.5%
Bing.dk	1.9%
Yahoo!	0.4%
Others	0.4%

Source: StatCounter: June 2011

Although Google held the biggest market share of search media in Denmark and Bing had a small amount of market share, there are several local players that you might want to consider for localized appeal, such as Jubii (see Figure 10.1) and Eniro, the latter based in Sweden and with sites also in Denmark, Finland, Norway, and Poland.

Google is the main point of entry to online Scandinavia and, for that matter, the whole Nordic region. There are local players in some of the Nordic countries, but they are all well behind Google, despite their niche strengths. Among them is the Scandinavian AdNetworks, formed by Eniro in mid 2011 to create the largest regional pay-per-click network outside the big engines. The sites in the ScanAd Network have their own systems for display ads, however many run their organic searches on customized Google results, adding to Google's share.

Scandinavia AdNetworks includes content sites such as MSN, Stateside, and SOL in Denmark, and more in Denmark, Sweden, and Norway, as well as search sites Gule Sidorna in Sweden, Kvasir and Proff in Norway, and other directory listings in Scandinavian countries.

Figure 10.1   *Danish search engine Jubii.dk—powered by Google.*

Profile of Finland Online

The Finnish online market has grown 20 percent since 2009, according to IAB. However, Finland's total online advertising as a percentage of total advertising is still at just 17 percent, meaning Finland has a long way to go before it can be compared with the United Kingdom or Germany, for example. In 2009–2010, the overall European search market was worth about $11 billion; of that amount, Finland accounted for only $101 million. The Finnish search market, however, grew about 17 percent year over year between 2009 and 2010, which is notable.

Despite its small size, Finland is remarkable because it was the first country to have a national wireless broadband network. Further, in July 2010, Finland became the first country to declare Internet access a legal right, with the government committing to a minimum of 1Mbps available to every household, increasing to 100Mbps by 2015.

> "Despite its small size, Finland is remarkable because it was the first country to have a national wireless broadband network."

Finland uses two main languages: Finnish and Swedish. Finnish is the most widely used (92 percent). The key to the Finns is Finnish, but when using that language as a part of your search marketing efforts, you will quickly find out that the character space provided by Google is not very useful because of the length of words translated into Finnish. Use keyword research to find alternatives and maneuver around the copy you are using for your English ads.

Finnish users numbered 3,349 million unique visitors in May 2011, according to comScore, and spent an average of 26 hours online, viewing 2,396 pages each.[2] In December 2010, Google Finland drew 3.2 million unique visitors, a 95.5 percent reach. These Finns viewed 985 pages on Google and spent on average more than 3 hours at the search giant. As in Denmark, Facebook drew more page views, and Finns on Facebook spent 50 percent more time on the social network. Facebook counted more than 2 million Finnish friends, close to 40 percent of the population. Video sharing is popular on Facebook, as are ancestry and genealogy. Mobile Internet

---

2. Source: comScore May 2011

connections in 2011 were increasing faster than fixed broadband, which suggested growing mobile Internet access.

Although there are more people 45 and older online, the 15–24-year-olds spent more than a third more time online than those older than 45, and one-fifth more time online than 25–44-year-olds.

Finnish advertisers spent around $242 million dollars online to reach the 85.3 percent of online Finns (about 4.5 million). Of the $242 million, 51 percent was spent on search engine advertising. Finland launched 4G services in 2010 to support high-speed video streaming and other advanced Internet technology.

Search Media in Finland

As you can see in Table 10.3, Google's market share in Finland is 98 percent. Unlike in its Scandinavian neighbors, Finland has no local contenders for a real share of the pie. Yahoo! has a Finnish version called Suomi (see Figure 10.2), but Bing in Finland is in English. These two, along with a tiny amount of Yandex use, make up the rest of the search engine media there.

Figure 10.2   *Yahoo! Suomi (Finland).*

Table 10.3   Search Engine Market Share—Finland

Search Engine	Percentage of the Search Market
Google	98.06
Bing	1.25
Yahoo!	0.53
Ask	0.02
Baidu	0.01
AOL	0.01
Other	0.12

Source: RealTimeStats.com: August 2011

Profile of Norway Online

Norway has close to 95 percent Internet penetration with some 4.4 million users. Like Sweden, Norway is one of the most connected countries in the world. More than 90 percent of households had Internet connections and 34.2 percent had broadband. Norway's broadband is the fastest in the world, reaching speeds of 46Mbps. By way of comparison, broadband in the United Kingdom reaches speeds of 26.6Mbps, and in the United States, only 14.4Mbps. Norway and Sweden were the first countries to offer 4G mobile broadband, making rich media and streaming video easy to access.

There were 3.2 million unique visitors online in Norway in May 2011, according to comScore, who spent an average of 26.5 hours online, viewing on average 2,156 pages. The biggest group online was people 55 and older, unlike many other regions. However, the most active group online was the 15–24-year-olds.

With plenty of wealth fueled by their oil industry, Norwegians had a GDP per capita of $52,238 in 2010, which is second highest in the world. Norwegians spend enthusiastically but wisely online. For example, budget carrier Ryanair was the top Norwegian search query in 2010.

Norway is known for being the expensive Scandinavian nation, and this is also true when it comes to online marketing agencies, whose fees are on par with the more expensive agencies in the United States. Even so, it is often worth the cost to get local guidance to maximize your effectiveness.

Advertisers in Norway have devoted 23.4 percent of their media spending to online advertising. Search engine advertising accounts for 24 percent of the overall online budget, which was estimated to be around $545 million in 2010.

Norway is one of the few countries in the world that does not sell its country domain extensions on the open market. To buy an .no domain, you need to be a Norwegian company with a Norwegian ID number. What also sets Norway aside from its neighbors is that Norwegian broadcasters have focused their efforts on building paid subscription services with most premium on-demand content available to subscribers only. Both practices indicate a culture of guarding assets and maximizing their value.

When it comes to reach, Google is truly the largest search engine in Norway, but when we look at overall online assets, Microsoft had more reach in mid-2011.[3] Microsoft had more unique visitors who spent more time online, but with far fewer page views (see Figure 10.3). Similarly, Facebook at 2.5 million, 54.43 percent of the population, held visitors for more time than Google did. Online Norwegians' interests trend toward music videos on YouTube, fitness, and Facebook mobile apps.

---

3. Source: comScore May 2011

Media	Total Unique Visitors (000)	% Reach
Microsoft Sites	3,040	95.2
Google Sites	2,897	90.7
Facebook	2,545	79.7
Schibsted (Anuntis-Infojobs-20minutos)	2,154	67.5
Eniro Sites	1,342	42.0
Wikimedia Foundation Sites	1,331	41.7
AS Avishuset Dagbladet	1,312	41.1
Telenor	1,299	40.7
Spotify	1,226	38.4
NRK Sites	1,036	32.4

Figure 10.3   *The true reach of the top 10 online properties in Oslo.*

Search Media in Norway

Google's grip in Norway at 93.16 percent share is similar to neighboring Scandinavian countries (see Table 10.4). Local player Kvasir (see Figure 10.4) has around 3 percent, Bing holds around 3 percent, and others barely register.

Figure 10.4   *The Norwegian search engine Kvasir.no powered by Google.*

Table 10.4   Search Engine Market Share—Norway

Search Engine	Percentage of the Search Market
Google.no	93.16%
Kvasir	3.3%
Bing	2.46%
Yahoo!	0.65%
AVG search	0.27%
Others	0.16%

Source: StatCounter: June 2011

Profile of Sweden Online

Sweden has one of the deepest Internet penetrations in the world, with more than 92 percent (nearly 8.4 million users) of its population online. Swedes accounted for 6.2 million unique visitors to the Web in May 2011, viewing 2,423 pages each, and spending an average of 25 hours that month online. More than 3.8 million Swedes (40 percent of the entire population) have broadband access.

Internet reach is pretty evenly spread across age groups from 15 to 54, but the 55+ crowd is greater by 25 percent.[4] However, all the younger age groups spend considerably more time online, with the youngest group spending 70 percent more time online than the oldest, accounting for the high interest in music videos.

Sweden is very well connected and boasts the third-highest online spending of all European countries, with 22.6 percent of all advertising money being spent online in 2009. That number was expected to reach 25 percent in 2011. Search as a marketing channel has around 27 percent of the overall online budget, estimated to be around $640 million in 2010.

Facebook had nearly 4.5 million Swedish friends in 2011, which is 49 percent of the people who live there. There were more than 6 million unique visitors to Facebook, making 6.4 billion page views in a month. This suggests Swedish Facebook visitors are following links on public profiles, further proof that Swedes pay attention to their fellow citizens. Be sure your marketing strategy includes reviews and recommendations. Similarly, Swedish social networking is not limited to Facebook. LinkedIn had 12 million pages views in 2011, and Twitter had 13 million.

Swedes also love video. YouTube draws 5.6 million unique visitors each month, who viewed an average of 970 pages for 28 minutes, mostly looking at online video, with a preference for rock, soul, R&B, and rap and hip-hop. By June 2011, the top two searches on Google for an entire year were "YouTube" and "Facebook," presumably navigational searches to find the networks. Successful online marketing in Sweden should indeed include both.

---

4. Source: comScore May 2011

Search Media in Sweden

StatCounter reported Google as generating more than 97 percent of referrals in November 2010 (see Table 10.5), while NetMarketshare tallied more than 94 percent of referrals for Google (see Figure 10.5) and gave Bing 2.28 percent and Yahoo! less than half a percent.

Table 10.5 Search Engine Market Share—Sweden

Search Engine	Percentage of the Search Market
Google.se	97.17%
Bing.se	1.96%
Yahoo.se	0.52%
AVG search	0.15%
AOL.se	0.08%
Others	0.11%

Source: StatCounter: June 2011

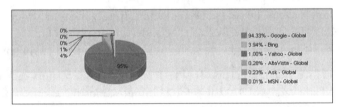

Figure 10.5 *NetMarketshare reports Google having a 94.33 percent of use in Sweden. Source: netmarketshare.com*

In Sweden, the scenario is a little better for the local players such as Eniro (see Figure 10.6) holding some ground. Eniro is part of the Scandinavian AdNetworks and the largest regional search engine, although it does not have a site in Finland.

Figure 10.6 *Swedish search engine Eniro.se.*

Common Mistakes

The most common mistake marketers make is to think that the Scandinavian market is all the same—that the similarity of the languages means all Scandinavians think the same. In reality, the languages are not the same, nor are the cultures.

Another common mistake is to assume that Scandinavians use English primarily. Though English is taught in most schools there from an early age, all the Scandinavian countries have their own individual languages, although Danish, Norwegian, and Swedish all have common linguistic bases. The odd one out is Finnish, which has closer ties to Hungarian and Turkish than any of the other Nordic languages.

> "Getting B2C lists in the Nordic region is close to impossible, and if do you get them, it is very likely that they are illegal..."

Another common mistake—something that most companies located outside the Nordic region do not realize—is that consumer and spam laws in all these countries are far stricter than in the United States. For example, you cannot send emails to people just because you have their addresses. You need to have their explicit permission to do so, especially in business-to-consumer (B2C) contact, although the rules are more relaxed in business-to-business (B2B) communication. Figure 10.7 shows results from one of the Yellow Pages directories. Although you can find information about people, the red box with the white X tells the searcher that he cannot contact the person without being in violation of consumer protection laws. Getting B2C lists in the Nordic region is close to impossible, and if do you get them, it is very likely that they are illegal and using them might get you into problems such as being blocked on spam lists.

The red X wards off unwanted contacts

Figure 10.7   *The boxes preceding the phone numbers in this directory mean contacting the person listed is in violation of consumer protection laws.*

Pay-Per-Click

Google AdWords is the biggest search advertising media and the most likely to be seen by your target audience. There also are some local networks that you might want to look at, such as Scandinavian AdNetworks.

Until recently, these local networks were closed to the outside world, but as we have seen in China with Baidu and in Russia with Yandex, the focus has increased toward international advertisers and providing English-language support. Scandinavian AdNetworks allows you to create an account and then use that account to manage your creative advertisements, advertisements' location, budget, and so on (see Figure 10.8).

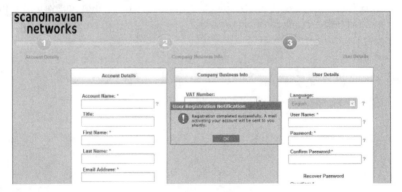

Figure 10.8   *Creating an account with Scandinavian AdNetworks is easy, and English is accepted as the user interface language for your account management.*

It is useful to know that when it comes to keyword research and PPC, Scandinavian AdNetworks has account managers whom you can easily call or contact; you can find their contact information on their contact pages. By going directly to your account managers with your questions, you are likely to obtain some bits of knowledge giving you the extra you need to be better than your competition. They don't have accounts like Google, so you need to contact them directly or go through a local agency that can help you get your ads on their sites. This approach works well because you get to talk to a person who can guide you in the right direction. This is in contrast to Google, where you need to figure things out yourself. You can use the knowledge you gain there to further your PPC efforts or vice versa.

If you do not want to go local, Google is your main contender.

The main problems likely to arise doing PPC in the Nordic region are poor translations and sloppy keyword research. For example, if you want to sell laptop computers in Denmark, the local word is "bærbar computer." In Norway, it is "bærbar datamaskin," and in Sweden (and the Swedish part of Finland), it is "bärbar dator" or "bärbar PC." "Laptop" is still used, but the local terminology accounts for close to half of all laptop searches, and if you look at the long tail, there are more searches using "bärbar"-related terms than "laptop" (see Figure 10.9).

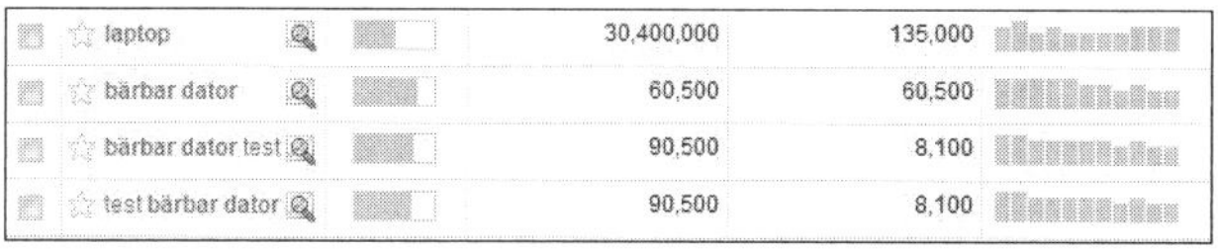

☆ laptop		30,400,000	135,000	
☆ bärbar dator		60,500	60,500	
☆ bärbar dator test		90,500	8,100	
☆ test bärbar dator		90,500	8,100	

Figure 10.9 *Using the Google Keyword tool yields the volume of search in Sweden.*

For PPC advertising, as mentioned previously, we have found that Finnish, known for its long words, is one of the most complex languages. Clearly, when you start a campaign based on an English strategy, you need to change that strategy to suit Finnish. The per-line character limits of 25, 35, 35 in Google AdWords can be very difficult to work with. We recommend that you create your Finnish ad copy from scratch with the help of a native speaker. To illustrate this, consider the word "laptop." In Finland, the translation would be "kannettava tietokone," changing a simple 6-letter word to 20 letters—including a space between the two words (see Figure 10.10).

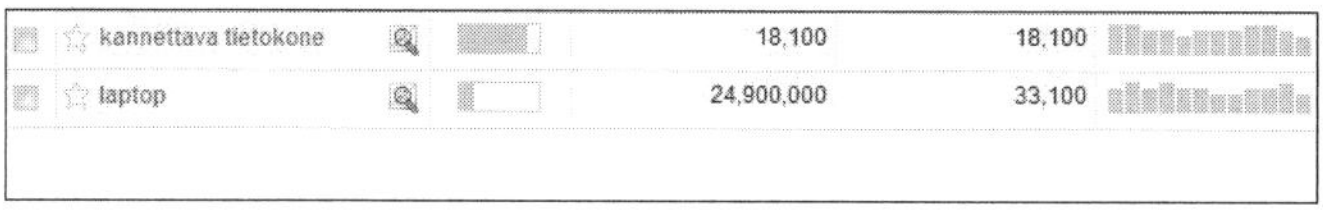

☆ kannettava tietokone		18,100	18,100	
☆ laptop		24,900,000	33,100	

Figure 10.10 *"Laptop" is more searched in Finland, but the local word, "kannettava tietokone," has a good volume.*

The other Nordic languages are easier to manage and adapt to from English. The reason is that many of the ads using the locally popular versions of words will likely draw more clicks and potential conversions.

Figure 10.11 shows two companies targeting an Icelandic audience with PPC. One ad is in English, and that might pass although, according to our experience, it is likely that using the native language (even if the landing page is in English) will be more effective. The other ad is in English with an Icelandic word squeezed in, thus creating an ad in two languages.

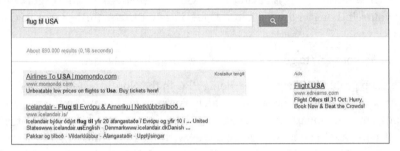

Figure 10.11   *An ad in English that targets an Icelandic audience is not as effective as one in Icelandic.*

Figure 10.12 shows a car rental search (bílaleigubíll) on Google.is, illustrating the same problem for all the other countries in this chapter. Here, not only are there spelling mistakes, but the letters used in some of the words are just plain wrong, making the accent wrong and making the ad, at best, a joke. Ads like these make the advertisers appear to have low esteem for these markets and are insulting to the people who see the ads.

Figure 10.12   *Ads for rental cars in Iceland make a joke of the language and perhaps also an insult.*

The question is this: If somebody in London searches for, say, a car rental using Finnish (something like "Autovuokraamo Lontoon") and gets a page saturated with car rental ads, is that person more likely to click on an ad in Finnish echoing the search term or on one in English?

Organic Search

Google holds the key to successful SEO in all the Nordic markets and, combined with the local players who use their results, is likely to give them access to more than 90 percent of the local market. The customary rules for good organic optimization we discussed in Chapter 2, "Common Territory: Search Marketing Without Borders," apply with all the search engines in this market.

Obtaining those all-important inbound links can be challenging and take more time and effort than in other regions because not one of the countries has a rich link exchange or link-building culture. An honest, transparent, and personal approach should take your linking efforts a long way. You can request links in English, although we recommend creating a translated version of your request email. You can then use Google Translate to get a rough idea of the responses you get by changing them back to English.

For content, let us repeat that although automatic translation tools are getting better, we do not recommend you use such tools as your only source when translating. Get a professional translator, and then if you want to be sure, get a second reader to review your content.

Press Releases

There are several options for online press release distribution focusing on the Scandinavian region. These are the channels that will help you with media and stakeholder communications. For media relations, Pressport.com supports all the languages in the region and has a vetted list of media you can select; however, it is not as effective for organic visibility (see Figure 10.13).

Figure 10.13   *Pressport is a Danish press release distribution service.*

For organic visibility, there are few native players: eNewsPR.com has some good services and so does NewsCertain.com. eNewsPR.com is based in Iceland, while NewsCertain.com is based in the United Kingdom. Both of these services allow you to publish releases in the targeted languages, in addition to English.

Another service worth mentioning for direct distribution to media is Marketwire, which has a good list of contacts you can send to. However, as of this writing, Marketwire does not support distribution in local languages for online visibility as well as it does in English.

Sites that might be useful when sending out releases in the Nordic languages are presport.dk (also in Sweden and Norway), News.Randburg.com (takes Finnish), and maybe Icenews.net (also takes Finnish) and eNewspr.dk, all sites that either accept press releases for free or have some minimal fee.

Analytics

For keyword targeting within the Nordic markets, the Google AdWords keyword tool is great, but there are other tools such as Keyword Spy that fit well with the Scandinavian market, especially Denmark, Norway, and Sweden. These tools give good insight into the markets and should help marketers get keyword ideas for both organic visibility and PPC.

Google also gives great insight into the market through its Search Trends tool. For onsite traffic and referral information, check out Google Analytics or Yahoo! Web Analytics. Both tools are free, and both are quite easy to access and set up.

In general, we have found Google Analytics and Yahoo! Analytics or other vendors such as Omniture or WebTrends are quite satisfactory for collecting data on Scandinavian web users. There are some local tools, such as the Finnish Snoobi shown in Figure 10.14, that we have little experience with, but tests indicate it is an existing high-end analytics tool.

Figure 10.14 *The Snoobi Analytics dashboard.*

Search Marketing Tips for Scandinavia

- Google is your main point of entry for Scandinavian countries for both SEO and PPC. Follow the procedures discussed in Chapter 2.

- Although Scandinavian languages are quite similar, be aware of differences in popular search keywords.

- Scandinavians are big social networkers and YouTube video consumers. Be sure to include them in your online marketing strategy.

- Similarly, they have a high adoption of broadband, especially mobile, so go ahead and use rich media and streaming video to reach them.

- Learn consumer regulations for each Scandinavian country, especially regarding privacy, so that your marketing efforts do not risk being blocked.

11

Netherlands

The Netherlands is one of the smaller markets in Europe when you look at it from a population standpoint only. However, with nearly 17 million people, it is still close in size to all of Scandinavia combined, and has a very lively Internet market. The Netherlands has a long history of international exploration and trade, and is home to multinational giants, such as Ahold and Philips. This global enthusiasm is expressed online as well. In 2010, nearly 89 percent—or 14 million people—of the Dutch nation was online. This means the Netherlands ranks seventh-highest in the world insofar as Internet penetration is concerned.

Profile of the Netherlands Online

The potential for marketing through search in the Netherlands is big. Not only is Dutch Web usage impressive, but according to comScore, the Netherlands leads Europe in online visit frequency. European Internet users age 15 years and older accessed the Internet on average 58.9 times in September 2010. The Netherlands ranked highest in Europe with 78.2 visits per visitor, nearly 20 visits per month higher than the European average, and surpassing such nations as the United Kingdom, France, and Spain.

Table 11.1 shows how Internet usage in the Netherlands compares to other countries.

Table 11.1   Top European Countries by Visits per Visitor

Country/Region	Average Visits per Visitor
Europe	58.9% (total Europe)
Netherlands	78.2%
United Kingdom	71.3%
France	68.4%
Spain	63.7%
Germany	61.0%
Poland	55.6%
Finland	54.6%
Turkey	53.7%
Russian Federation	52.3%
Sweden	49.8%

Source: *comScore Media Matrix, September 2010, Age 15+, Home and Work Locations*

In a study done in the second quarter 2010, the Consumer Commerce Barometer found that 61 percent of Dutch respondents turned first to the Internet when researching before buying a product or service. Further, 59 percent started their purchases with search engines. Technology, travel, and finance products were the most-often-purchased online. NewMedia TrendWatch reported that 55 percent of Dutch 12–74 years old bought online in 2010—a half million more than the year before. Seven in 10 said they were frequent online shoppers.

The most popular method for online payment is iDeal (see Figure 11.1). iDeal was set up by a consortium of Dutch banks and was preferred by 54 percent of Dutch customers in 2010. iDeal is trailed insofar as popularity is concerned by AcceptGiro, which is similar to writing a check. AcceptGiro is preferred by 22 percent. Using standard credit transfer was preferred by 8 percent. Credit cards and PayPal were nearly last at 5 percent each.

Figure 11.1 *You'll find the most popular Dutch payment method at ideal.nl, which provides information in English via the UK flag at the top right, where you will be able to navigate to instructions for applying to include iDeal on your ecommerce site.*

As you can see in Table 11.2, the Netherlands has more Twitter and LinkedIn users than anywhere else in the world, according to comScore data from March 2011. More than a quarter of all Dutch online users reported using LinkedIn and Twitter. More impressive still, 96 percent of all Dutch people online use social media sites.

"...Netherlands has more Twitter and LinkedIn users than anywhere else in the world..."

Table 11.2 Top 10 Countries in Internet Penetration for LinkedIn and Twitter by Reach (%)

LinkedIn	% Reach	Twitter	% Reach
Netherlands	26.1%	Netherlands	26.8%
Ireland	21.0%	Japan	26.6%
United States	17.6%	Brazil	23.7%
Canada	15.6%	Indonesia	22.0%
United Kingdom	14.9%	Venezuela	21.0%
Denmark	14.4%	Canada	18.0%
Australia	13.1%	Argentina	18.0%
New Zealand	12.9%	Turkey	16.6%
Belgium	12.6%	Philippines	16.1%
Singapore	12.0%	Singapore	16.0%

Source: comScore Media Matrix, March 2011, Age 15+, Home and Work Locations

Search Media in the Netherlands

As you can see in Table 11.3, Google has near total control of the market in the Netherlands. Among other search engines, only Bing has more than a one percent share of market.

Table 11.3 Search Engine Market Share—Netherlands

Search Engine	Percentage of the Search Market
Google.nl	97.8%
Bing.nl	1.3%
Ask.com.nl	0.3%
Yahoo.nl	0.3%
Other	0.4%

Source: StatCounter: June 2011

Although the Netherlands might not be the biggest market, the people do use search engines heavily. As you can see in Table 11.4, the largest, most-visited sites are search engines or social media sites.

Table 11.4   Most Visited Sites in the Netherlands

1	google.nl
2	google.com
3	youtube.com
4	facebook.com
5	live.com
6	hyves.nl
7	linkedin.com
8	twitter.com
9	nu.nl
10	wikipedia.org

There have been some changes over the past years. Local players such as Ilse (see Figure 11.2) used to have some market share but lost almost all of it to Google, as seems to be the trend throughout Western Europe.

Figure 11.2   *The Dutch search engine ilse.nl.*

According to the comScore Media Matrix, Google sites claimed 11.3 million unique visitors aged 15 or older in December 2010. Microsoft was second with its network and third was a local, social media site, Hyves, (see Figure 11.3).

Figure 11.3 *Hyves is one of the leading social platforms in the Netherlands, and as you can see, it's very "English" friendly. If used well, it's a good source of information and organic traffic.*

What is interesting is where Facebook stands in this. Facebook had 6.6 million unique visitors by March 2011, compared to Hyves's 7.6 million. Facebook grew in popularity by 76 percent in 12 months. Both social network sites offer marketers increased exposure to the Dutch online.

Another similar resource might be Marktplaats.nl, the Dutch eBay, which is a great source if you want to sell products in the Netherlands. Signing up is little more complicated than Hyves because the site is written in Dutch, but if you contact the site directly using the contact page information, you should get the help needed to start using the site. Note: The Dutch use the same word for "Contact" as is used in English.

Figure 11.4 *Marktplaats.nl, owned by eBay, is a great source if you want to sell products in the Netherlands.*

Most Common Mistakes

"Thinking of the Netherlands as being the same as Belgium or, even worse, Germany, is a common error."

Thinking of the Netherlands as being the same as Belgium or, even worse, Germany, is a common error. Another common pitfall is thinking only of Amsterdam. The Netherlands is a very Web-savvy country with several different districts.

As in most of the "smaller" nations in Europe, many Dutch people speak more than one language: 70 percent speak English, and 60 percent speak German. But that does not mean you can target the Dutch using English. Although internationally focused, they are very proud of their language and everything Dutch. Although you might get away with using English to target more cosmopolitan searchers, if your website is geared for mass Dutch appeal, it will gain more trust if it speaks their language.

The Netherlands has two official languages: Dutch and Frisk. Frisk is spoken in only one specific area, and there they also speak Dutch. There are more dialects in Holland, but Dutch is the official language in the country.

It is also good to keep in mind that the Netherlands is not just Holland. North and South Holland are two of 12 provinces in the country. Some people in the Netherlands are offended when their country is referred to as Holland, a common mistake made by many.

Pay-Per-Click

As in many of the European nations, Google is in the lead with close to 98 percent of the market share, so penetrating the market with PPC should be easy. You can set up a Dutch campaign in your Google AdWords account and use location targeting to display your ads in the Netherlands, based on postal codes or defined location by drawing on maps.

Google Trends and the Google keyword tool are great research tools for finding Dutch keywords. If you are using Google Translate to assist with evaluating keywords and how their cost-per-click and click-through rates will affect the daily budget you have set for your campaign, remember that Google's translation will be acceptable, but it is not likely to understand slang usage. Local slang may draw more clicks and larger expenditure, depending on their cost.

As you set up your campaign, remember the Dutch like a good deal. Make sure when you write ads that you have clear calls to action if you want to sell and make sure that the ads reflect a special deal in the offer.

Organic Search

Your website should, of course, follow all the best practices for architecture, keyword research, and content. Google.nl results pages include plenty of images and videos, so be sure to optimize and tag them with your targeted keywords.

When it comes to link building, Holland has a fairly mature market. By searching for **"link exchange" site:*.nl**, you will find close to 20,000 sites that are willing to exchange links (see Figure 11.5). Though that might not be the most effective way to get links to boost Google ranking, it shows that Dutch webmasters are thinking about link exchange.

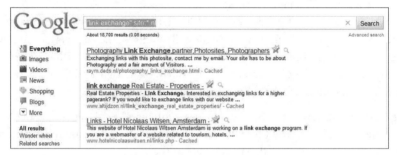

Figure 11.5   *Looking for link exchange in Holland is easy.*

Even better, look for "Link ruil" or "Link uitwisseling," the Dutch terms for "link exchange" (see Figure 11.6).

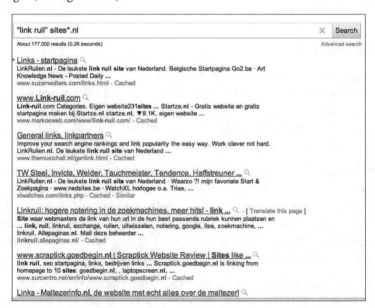

Figure 11.6   *You can search for links in Dutch.*

Though Google has a huge market share, many small search engines share the balance. For a general to niche marketing focus on the Dutch market, you should be fine using only Google to identify link sources. If you decide to dive deeper, Startpagina.nl is the largest local site with about 3.5 percent of the market (see Figure 11.7). Search marketers from outside Holland often forget to include links from Startpagina.nl. For visibility on Startpagina.nl, make sure to get about 20 links for a proper link profile.

Figure 11.7 *Startpagina.nl is a good source of links in the Netherlands. Use Google Translate (see the top of the image) to navigate it.*

Analytics

When it comes to analytics, the Dutch don't like cookies, especially cookies that track the users' visits and activities. The Dutch value their privacy very highly, indeed as much as Germans do. In 2009, a Forrester Research study found these two countries stand apart in their interest in protecting citizens from prying eyes—or tracking codes that record their activities online.

As shown in Figure 11.8, only 3.1 percent of Internet visitors surveyed in the Netherlands support cookies, and 3.38 percent did not support JavaScript. These are similar numbers to traffic from the United States and far less than Germany, where close to 5 percent of those surveyed had disabled JavaScript.

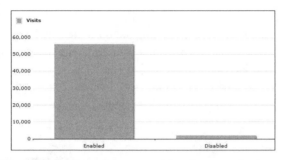

Figure 11.8   *In this test, only 3.38 percent of Dutch visitors had JavaScript disabled, with the majority allowing JavaScript and analytics tracking that use it.*

Online Public Relations

Traditional public relations came to the Netherlands after World War II ended. In 1953 Max Beauchez started a company called Beauchez Public Relations in The Hague, with Coca-Cola as its first customer.

After nearly 60 years, the PR industry in the Netherlands is now quite mature. Though we always recommend using the local language, the Dutch will accept press releases in English.

For distribution, there are some great services out there that focus on the Netherlands. We have found Marketwire to be really useful, and you can also test NewsCertain and eNewsPR. All of these have some good direct-to-media and online capabilities.

Search Marketing Tips for the Netherlands

- Dutch people have a wide-ranging global focus, but you will get a bigger response if you appeal to them in Dutch.
- When it comes to search, Google is the main player and should be your focus.
- The Dutch love a good deal, so be sure to make your offers and calls to action clear and appealing.
- The most popular payment systems are iDeal and AcceptGiro; PayPal and credit cards are much less preferred.
- There are many smaller directory sites, such as Startpagina.nl, which make good link sources. Use Google Translate to navigate sites.
- The Dutch online are active Tweeters and engaged heavily on other social networks, including their local social media network, Hyves. Use these to boost your visibility.

12

France

According to the Census Bureau, there are nearly 65 million people living in France. Of those, the International Telecommunication Union says that 68.9 percent—or 44.6 million—are online, making this country the ninth-largest Internet market in the world and the third-largest in Europe, behind Germany and the United Kingdom. France's online community has exploded in the past 11 years, having jumped from just about 8.5 million people in 2000.

French isn't spoken only in France. French is spoken in other countries in Europe, such as Belgium, Switzerland, and Luxembourg. We estimate that just over 70 million people speak French as their first language in Europe, and close to 200 million speak French worldwide, making for a sizeable market opportunity. French is spoken and influences of French culture can be found in former French colonies such as Algeria, Morocco, and Tunisia, as well as in large parts of western Africa. In total, there are 29 countries in which French is an official language, including Canada (see Chapter 15, "Canada").

Profile of France Online

In France, 95 percent of French Internet users go online daily. *Le Journal Du Net* reported in October 2010 that 72 percent of French Internet users had shopped online. It is important to note that 60 percent used price comparison websites when looking for services and products, mainly multimedia products and appliances. In 2010, 42 percent of French respondents to a Eurostats survey answered affirmatively to the question, "Have you bought something online in the last three months?"

French ecommerce is projected to grow 31 percent according to Kelkoo, the popular shopping comparison site. For payment, the French prefer bank cards (including *Carte Bleue*, private cards or store cards. and France had 8 million PayPal accounts in 2011, the third-largest number in Europe after the United Kingdom (21 million) and Germany (10 million).

French online shoppers are set apart from the rest of Europe by the importance they place on product pictures, which allow then to evaluate the quality of items. So said a 2010 study by agency Yuseo of 1,574 French online consumers looking for fashion, food, banking, and travel online.

> "French online shoppers are set apart from the rest of Europe by the importance they place on product pictures."

Le Journal Du Net also reported that despite the fast development of the Internet, old-school text messaging still keeps growing in France with more than 24 billion text messages being sent during the second quarter of 2010. Seven million mobile phone users in France accessed the Internet on their mobile phones in 2010, which represents 17 percent of mobile phone users in France. Mobile is definitely worth incorporating into your marketing in France.

According to Interactive Advertising Bureau's 2009 European Online Advertising Expenditure Report, published in 2010, search advertising spending is number two behind classified advertising at 40 percent and ahead of display advertising at 26 percent.

It is also worth noting that according to a study done by ESOMAR in 2009, 90 percent of French Internet users worried about the privacy of their personal data. This concern echoes other European nations, such as Germany and the Scandinavian countries.

Search Media in France

As you can see in Table 12.1, Google maintains a strong hold on the market in France with nearly 96 percent of the market. Bing and Yahoo! jointly have about 3.5 percent. Among the remainder, there is no local player—for example, voila.fr, shown in Figure 12.1—with even 1 percent share.

Figure 12.1   *Voila is one of the small local search engines; it has a tiny percent of the market.*

Table 12.1   Search Engine Market Share—France

Search Engine	Percentage of the Search Market
Google	95.87%
Bing	2.06%
Yahoo!	1.23%
Voila	0.37%
Ask	0.25%
Other	0.22%

Source: http://gs.statcounter.com/#search_engine-FR-daily-20110601-20110630-bar *and Stat-Counter: June 2011*

Most Common Mistakes

French people are very particular when it comes to their language and are not likely to use English. That means it is very important to understand the French culture and behavior. A Forrester Research study clearly showed that it is important to use the French language when it comes to ecommerce.

The French use the Latin alphabet with the addition of five accents. It is these accents that represent the greatest challenge for the French-focused search marketer. On top of that, there are opportunities missed by translating text and not doing any keyword research. In our experience, foreign marketers are very likely to allow "dry" translations to go through without any second guessing and therefore lose valid traffic in the process.

A good example of this might be "mobile phone," which is searched in France about 650,000 times each month. "Mobile phone" is often directly translated as "téléphone mobile." However, if you fail to also include the keyword "portable," you are missing out on about 4 million monthly searches.

A longer query, such as a search for a "cheap mobile phone," which would translate to "téléphone mobile pas cher," returns about 40,000 monthly searches. However, "portable pas cher" is searched about 200,000 times each month.

> "French people are very particular when it comes to their language and are not likely to use English."

Pay-Per-Click

With Google's dominant hold on French market share, there is little need to venture out of the comfort of the tools it provides. Google AdWords, Analytics, and Webmaster tools should prove to be all you need to successfully implement a PPC campaign by targeting France from your AdWords account.

According to a 2009 Forrester report, a growing number of mobile users in France access the Internet on their devices. Forrester projects this number to rise to 41 percent by 2014. Furthermore, 67 percent of French advertisers say they plan to have a mobile

> "With Google's dominant hold on French market share, there is little need to venture out of the comfort of the tools it provides."

app in the near future. You should focus some part of your budget toward mobile advertising because these advertisers are your competition in the French market.

It is also worth mentioning Facebook advertising as a growing opportunity. This is evidenced by the fact that Facebook opened a sales office in Paris. No need to go there to purchase ads, however; you can purchase ads at Facebook from wherever you are, and target them to the marketplace section on Facebook.fr.

Organic Search

Given the European dominance of Google, you should optimize for Google. As you can see in Figures 12.2 and 12.3, both Google and Bing show images, news, and video results, so be sure to include those in your optimization tactics.

Figure 12.2 *Google France displays images, news, and videos in results pages.*

Figure 12.3 *Bing.fr also includes many images, news, and videos in search results.*

With Google being as pervasive as it is, it should be relatively easy for you to get your message across in France, as long as proper research is done into the keywords used and if content and domains are localized—in French, of course.

Getting links from an .fr site in French is crucial because Google.fr puts emphasis on local inbound links, as everywhere else. This can be done through syndicating articles, requesting links, and exchanging links. In general, French website owners are very open to link exchanging, especially when webmasters are approached in their own language.

The best way to find link exchange partners is to open Google and start searching in English, using query strings such as **"web directory" site:*.fr** (see Figure 12.4). This search will return a number of good directories, starting with the Google-owned Open Directory Project.

Figure 12.4   *When doing link building in France, try searching Google using this search string: **"web directory" site:*.fr***.

Analytics

As in the rest of the developed Internet world, most web analytic tools work. Google's French data is very reliable, as is much of the data from most of the other vendors such as Yahoo!, Omniture, Webtrends, and Unica.

Be sure to check out XiTi, which is a French analytics tool (see Figure 12.5). XiTi also is available in English, German, and Spanish.

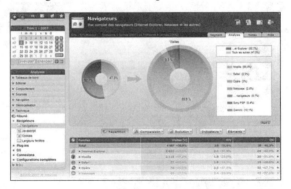

Figure 12.5   *The French web analytics tool XiTi, which is also available in English.*

Online Public Relations

France is very mature in terms of public relations. Journalism is lively there, and some of the leading publications of the world have their origins in France. All the big service providers offer distribution into France. Marketwire offers distribution to major traditional media and websites in France, and it includes French translation among its services.

There are also good local players, such as Augure, a French company that provides excellent distribution and listening services as well as local knowledge that can often be key to the market. Augure has sites in English and Spanish, and offices in London and Madrid (see Figure 12.6).

Figure 12.6   *Augure is a French company that provides press release translation into French, Spanish, and English. Augure provides its service in Spain and the United Kingdom.*

Search Marketing Tips for France

- Understanding and respecting French pride in their language and culture is the key to success.

- Sixty percent of French online shoppers use price comparison websites, such as Shopzilla, Kelkoo, and local favorite, Acheter-moins-cher.

- Using Google AdWords, Webmaster Tools, and Analytics will cover 90 percent of the online pay-per-click advertising market for you in France.

- French webmasters are likely to exchange links with you, more so if you approach them in French.

- Most U.S. analytics tools you already know work well in France.

13

Spain

According to the U.S. Census Bureau, the Kingdom of Spain is one of the biggest countries in Europe, with just over 46.5 million inhabitants. Spain is the fifth-largest Internet market in Europe, and in the top 20 worldwide. According to a Nielsen study done in June 2010, just over 29 million, or 62.6 percent of the total population, use the Internet. This is an increase from around 5.5 million users in 2000. In a typical week, 20.2 million, or 58 percent of the population, use the Internet.

Profile of Spain Online

As you can see in Table 13.1, Spanish Internet users are content readers, and the results of the data from comScore show that Microsoft portals were the most popular website category, reaching close to 99 percent of web users in Spain. In second place were the search engines and then social media networks such as Facebook. Facebook reached 48.8 percent of the Spanish online population with 14.2 million unique visitors in September 2010. Facebook and local social network, Tuenti, both were the big gainers that year, by 49 percent and 21 percent, respectively.

Table 13.1   Top 10 Web Properties in Spain—Millions of Unique Visitors

Site	September 2009 (in Millions)	September 2010 (in Millions)	% Change
Total Internet Persons	19,836	20,910	5%
Microsoft Sites	15,592	20,866	34%
Google Sites	16,756	19,625	17%
Facebook.com	9,527	14,177	49%
Yahoo! Sites	10,143	10,722	6%
Wikimedia Foundation Sites	7,578	9,013	19%
Grupo Prisa	7,766	8,757	13%
Schibsted	7,604	8,716	15%
RCS Media Group	7,791	8,693	12%
Terra–Telefonica	7,241	8,620	19%
Tuenti.com	6,854	8,285	21%

Source: comScore, Total Spanish Audience, Home and Work, Ages 15 and Up, September 2009 vs. September 2010

The comScore study found Spanish Internet users engaging more and more with social media sites and networks, with a stunning 90.1 percent of the Spanish online population now being reached via social media such as Facebook and Tuenti (see Figure 13.1).

Figure 13.1   *Tuenti is one of the leading social media platforms in Spain and is avail-able in Castilian (Castellano), Catalan, English, Basque, and the Galician languages.*

Spain has one of the most mature mobile markets in the world, with 3G licenses available for more than a decade. Spain's mobile market also is one of the largest in Europe. The effect of the Spanish people's strong ties to their smartphones and tablet devices was made clear in a 2010 Zed Digital study in Spain of 16,000 consumers ages 14–44. This study found that 54 percent of the respondents access the Internet via mobile devices (smartphones and tablets, for example). One of the principal activities was using search, but checking emails, entering social networks, and instant messaging were also strong. Accessing social networks on mobile devices by 16–44-year-olds grew 275 percent in 2010.

The Spanish language is key. According to a 2005 study called the Eurobarometer, conducted by the European Commission, only 44 percent of Spaniards said yes when asked if they spoke a second language well enough to have a conversation. What's more, you may need to choose among four recognized regional languages depending on which part of Spain you're targeting:

- **Castilian Spanish**—Spoken by 74 percent of the population and the official language nationwide
- **Catalan/Valencian**—Spoken by 17 percent and official regionally
- **Galician**—Spoken by 7 percent and official regionally
- **Basque**—Spoken by 2 percent and official regionally

 Note

See more about differences among various versions of the Spanish languages and how those differences spell the difference between success and failure in Spain in the section "Organic Search," later in this chapter.

Other than Basque, the regional Spanish languages are similar in the way that Scandinavian languages are. However, each region has a strong identity and distinct cultural differences, such as you'd find in Sweden, Denmark, and Norway. More than merely dialects, these differences set each region in Spain apart from its neighbors. Even though people in each region can understand each others' version of Spanish, they will respond more readily when addressed in their own.

Video sites are extremely popular with Spaniards. In fact, they are second only to France among European nations. According to research published by comScore, 83.1 percent of Spaniards online watched a video in October 2010, representing 19.2 million Spanish viewers, who watched 2.9 *billion* online videos. As you can see from Table 13.2, more than 8 out of 10 of those who watch video did so on YouTube, which supplies nearly all the videos watched on Google in Spain. Owning both the most-used channels for search and video online grants Google enormous influence over Spanish Internet users, and provides a large opportunity for your marketing message. You can use YouTube for both PPC advertising and video uploading for visibility in Google universal search results.

Table 13.2   Top Spanish Online Video Content by Unique Visitors

Media	Total Unique Viewers (000)	Videos (000)	Total Hours (MM)	Share of Audience
Total Internet Audience	19,222	2,912,947	311.3	100%
Google Sites	16,711	1,205,023	55.2	86.9%
Vevo	3,868	23,309	3.0	20.1%
Dailymotion.com	3,531	17,291	1.8	18.4%
Microsoft sites	3,355	20,407	0.7	17.5%
Facebook.com	3,215	13,971	1.0	16.7%
RCS Media Group	3,075	21,230	0.5	16.0%
Grupo Prisa	3,034	18,024	0.8	15.8%
Viacom Digital	2,386	10,225	1.7	12.4%
Hispavista Sites	2,144	29,716	1.7	11.2%
Rtve.es	2,078	20,434	3.5	10.8%

Source: comScore Video Metrix October 2010

The Spanish version of YouTube is shown in Figure 13.2. Other video sites that should not be overlooked are Vevo and Dailymotion; both are in English. There are other local and global players with significant share, too, as you can see in Table 13.2. Clearly Google's YouTube accounts for much, much more video watching than other sites in Spain, but it is not exclusive. The shares of audience add up to more that 100%, which tells us that Spanish viewers visit more than one site to watch videos. This means the other sites can be additional opportunity for you to show your video content to Spanish audiences.

Figure 13.2   *YouTube can play a hefty role when it comes to marketing in Spain.*

The Spaniards' affinity for video sites aside, multitasking is apparently not as popular in Spain. Only 54 percent use at least two different media at the same time—also known as "media meshing." This is well below the European average of 76 percent who media mesh, as it were.

Similarly, according to research done by Affilinet in June of 2010, Spanish online shoppers shop less frequently online and spend less than their European neighbors. However, Spaniards do use social networks far more than others in Europe to research online purchases. People in Spain also are likely to gather more research overall before making a purchase; 50 percent indicated they use three or more sources to make buying decisions. Furthermore, 21.6 percent said they use Facebook or Twitter to investigate product satisfaction among people in their networks before buying.

Search Media in Spain

As you can see in Table 13.3, Google is by far the most popular search engine in Spain with 97.5 percent market share. Bing follows with just over 1.3 percent and Yahoo! has less than 1 percent.

Table 13.3   Search Engine Market Share—Spain

Search Engine	Percentage of Search Market
Google.es	97.5%
Bing.es	1.3%
Yahoo.es	0.7%
Terra	0.5%

Source: StatCounter: June 2011

As you can see, Google's market share is near-total in Spain. Terra is the only local player in Spain, but it has less than 1 percent. Terra is shown in Figure 13.3.

Figure 13.3   *Terra has 0.7 percent market share and is powered by Google.*

Terra uses search results from Google, which gives Google near total dominance over the Spanish online market. Clearly, search marketing in Spain is all about Google, whether you are looking for better paid or organic listings. The tactics we discuss in chapter are your best bet.

Most Common Mistakes

The biggest mistake we have seen companies make is to target Spain with a single European campaign, using English only and treating Europe as a single country. Remember, there are 27 countries in the European Union alone and Spain is just one of them.

Another common mistake is to group "similar" countries into buckets. For instance, putting Italy, Spain, and Portugal in the same bucket. As you might imagine, companies who do this see less than beneficial results.

Finally, some companies roll out a single website to target Spanish-speaking countries. Yes, it is true Spanish is the native language of 332 million people in the world, as well as the official language of 22 countries. It is also widely spoken in several other nations, including Canada, Morocco, the Philippines, and the United States. Also true: Spanish is the third most-spoken language online after English and Chinese (though fewer than half of those speaking Spanish are in Spain).

> " ...the Spanish language spoken in Spain is surprisingly different from Latin American Spanish and that from U.S. Hispanic Spanish..."

However, the Spanish language spoken in Spain is surprisingly different from Latin American Spanish and that from U.S. Hispanic Spanish, and so on. Often U.S. companies think it enough to get a person who speaks Mexican Spanish to do their translation. This is a problem because aside from accent, many random words are used differently in each country, and that can lead to all kinds of problems. For example, in Spain, the word "cojer" means to pick up, as in "Please pick up an order at the store." However, in Mexico, "cojer" has a far less pleasant slang meaning not suitable for repeating in this book. The word to use in Mexico would be "recojer" for picking up an order at the store.

For example, when Mazda came out with its Laputa minivan, the company failed to realize that "puta" is the Spanish word for prostitute. You can imagine the stir this caused when the Laputa minivan was introduced in Spain. Distributors in Chile went so far as to ask Mazda to change the name of the minivan to a less offensive term. Other similar unfortunate vehicle names include the Mitsubishi Pajero and the Nissan Moco; both do not translate very well into Spanish (meaning both have negative or sexual connotations). In Spain, the Pajero is now known as the Montero. The Moco is no longer sold in Spain, though it is sold under different names in other countries.

 Note

It would be suitable to use an educated person from Mexico to translate your campaign aimed at Spaniards as long as you are certain the person understands the nuances between the various versions of Spanish.

Pay-Per-Click

Google is the most-used search engine in Spain. You can also target Spanish searchers through Google's vast advertising network of sites within Spain. Google has hundreds of sites where you can get your ads displayed.

This capability is important mainly because the Spanish spend their time browsing between sites when online, in fact more so than in the U.S., where our web use tends to be results-directed. Getting your message on as many sites as possible will increase the chances of browsing Spaniards seeing it. These can range from news sites such as HERALDO.es or Publico.es, to entertainment sites such as KissFM.es or Musica.com. On top of that, some of the most-visited news sites in Spain have their internal search powered by Google; Elmundo.es—the most-used Spanish news site according to a comScore study done in February 2009—uses Google to power its internal search capabilities.

PPC for the Spanish market can be done from the comfort of your chair wherever you are located, whether you are targeting through Google or Yahoo!. As of this writing, the Bing/Yahoo! alliance had not reached Spain but is likely to do so by 2012. Figure 13.4 shows how similar Google PPC ads are to those in the United States.

Figure 13.4   *PPC focusing on Spain can be done through Google.*

Because Terra is Google driven, you can easily reach most Spanish-based searchers by using Google only. In fact, you can reach nearly 100 percent of searchers this way.

Another issue worth noting when it comes to PPC is that by using Microsoft's ad network, you can reach nearly every Internet user in Spain. Microsoft sites received close to 21 million visitors, meaning nearly all Spanish Internet users have visited Microsoft sites. Google websites, which include YouTube, are increasing in popularity. Google sites have grown by 17 percent to 19.6 million users.

Organic Search

As we discussed in Chapter 2, to build online visibility in Google, you need to provide clear signals identifying the country you are targeting. Because Spanish is spoken in many countries, marketing in Spain must employ at least at least two of the following, and all three would be even better:

1. Use the Spanish language, preferably the right Spanish language—Castilian, Catalan, and so on.

2. Use the .es extension for your domain.

3. Use links from sites within Spain, or at minimum, links from sites written in Spanish.

For search engine optimization (SEO), it is important to have in mind the different dialects spoken in Spain. Though Spanish is the official language of Spain, there are various dialects. You will find people who speak Spanish (Castilian), Galician and Catalan from Latin, and Basque (of uncertain origin). There are even other historical dialects that cannot be considered official languages but are widely used nonetheless. The big ones—like Catalan, Galician, and Basque—each boast dedicated TV and radio stations, newspapers, and magazines. As you can see in Figure 13.5 and Table 13.4, an English word might be a completely different word from one language in Spain to the next.

> "Although Spanish is the official language of Spain, there are a variety of dialects."

Table 13.4 Examples of How Words Translate Differently Among Spanish Languages

English	Castilian (Castellano)	Catalan (Català)
Brick	Ladrillo	Maó
To go	Ir	Anar
Lightning	Relámpago	Llampec
To eat	Comer	Menjar
Bottle	Botella	Ampolla
Chair	Silla	Cadira
Bed	Cama	Llit
Table	Mesa	Taula

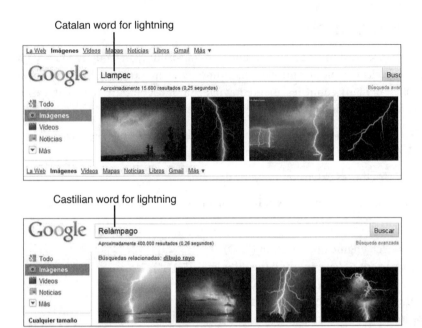

Figure 13.5   *The two images illustrate the difference between a search for "lightning" in Catalan versus Castilian.*

Another good example of language differences in Spain is how the word "mobile" (as in "mobile telephone") translates. In Spanish (Castilian), it is "Móvil"; in Catalan, it is "Mòbil"; and in Basque, it is "Mugikorra." You need to carefully research these differences and build them into your marketing efforts in Spain to maximize success.

As we know from basic SEO, search engines are very literal and evaluate relevance according to the exact search phrase they are given in a query. Search bots will not make connections between synonyms. This of course, is equally true in languages other than English. As with all search marketing, your best path to visibility is to use the exact terms your targeted searcher would use.

When it comes to link building, there is some low-hanging fruit at the Open Directory Project, also known as Dmoz (see Figure 13.6). Do your homework to find the right category within the site.

Figure 13.6   *Dmoz can give you a helpful first link.*

It should be easy to find more sources for links, such as directories, forums that are addressing issues related to your services, and so on. Use the Google search string **"web directory site:*.es -google"** to find directories in English. This will take you to local directories, such as Linkadoo (see Figure 13.7) and webbarato.es.

Figure 13.7   *Linkadoo.es is a good source for inbound links in Spain.*

Analytics

The top free tools such as Google Analytics and Yahoo! Analytics work well in Spain. If you want to keep your data private, it is worth looking at both Webtrends and Omniture. As marketers, we (the authors) have had no experience with analytics tools created and sold out of Spain, and when trying to find a tool, we could not find any.

Online Public Relations

Spain is a fairly mature public relations market, when it comes to traditional PR. However, when it comes to online PR, there are not many channels that work. There are local teams that can help you with your PR efforts, such as Marco de Comunicación. We have found both the eNewsPR network and Marketwire to have proven quite successful. With eNewsPR and Marketwire, you can send direct to media, which targets the inboxes of local journalists.

Search Marketing Tips for Spain

- Use Spanish and pay attention to the different dialects. Choose the one spoken in the market you are targeting because most searchers do not comfortably speak a second dialect.
- Use social media. Ninety percent of those on the Internet in Spain participate in Facebook or local social networks such as Tuenti.
- Be sure to include videos in your online strategy.
- Dmoz is a good place to start for links from Spain.
- Use Marketwire and eNewsPR to send your press releases directly to Spanish journalists.

14

Italy

Italy and the Italian market are a world in themselves, just like other European countries. Italy is one of the most populated countries in Europe with nearly 61 million inhabitants stretched across the boot in the Mediterranean Sea. Italy's endless beaches and long sunny days make it a natural travel destination—not only for the fine weather, but also for its world-class food and fashion industry.

Slightly more than half of Italy's population is online (51.7 percent). This makes Italy the fifteenth-largest Internet population in the world and the fourth-largest Internet market in the European Union.

Globalization has considerably changed Italy, and it is no longer the conservative country it was when it had clan-structured families. Immigration has had a considerable impact with nearly 5 million people having immigrated to Italy from many parts of Eastern Europe and Africa. These recent immigrants account for more than 8 percent of the population.

It's no myth that Italians are great talkers. They enjoy engaging in conversations and pleasant evening walks with friends they meet for an aperitif (an alcoholic drink served as an appetizer). They enjoy traveling and are very open to new ideas, trends, and cultures. That said, they don't speak foreign languages very well, although this is changing rapidly with the younger generations.

Profile of Italy Online

Italians are very active online. An estimated 67 percent—8 million users—of people ages 25–54 are online on any given day. The most active age group is the 35–54 age group, while the nearly 2 million people from the "older" generations (55–74) are online every day.

According to Audiweb by NetNielsen:

- In January 2011, 28.5 million Italians surfed the Web at least once, which is an 11.6 percent increase from the year before.
- Italy has one of the highest growth rates in Internet use. Internet usage reached 51.7 percent in 2008, which is up 15 percent.
- About 12.6 million go online daily: 7 million males, 5.6 million females.
- Average time spent online is 1 hour and 40 minutes. During that time, the average Italian visits 201 pages.
- Nearly one-third (30.4 percent) of those active online are located in southern Italy.
- Nearly half (46.6 percent) of Italy's online population is aged 35–54.
- Italians use the Internet mostly in the afternoon and evening, with many users being night owls. The daily Internet audience peaks at 6.6 million in the early afternoon (noon–3 PM) and remains stable until 9 PM, where it holds steady at 5.2 million until midnight.

However, the Internet is most definitely not the only way to reach Italians. Italy has the highest percentage of people watching TV at 98 percent (matched only by Belgium). The Italian population is above the European average for meshing media—combining use of the Internet on PC or mobile, TV, and magazines or newspapers to find what they want. Of Italians, 82 percent mesh their media, compared to 58 percent in France and Germany, 96 percent in Norway, and 94 percent in Belgium.

You can find out a lot more about Italians online at Audiweb (www.audiweb.it), an updated list of the most popular portals and online news media (see Figure 14.1). Using the data section of the portal requires registration, which is free. There is an English version you can use to register and access the lists (see Figure 14.2).

Figure 14.1   *Audiweb is a good source for data about Italians online aggregated from media, portals, and online publications. There is an English version, shown in Figure 14.2.*

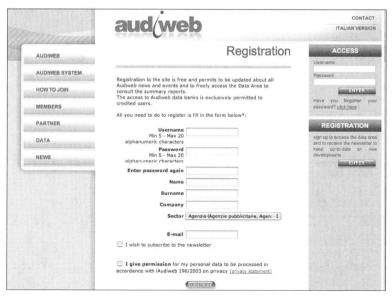

Figure 14.2   *Italian portal directory Audiweb provides a registration page in English for your convenience.*

The Italians' "gift of the gab" makes it only natural for them to embrace and engage with others on social media platforms. Facebook is widely used by Italians of all ages, rising to 20.5 million members in November 2011, making the Italian Facebook community the eleventh-largest in the world. This love of talking could also explain why Italians have been such early adopters of mobile communication right from the start—even in the early 1990s when mobile phone communications were very expensive. Today it is not uncommon to ride on a bus for hours and see people talk on the mobile phone for the entire journey.

Ecommerce plays a significant role in planning activities and purchases in Italy. Though Italians are well known to be among the biggest online gamblers in the world, they tend not to use credit cards very much. In fact, it is quite common to find online retail sites offering a variety of payments and cash on delivery (COD).

> "The Italians' 'gift of the gab' makes it only natural for them to embrace and engage with others on social media platforms."

Search Media in Italy

Google.it is king of search in Italy with nearly a 98 percent share in 2010 followed by Virgilio.it, a local portal, with 3 percent. Bing/Yahoo! holds 1 percent of the market.

Table 14.1 Search Engine Market Share—Italy

Search Engine	Percentage of Search Market
Google.it	97.8%
Virgilio.it	3.0%
Yahoo.com.it	1.0%
Arianna.it	1.6%
Others	0.7%

Local portal Virgilio is popular enough to outpace Microsoft's Bing/Yahoo! collaboration, but Google has near-total market share. Virgilio shows results provided by Google, which makes it easier for search marketers, as the methods for success are familiar (see Figure 14.3).

Figure 14.3   *Virgilio.it is Italy's local portal and displays Google results.*

Most Common Mistakes

Italians are fond of good looks and elegance. Keep this in mind at all times when you are planning your website. Thorough and complete localization is a must. Remember Italians aren't very good with English and foreign languages in general. Unless you are targeting a very specific and technologically advanced market segment, your web presence must be in Italian. In this respect, Italians are very much like Germans in that TV shows in their countries are not dubbed in English, but only subtitled, unlike in most other northern European countries. This means English is not as easily learned as a "native" second language for Italians as it is for many Europeans.

Italian itself is a complex and very colorful language with difficult verb conjugations and long individual phrases. To be sure your website and search advertising messages are clearly understood, have your website localized by reliable professionals.

Italians tend to be formal and keep a distance from people they do not know, and use "il lei" (in English, the ancient "thou~you") also as a sign of respect toward an older person during a conversation. They are very wary of newcomers, and you need to win their trust. However, once you earn their trust, you might've just earned a friend for life.

When localizing your website, keep in mind who your typical readers are and their ages. Direct and informal might not be the right way to go if you are addressing a mature and sophisticated audience. If your target audience is under age 50, your approach could be more direct and informal. Knowing your demographics is a key element in creating empathy and establishing a connection with your audience. Younger generations make more use of the Web and have had greater exposure to an innovative online culture, one of direct and informal contacts that differs significantly from the much more formal traditional Italian culture. This may vary significantly by sector. For example, lawyers and public servants tend to be more formal, and businesspeople in corporations less so because they are accustomed to dealing with international partners and clients.

Aggressive web marketing with "loud" language typical of long-landing page copy may not reward your efforts. The Italians' approach to everyday life differs from the U.S. lifestyle, and they respond less to hype and boisterous attitudes. Don't just translate your landing pages, but localize them, taking into consideration a typical persona, gender, and age to make the most of your web marketing efforts.

> "Don't just translate your landing pages, but localize them..."

Make payment by credit card an option, not a mandatory method of payment. Italians are very cautious about using credit cards on the Web. They will often use PayPal (see Figure 14.4). Online banking is very popular and inexpensive. For Business-to-Consumer (B2C), online banking is regularly used and is a preferred means of payment. Indeed, there are many portals that do not accept credit card payment at all!

Figure 14.4   *Translate Paypal.it to English using Google Translate.*

Note

Internet scams offer the opportunity for great headlines in news and papers and TV shows, increasing suspicion and distrust. Put a great deal of effort in reassuring and building a reputation for your website. An essential starting point toward establishing trust would be placing a policy endorsing consumer rights as regulated by the EU Directive 97/7/EC converted into law in Italy (d. lgs. n. 185/1999, later replaced by d. lgs. n. 206/2005 known as the "Codice del Consumo").

To further build trust, include a page prominently reachable in your high-level navigation called "Condizioni di vendita" ("Terms and Conditions") providing full disclosure on all the following:

- Product characteristics and vendor details
- Preferred methods of payment
- Money-back guarantee (within 30 days), no questions asked if buyer decides to return merchandise within 10 days of purchase
- Two-year warranty

Pay-Per-Click

Because Google controls about 96 percent of the Italian search traffic, Google is a natural starting point for your pay-per-click (PPC) campaigns. There are no significant differences from U.S. campaign management. Set up separate ad groups and campaign in your Google AdWords account and geo-target for the regions you want. You can drill down to minor cities and municipalities a notch to an individual province or to regional coverage. As with an organic search, the real challenge lies in the correct selection of keywords and campaign management. It is universally known that poorly managed PPC campaigns can devour budgets. This is true in Italy as well.

Organic Search

The basic rules for properly achieving organic visibility on Italian search engines are fundamentally the same as in the United States. Despite the similarities, those approaching the Italian market may find it hard to implement web marketing strategies. Experience has taught us that foreigners can find it difficult to establish a network of contacts among the market in Italy of many small search engine optimization specialists (SEOs) and only a handful of structured web marketing agencies. The difficulties of working with SEOs who are often individualistic with an artistic vein may create misunderstandings that can founder partnerships. Remember, Italians aren't very good at speaking or writing English, so it is important to be clear about your intent and goals, and make sure you are clearly understood, whether you are communicating in Italian or English.

At the time of this writing, Google.it search engine results are rich in images, video, and news. However, they do not include real-time results. This will most likely change at some point in the not-too-distant future, with real-time information being integrated in the Google.it results as well.

A search for information about Libya on the U.S. version of Google (see Figure 14.5) shows images and video results. However, Italians searching on Google.it in Italy do not see real-time results (see Figure 14.6).

Click here for real-time results

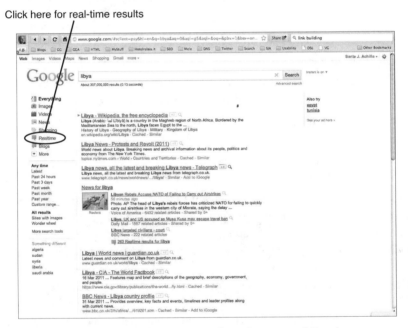

Figure 14.5   *Google.com results as seen in the U.S. version of Google.*

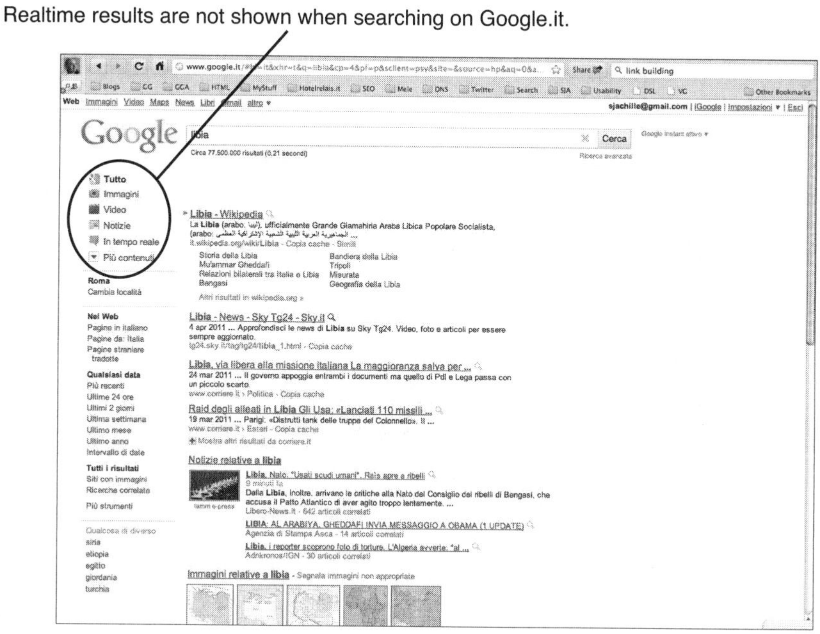

Realtime results are not shown when searching on Google.it.

Figure 14.6   *Italian searchers do not see real-time results on Google.*

A search on Bing at the same time shows that many of the features you may have seen on Bing in the United States, such as images and videos incorporated into the search results page, had not made it to Italy (see Figure 14.7).

Figure 14.7   *Bing.it results show none of the newer features available on Bing.com in the United States.*

Directories can be a starting point in your link-building efforts. There are approximately 100 directories where a website can be submitted. Some require a return link, but on the whole, Italians are very reluctant to host return links, and this continues to be an unexpected problem. Linking is done much more easily among U.S. webmasters. You will do better by looking for portals, publications, and associations from which you may be able to get a link by joining or submitting content.

Figure 14.8 shows a sample from the list, Pubblicitaonline.it. Registration is free, and required to get at the data.

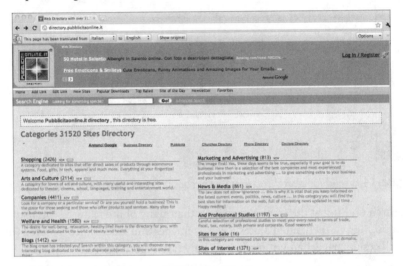

Figure 14.8 *Sample link source Pubblicitaonline.it.*

Analytics

Google Analytics are the de facto standard for measuring web performance in Italy. Every web agency and Small Office-Home Office (SOHO) SEO in Italy uses Google Analytics.

Be aware that using web analytics software that requires log file analysis can be a challenge for domains hosted in Italy. Log file analysis will almost certainly require a personalized configuration, which most providers will not offer for hosting "out of the box." This type of web analytics solution never gained traction in Italy, and log files remained a mysterious entity. One reason may be that legislation on privacy and protection from hacking requires system administrators to save and maintain these files for up to five years. If you are going to use analytics software other than Google, you will find it easier to work with one that tracks with page tags, JavaScript, or cookies.

Online PR

As in other regions, press releases are a viable solution to distribute your content and gain organic visibility. There are a number of free press release outlets that allow you to post followed links and upload images as well. Almost all press release portals are made with WordPress. You'll have to create an account for each one of them. Few offer desktop publishing via an XMLRPC interface. This means you will have to log on to each portal, write and configure your article, and then publish each, because desktop blogging tools such as Microsoft Live Writer for Windows or Ecto on Mac (just to name a few) do not provide the functionality to manage your press releases across all publications.

There are several press release portals within Google News (see Figure 14.9) offering great opportunity for maximum exposure. Following are several free press release portals in Google News:

- a-zeta.it
- comunicati-stampa.net
- informazione.it
- itnews.it
- notiziefresche.info

As you can see in Figure 14.9, Google returns images with some of the results. Be sure to optimize your images for Italy as you would for Google.com to take advantage of the additional attention an image in search results can draw.

Figure 14.9   *News.google.it contains several press release portals—for example, a-zeta.it, the first result for this search result page.*

PRLog (www.prlog.org), shown in Figure 14.10, is a free international press release outlet, which works very nicely in Italy, providing excellent visibility.

Figure 14.10   *PRLog.org is a free international press release outlet.*

As you can see in Table 14.2, there are approximately 20 press release portals that vary in quality but can be used in an effort to promote your website.

Table 14.2   Italian Press Release Portals

Area-press.eu	Comunicatistampa.net
Comunicato-stampa.info	Comunicatistampa24.com
Comunicalanotizia.com	Comunicatistampaweb.it
Comunicati-stampa.biz	Divietodispam.com
Comunicati-stampa.cc	Eventi-italia.net
Comunicati-stampa.com	Fainotizia.it
Comunicati-stampa.eu	Joyfreepress.com
Comunicati-stampa.info	Maiamagazine.it
Comunicati-stampa.ws	Nelweb.biz
Comunicati.net	Notizie-oggi.it
Comunicati123.com	Notizieflash.com
Comunicatimprese.it	Notizieoggi.net
Comunicatistampa.name	Sitoqui.it

Note

Most free press releases expire in a matter of months, and are often deleted after six months unless you are willing to pay a fee of about €5.00 (about $7.50 US) per each to grandfather it. Then it will remain online indefinitely.

Another issue with Italian press release portals is that you need to allow time for editorial delays. Most portals will put your press release on hold until an editor reviews it and decides to publish it. This can take anywhere from few hours to several days—and that's after you have published a few posts and proven that you are trustworthy. Many portals do not tell you when your release has been published, so you'll have to check in from time to time and see the status of your post.

Search Marketing Tips for Italy

- Italians are classy and sophisticated and take being stylish seriously. Don't make your website look and sound like a party animal wearing a Hawaiian shirt. They won't like it.

- Italians are a bit standoffish until they get to know you. Gaining cooperation from other websites for reciprocal linking might prove to be a challenge at first. Work to build trust with the italian webmasters you contact . . . and don't give up.

- Choosing a local partner can be a challenge. There is a very large number of very small SEO entrepreneurs who are hard to follow and difficult to understand. Look for referrals and ask to see results.

- If you are selling online, be sure to offer PayPal as an option; many Italians do not use credit cards online.

- Consider paying the fee to prevent losing a link because your press release expired.

15

Canada

According to the U.S. Census Bureau, there are just over 34 million people living in Canada. According to the International Telecommunications Union (ITU; the UN agency for information and communication technologies) about 79 percent—or just under 27 million—Canadians are online.

According to the most recent Canadian census conducted in 2006, Canada has two official languages:

- English—Spoken exclusively by 58.8 percent of the population
- French—Spoken exclusively by 23.2 percent of the population

However, fewer than 18 percent of Canadians speak both English and French. Eighty-five percent of French-speaking Canadians reside in Quebec. In addition, Canadian French is a term that also includes distinct varieties of the language spoken by Quebec French, Acadian French, Métis French, and Newfoundland French.

Canada's strategic location and its relationship with its powerful neighbor, the United States, have helped define its economy. Nearly 90 percent of Canadians live 125 miles or less from the U.S. border, according to the BBC. Canada indeed shares a very strong trading relationship with United States; it is said to be the largest of its kind in the world. This clearly shows why the potential for U.S. online retailers to branch out and invest in the Canadian markets has been quite promising. Although many aspects of marketing to Canadians is the same as marketing to U.S. Internet users, there are a few key differences. Perhaps the most significant difference is that when creating national marketing campaigns, you must have one website in English and one in Canadian French to satisfy the bilingual culture. Figure 15.1 shows an elegant way to toggle between the two languages.

Click here to toggle between
English and French

Figure 15.1 *In Canada, national campaigns must be done in English and Canadian French. This is most often done as shown, with a link to "English" in the upper left that toggles to the French site.*

Canada, with its stable currency, is one of the most prosperous countries on the planet, and one that managed to avoid the banking crisis that befell much of the rest of the developed world. As you will see, Canadians enjoy robust connectivity and top many other countries for engagement online. Even so, online shopping has been slow to catch on, for reasons we discuss later, but it is not surprising that foreign retailers, especially from the United States, have decided to play in the Canadian online retail industry.

Profile of Canada Online

According to a 2010 study by comScore, the two age groups that make up the largest share of the total online population are 18–34 and 35–44 years of age. However, the fastest-growing group is made up of those 55 and older, and it is also the fastest-growing group on social media. Some facts about the daily online activities of Canadian users reveal that

- Email is the most popular online activity among English-speaking Canadians (70 percent). The percentage of French-speaking Canadians who frequently use email is 56 percent.

- Online searching on Google, Yahoo!, and Bing ranks second, with 59 percent of English-speaking Canadians and 54 percent of French-speaking ones searching on at least one of them.

- Social networking is the third most-popular online activity online, with 41 percent of English-speaking and 38 percent of French-speaking Canadians regularly logging in to these sites.

- About a quarter of Canadian Internet users read blogs and watch online videos on a daily basis.

- Eighteen percent of Canada's Internet users research online before making a purchase offline.

- Other regular online activities include reading news, instant messaging, gaming, accessing online magazines, and listening to radio.

Internet usage statistics in Canada reveal some very impressive figures:

- Canadians were the most engaged online worldwide in 2010, with more average visits per visitor, who stayed for more average hours per visit than any other country, according to comScore.

- Household broadband penetration was 72.2 percent in 2010, ahead of the United Kingdom (69.7 percent), the United States (67.3 percent), and Japan (66.8 percent), according to eMarketer.

- Canadians ranked first in online banking worldwide with 64.8 percent usage rate in ages 15 and above (comScore Media Metrix, October 2010), and two-thirds of the online banking customers used online bill payment in the first quarter of 2011 (comScore).

- Social networking ranked sixth worldwide, with time spent on social media sites per user at 5.8 hours per visitor (comScore Media Metrix, December 2010).

- Group buying ranked seventh worldwide in number of unique visitors to Groupon (Advertising Age, December 2010).

- Online videos were watched by 70 percent of Internet users in Canada, compared to 65 percent in the United States and 60 percent in the United Kingdom, according to Angus Reid Public Opinion (December 2010).
- The Retail Council of Canada reported two-thirds of medium to large Canadian retailers surveyed in May 2010 already had an ecommerce site, with most of the remaining respondents saying they would launch one within five years.

Despite all the foregoing, Canadians trailed quite a few other countries in online shopping, with a meager 46 percent of those online buying there in 2009, according to Forrester research. However Canada's online shopping population is squeaking upward, reaching 52.7 percent in 2010, and spending C$16.5 billion (Canadian dollars) that year. Online buyers each spent C$1,460 on average in 2010. The most popular products purchased were travel services, books, and event tickets. By 2011, consumers in Canada were buying home electronics, apparel, luxury items, and even bulk-packaged common household goods on the Internet. Web retailers reported that demographics for the online buyers were also becoming more diverse with older and more affluent middle-aged buyers discovering online shopping. Furthermore, Canadians happy with an online shopping experience were recommending it to their friends on social networking sites.

Young adult consumers are expected to be the main propellers of the growth of ecommerce in Canada. According to an April–May 2010 study by consumer market research firm NPD Group, online users ages 25–34 made the maximum number of online purchases across all retail categories. Plus, those ages 18–24 years of age were the most active online users, adding up to more than 17.9 million online shoppers. Experts predict that the number of online buyers is bound to grow steadily at the rate of 3 percent every year, reflecting the dramatic influence this new group of buyers is bound to have on Canadian ecommerce as their earning potential continues to rise.

Mobile Internet access, while lower than in other countries, is expected to grow in Canada. Thirty-seven percent of smartphone users and 16 percent of other mobile users in Canada went online in 2010 for searching and social networking. As the popularity of mobile continues to increase, mobile advertising spending is also on the rise, with 63.1 percent of marketing professionals in Canada reporting they are willing to allocate up to 15 percent of their marketing budget to mobile marketing. Advertising Expenditure Forecasts by Zenith Optimedia predicted the total spending on mobile advertising would be $C55 million by the end of year 2011, an increase of C$25 million over 2010.

Clearly, consumers in Canada have the technology and the mindset to be active online, from researching product reviews to banking online to using social networking sites such as Facebook and Twitter to comparing services such as travel. However, when it comes to actually buying products or services online, Canadians appear reluctant. Several factors are responsible for the delta between Internet use and online buying in Canada:

- First, Canadian buyers like to "touch and feel" a product before buying it and prefer real stores, where they can look at the product options and make an informed choice. Although Canadian shoppers do research for products and services on the Internet, they would rather spend their money in a bricks-and-mortar store, which allows them to see and feel the product and even return it conveniently.

> "While Canadian shoppers do research for products and services on the Internet, they would rather spend their money in a bricks-and-mortar store...."

- Next, Canadian consumers are fairly conservative about security. In a study conducted by the NPD, almost 51 percent of the Canadian population were wary of making online transactions, even though Canadians are avid online bankers. Middle-aged people in Canada are concerned about the security of their credit cards and about the security of credit card payments online. Similarly, new online users, surveyed after less than five years online, are also distrustful when it comes to making online transactions or providing their card details.

- Last, shipping costs can be a problem. The NPD study in 2010 revealed that more than one-third of online shoppers in Canada did not go ahead with a checkout because of high product shipping costs. Nearly 50 percent of the Canadian online shopping population cited a lack of shipping options as a factor dissuading them from buying online. Three-quarters of the online shopping population in Canada indicated they would be in favor of the idea of free shipping even with a slower delivery. Foreign retailers who wish to capitalize on the evolving online shopping trend in Canada would be wise to devise creative ways to remove the barriers to completing purchases, including free shipping, in-store pickup, or a greater variety of product options than are available from Canadian online retailers to make the cost of shipping worthwhile.

Search Media in Canada

As you can see in Table 15.1, Google is the leading media in Canada, with a larger market share there than in the United States. According to RealTime Stats in November 2011, Google.ca and Google.com held just over 86 percent share, Bing had just under 8 percent, and Yahoo! had 4.43 percent. Local search media include 411.ca, shown in Figure 15.2.

Table 15.1   Search Engine Market Share: Canada

Search Engine	Percentage of the Search Market
Google.ca	86.10%
Bing	7.88%
Yahoo.ca	4.43%
Ask.ca	1.06%
Others	1.6%

Source: marketshare.hitslink.com, November 2011

Figure 15.2   *411.ca is one of Canada's local search engines.*

As you might expect, the Canadian version of Yahoo! is similar to that found in the United States (see Figure 15.3) although the language is different on Yahoo! Quebec (see Figure 15.4). Curiously, there is no obvious link to toggle between the two. Having a link is an common way national websites ease switching back and forth in bilingual Canada.

Figure 15.3 *Yahoo! Canada in English looks pretty much the same as in the United States.*

Figure 15.4 *Note the bank display ad in French on the right on Yahoo! Quebec.*

Common Mistakes

A common mistake is using French as spoken in France to reach French-speaking Canadians. Although the French-speaking Canadians might have similar roots, the French spoken in Quebec has evolved on its own over the years. There are differences not only in the accent, but also in the way words are used. For example, naming daily meals can get very confusing:

"Breakfast" is "petit-déjeuner" in EU French but is simply "déjeuner" in Quebec.

"Dejeuner" in France means "lunch," but lunch in Quebec is "dinner."

And the evening meal in France is "le dîner" (similar to the English word), whereas most French speakers in Canada will say "souper."

Furthermore, "email" is the same in France as in English, but most of the Canadian French-speaking population is likely to use "courriel." The differences in vocabulary are broad enough that you risk missing the mark in Canada, and you could damage your brand if you use a copywriter who knows only European French to write your website or your search ads for French Canadians. It is essential to localize your French content for Canada.

> "...you could damage your brand if you use a copywriter who knows only European French to write your website or your search ads for French Canadians."

And last, but certainly not least to go shopping in France is "faire du shopping," but in Quebec they would say "magasiner," so while the EU French are more likely to search for "shopping en ligne" (online shopping) the Canadian far more likely to use "magasiner en ligne" (see Figure 15.5)

Télécharger ▾	Afficher sous forme de texte ▾	Autres résultats similaires ▾	Canada		Trier par Pertinence ▾	Colonnes ▾
	Mot clé	Concurrence	Recherches mensuelles dans le monde entier ⓘ		Recherches mensuelles dans les zones ciblées ⓘ	
☐ ☆	shopping en ligne	Moyen		14 800		480
☐ ☆	magasiner en ligne	Moyen		2 900		2 400

Figure 15.5 *As data taken from Google's Keyword Tool shows in the column to the right, the difference between use of two keywords in French for "shopping online" in Canada is significant.*

For English-speaking Canada, there is no real difference between the language spoken there and in the United States. However, seemingly small cultural discrepancies can disappoint Canadian customers. Taking care of small details such as writing "Postal Code," which Canadians expect to see instead of "ZIP Code," and having a Canada-centric FAQ section that addresses all the questions that a local consumer might have, especially related to shipping and delivery, are some minor but effective ways to improve the experience of online shoppers in Canada.

Another mistake by U.S. retailers is stating taxes and duties at checkout in U.S. dollars, instead of Canadian, which means, depending on the exchange rate, customers may be surprised with extra charges in their own currency upon delivery.

Speaking of delivery, a good practice is to offer shipping via U.S. Postal Service, because the USPS has agreements in place with Canada Post to expedite shipping and usually does not charge duty management fees, which other shipping services do charge and pass them on to customers. It is also a good idea to state clearly that you ship to Canada. Many websites overlook this point.

Pay-Per-Click

As mentioned before, campaigns for Canada must always be done in two languages—English and Canadian French. This is true not only for campaigns intended for users in Quebec, but also those for nationwide audiences. Treat your Canadian campaign in French as you would any other foreign language. This means you should set up a separate campaign within your AdWords account and then geo-target it to Canada. Chapter 2, "Common Territory: Search Marketing Without Borders," explains how to manage AdWords campaigns in multiple languages.

Note, although it is possible that Google could display your ads written in European French in response to queries in Canadian French because of similarities in the two forms of the language, this would not be your most effective marketing because the vocabulary differences could confuse your searchers. This is why it is important to set up a separate campaign and use the function in your AdWords account to specify the country where you want the ads to be seen.

Organic Search

Nearby Canada is home to world-class search engine optimizers, many of whom have clients in the United States as well as clients in Canada who are targeting the U.S. They know their stuff; do not underestimate the expertise you will find competing with you for visibility in the Canadian online market. As we have noted for similarly mature search marketing industries in the United Kingdom and Germany, you need to use all the tools in your arsenal to be successful.

The tools and techniques for SEO are the same you would use elsewhere; however, there are certain things you must know especially with regards to Canada: Google has at least one separate index to store sites intended for Canada, even the ones in English. This means that results for queries in Canada are served up first from the sites in the Canadian index, so if you want to rank well for Canadian queries, you need to be in that index. To be listed there, you should use as many of the signals as possible to clarify for Google that your content is intended for a Canadian audience, as we discussed in Chapter 2, including a Canadian top-level domain, inbound links from Canadian sites, and even hosting in Canada. Google tends to favor websites hosted in Canada or websites with .ca domains, for example.

Although it is possible that your U.S. .com site may turn up in Canadian results, and indeed, many get traffic from Canada, the bias we mentioned previously toward sites Google identifies as Canadian means that they are considered more relevant to Canadian queries and therefore are returned higher up in the results.

Though usability is beyond the scope of this book, we have to mention the most common practice for websites in Canada is to offer users the choice of "English" or "Francais" on the home page. Sometimes this link is easier to find than others. From a usability standpoint, putting the link to toggle between the two where users can find it easily makes sense—for example, near the top of the page rather than on the bottom where users have to scroll to find it. Putting it near the top also makes the site easier for search engine crawlers to find and follow it if they are looking for content in one language or the other. So does creating a URL structure that builds out URLs in French for your Canadian French site, as shown in Figure 15.6.

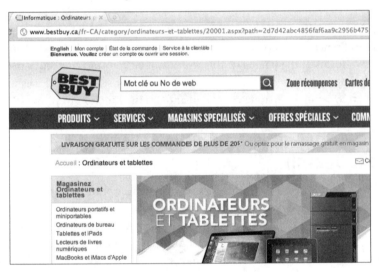

Figure 15.6   *The Best Buy page in Canadian French uses the French terms in its URL. This helps guide Google to the content.*

Public Relations

Online public relations is quite mature in Canada, both for English and French. Tools such as Marketwire and PR.com work well there, as they do in the United States. When we searched for online PR services in Canada, we found a lot about "Application for a Permanent Resident Card (PR Card)"—not to be confused with "public/press relations." There are good local channels such as Newswire.ca, which has the ccTLD and is hosted in Canada and therefore likely to get good ranking in Google.ca (see Figure 15.7).

Figure 15.7   *Distribution through Newswire.ca is picked up by Google News.*

Analytics

The analytics tools you are already using in the United States work fine for Canada. One caveat is that because of Google's Canadian index, if you are using a rank checker, you need to specify the geo-location in the URL that is passed to Google by including "&GL=CA" in the URL.

Search Marketing Tips for Canada

- Canada has two official languages, so all your national campaigns need to be done in both English and French.

- Be sure to use Canadian French, not the language as it is spoken in France, for your keyword research, web copy, and ads.

- Geo-target your Canadian French copy and ads to Canada in both Google Webmaster Tools and Google AdWords.

- Set up a separate campaigns in AdWords for your English content and your French Canadian content.

- Offer customers a choice of shipping options, such as USPS or even free shipping.

16

Brazil

Brazil is the fifth-largest country in the world in both area and population. With nearly 76 million Brazilians online, Brazil is also the fifth-biggest country in Internet usage and growing fast. According to the International Telecommunication Union, nearly 38 percent of the nation's population was online in 2010. A June 2010 study by comScore found that nearly 73 million of about 200 million Brazilians use the Internet. This is up from about 5 million users in the year 2000. That's a growth rate of 1,360 percent in the decade.

Brazilians also spend a good deal of time online—about 1,500 minutes per month, which is consistent with the average online time in Britain. While online, the average Brazilian looks at about 2,500 pages. Brazil ranks fourth worldwide for monthly page views per user, totaling about 33.4 billion viewed pages in 2009. Sixty percent of Brazilian Internet users identify themselves as "heavy users."

Profile of Brazil Online

Brazil offers huge opportunity for Internet marketers, both from a search engine and social media point of view. The Brazilian audience is highly engaged and growing. By the middle of 2010, Brazilian online shopping had grown 40 percent from the same time the year before. According to ecommerce research firm, eBit, 20 million people bought online at least once, spending on average $379, for a total of $6.7 billion. With growing confidence evidenced by online customer satisfaction at 86 percent, Brazilians scooped up books and subscriptions, appliances, cosmetics, medication, and electronics. (Sales of electronics were boosted by the World Cup football finals; many Brazilians wanted to watch on new flat-screen televisions.)

Brazilians online are a predominantly young audience, with 68 percent ages 6 to 34, which is much more than the international average of 54 percent. A comScore study released in mid-2010 found that Internet visitors 6–14 years of age accounted for 12 percent of the total online population in Brazil in May 2010, spending the majority of their time on entertainment, instant messaging, and social networking sites such as the Google-owned Orkut. These young folk are growing up Internet and social media savvy, and will be the next generation of online shoppers. Table 16.1 shows a breakdown of Internet usage by age.

Table 16.1   Brazilian Internet Consumption by Age (May 2010)

	Total Unique Users (000)	% Unique Visitors	% Share of Pages Viewed	% Share of Time on Site (Minutes)
Total Internet	40,713	100%	100%	100%
Persons 6–14	4,825	11.9%	1.8%	1.9%
Persons 15–24	10,421	25.6%	32.4%	32.6%
Persons 25–34	12,408	30.5%	31.6%	31.0%
Persons 35–44	7,641	18.8%	20.6%	20.8%
Persons 45–54	3,782	9.3%	9.8%	9.8%
Persons 55+	1,636	4.0%	3.8%	4.0%

What makes Brazil a bit of a dark horse is the big contrasts between living standards, depending on where Internet searchers live in the country. The southeast region of Brazil accounts for more than 60 percent of online content consumed. This is also where the largest cities are located, Sao Paulo and Rio de Janeiro, and most of the nation's wealth. There, around 50.5 percent of the population holds 74.5 percent of total GDP population. This region has developed a strongly diverse multicultural population.

However, we can say for sure that Brazil is a young nation with a fast-growing middle class with money to spend (see Figure 16.3). Purchasing power is on the rise with improvements in income distribution throughout the country. This has, among other things, led to a rapid increase in credit card usage, 800 percent from 2003 to 2008.

Brazilians spend roughly the same time using search engines as they do on their email, previously the most popular use of the Internet. What also sets Brazilians apart from others is how they use Google. According to ComScore, Brazilian web users spend close to twice the average time on Google as others worldwide. Further, Brazilians spend about 30 percent of their total online time on Google. Likely, the reason has to do with the popularity of Google's Orkut social network. Orkut is also popular in India, where web users also spend twice as much time as other countries do on Google.

Similarly, Brazilians use Twitter more than any other country. In fact, 23 percent of Brazil's Internet users used Twitter in 2010. This is more than twice as many as in the United States. Both Orkut and Twitter should be on your list to market online in Brazil.

Also, many Brazilians are migrating to Facebook, which increased 294 percent between 2010 and 2011, making Brazil the second fastest-growing country market in the world after Russia. Because of Brazilians' fondness for social networking, these platforms can provide you with diverse consumer profiles for the regions and interests you are targeting.

If you are selling consumer goods in Brazil, you will want to market your goods to women. According to a Sophia Mind survey, Brazilian women controlled 66 percent of Brazilian family consumption in 2010. You'll want to keep that in mind in your wording of the text in PPC ads, as well as when you're designing copy and the look and feel of your site. Also, according to eBit, more than half (55 percent) of the purchases motivated by social media were by women—something to consider in the marketing mix.

When Brazilians shop online, they care most about product quality, customer service, and ease and security of their shopping experience. Be sure to emphasize these points in your messaging and your choice of platforms, such as mobile.

Brazil is big in mobile phone usage: fifth in the world in 2011 according to the ITU. Brazil has more than 200 million mobile phones. Landlines are estimated to number far fewer, around 41 million. Clearly, Brazilians are more likely to have access to mobile connections, such as 3G and 4G, rather than wired. Indeed, Google reports seeing a 500 percent increase in mobile access in the past two years.

Search Media in Brazil

According to research done by Forrester, Internet Stats, and other research companies, Google leads the way as the biggest search engine in Brazil. As you can see in Table 16.2, Google search and Google image search hold more than 97 percent of the market. Bing and Yahoo! and the local players have far less.

Table 16.2   Search Engine Market Share—Brazil

Search Engine	Percentage of Search Market
Google.com.br	97.6%
Bing.com.br	1.7%
Yahoo.com.br	0.5%
Others	0.3%

Source: StatCounter, June 2011

One local search engine is UOL Busca, driven by Google (see Figure 16.1).

Figure 16.1   *UOL Busca is one of Brazil's local search engines.*

Brazil is one of the most social-networked countries in the world, and there are some good advertising options on the most popular platforms—Facebook and Orkut (see Figure 16.2). By far, Orkut was more popular, with 30 million members in 2011 compared to Facebook's 17 million.

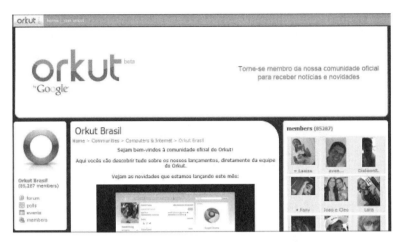

Figure 16.2   *Orkut is the leading social media network in Brazil.*

Most Common Mistakes

The most common mistake is to apply Portuguese marketing tactics to Brazil. Though the official language of Brazil is Portuguese, the culture is clearly different. While Portugal is one of the smaller countries in population, Brazil is fifth-largest country in the world, and the Brazilian culture has evolved in a multicultural environment of immigrants from many different regions and ethnicities.

Around 15 percent of the Brazilian Portuguese language is different from the language spoken in Portugal. The difference is limited mainly to words for flora, fauna, foods, religion, music, and so on. The lexicon and most of the grammar rules remain the same. Brazilian Portuguese is further flavored by the Amerindian tongues of the indigenous peoples there, then the various African languages brought by slaves, and finally those of the of European and Asian immigrants. You will mainly find that words related to technology, modern science, and finance have come lately from English. They include such as words as "layout," "designer," and "computer."

> "The most common mistake is to apply Portuguese marketing tactics to Brazil."

Roughly put, the differences between European Portuguese and standard Brazilian Portuguese can be defined as comparable to the difference found between British and American English.

A prime example of the differences between the language is to look at how the word "mobile" is translated to each. In Portugal, it translates as "telemóvel," whereas in Brazil it translates as "celular" (see Figure 16.3). If you go only with the Portuguese version, you will get only a fraction of the visibility as if you had used "celular." Note that even though the term is adapted from the American version, it is not spelled the same.

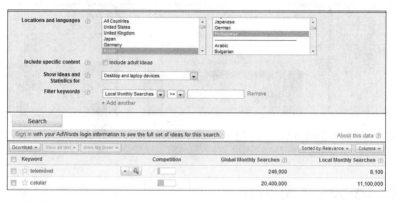

Figure 16.3 *Would you use the keyword "telemóvel" or "celular"? You can see here why you not only need to translate but also localize.*

Pay-Per-Click

Brazil is another one of the countries you can geo-target from within your Google AdWords campaign. For the broader market, you will, of course, target keywords in Brazilian Portuguese and write your ad text in it as well. That said, the International Advertising Bureau Latin American chapter suggests that using French or German in the text of ads for upscale goods may bring you better conversions among the Europeans who have settled in Brazil.

Though Google is strong in search and social, Microsoft has a good foothold in the Brazilian market through pay-per-click ads and Instant Messenger SMS, with a reach parallel to the social media networks, such as Orkut. Targeting your audience through IM might be an option worth exploring.

Microsoft reports 52 million active Instant Messenger accounts in Brazil. You can learn more about advertising opportunities by contacting Microsoft Advertising there. You'll find more information on its site, http://advertising.microsoft.com/brasil/wlmessenger, and using Google Translate if you need to (see Figure 16.4).

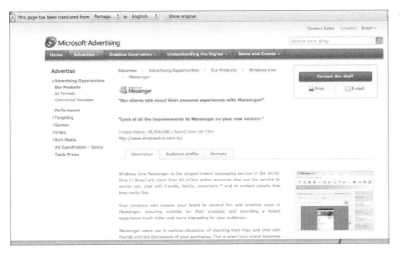

Figure 16.4 *Microsoft Advertising is a source for tapping into the lively and large Brazilian texting market.*

Organic Search

When you're optimizing for Brazilians, the Google Webmaster guide is a good benchmark of what you should and should not do. Localized links are a key factor and, on top of that, localized content in Brazilian Portuguese. The domain should include a country code top-level domain (ccTLD) such as .com.br.

 Note

The extension in Brazil can and often does include a "com.br" rather than ".br" alone.

With well over 100 million Web users expected in this decade, Brazil is likely to be one of the leading countries online. Google is likely to roll out algorithmic changes more rapidly in Brazil. For this reason, your best bet is to stay current with Google best practices, as you do for U.S.-targeted sites. In short, sloppy search engine optimization (SEO) tactics you may have been getting away with elsewhere might not fly in Brazil, any more than they do in the United States or United Kingdom, especially as Google refines its efforts to reduce clutter in its index.

The link-building practice is not as mature in Brazil as you are accustomed to in the United States. Exchanging reciprocal links is a commonly accepted practice. Identifying authoritative sites to link to your content would be even more effective for gaining visibility in Google in Brazil. Some low-hanging fruit might be the Brazilian section within Dmoz (also known as the Open Directory Project). As you can see in Figure 16.5, another option is to seek out local directories you can find with a search query on Google.com.br using this search phrase: **"web directory" site:*.com.br -google**.

Figure 16.5   *You can play around with Google to find directories to which you can submit your site.*

Also keep in mind Google owns both the leading video and social media platforms, which are enormously popular among Brazilians, giving you many other opportunities to reach them. On top of that, the biggest local search engine, UOL, uses Google results to power its own, so optimizing according to Google standards will be effective there, too.

Analytics

Through our research, we did not find any local tool that could replace Google Analytics or any of the other analytics providers. Both the well-known free tools—Google Analytics and Yahoo! Web Analytics—work well in Brazil and should help monitor any campaign activities into the Brazilian market.

One thing we would recommend when looking at the analytics is to consider where visitors are coming from. This will help you target the regions with better opportunities generated by greater wealth of the people there. You can filter your results by geographic area in Google Web Analytics.

Online Public Relations

When it comes to online PR, there are not many options in Brazil. Marketwire has proven to be useful, and NewsCertain and eNewsPR provide services in the region. You need to localize your language and understand the difference between Portugal and Brazil when it comes to languages and tone of voice.

"The Brazilians speak Portuguese, not Spanish, and their own version of Portuguese at that."

The Brazilians are very family oriented and heavy users of social networks. Because of this, online PR or content seeding should be an important part of your organic strategy because it is likely to feed into the lively Brazilian social media stream, helping you to push your brand and/or services in a very cost-effective way.

Search Marketing Tips for Brazil

- The Brazilians speak Portuguese, not Spanish, and their own version of Portuguese at that.
- Brazilians use social media heavily, especially Orkut, Twitter, and IM, with Facebook gaining ground. Consider those platforms for your messaging.
- When marketing consumer products or services, keep in mind women represent more than 50 percent of all users on social media sites and users of collective purchasing sites.
- Use press releases to seed content, and it will often reach sociable Brazilians though their networking sites.
- Likewise, optimizing video for YouTube is a big opportunity in Brazil.

17

South America: Spanish-Speaking Markets

Too often in the past we have heard that Latin America markets are not worth our attention because not much money was spent online. No longer can this be said. Rather, South America was something of a sleeping giant that woke up when several trends combined to create more rapid growth in Internet use and also search engines and social media use. In 2010, the Interactive Advertising Bureau (IAB) noted online spending in all of Latin America was not even 5 percent of all ad spending. However, the IAB identified lots of room for growth, predicting 10 percent participation by 2016.

Profile of Spanish-Speaking Latin America Online

According to Internet World Stats in June 2011, with just 8.4 percent of the world's population, Latin America makes up 10 percent of the world's Internet population. That means 1 of every 10 people online worldwide is in Latin America. With 162.8 million users, 40.7 percent penetration, the proportion of the South American population online in 2011 was well above the rest of the world average of 30 percent. Further, one-third of all Internet users in all the Americas are in South America.

South American Internet use grew 1,039 percent between 2000 and 2011, more than twice as fast as the rest of the world at 457 percent. That was more than Asia, more than Europe, and definitely more than North America. Although Western Europe is approaching saturated growth, countries such as Brazil, Colombia, Chile, Venezuela, Peru, and Argentina have a long way to go before maxing out their potential online.

The Net market in Brazil is by far the largest in South America, and was covered in the preceding chapter. In Brazil the official language is Portuguese, unlike all the other South American countries, which use Spanish. Even without Brazil, the rest of the region represented 54 percent of the region's GDP in 2011, according to fnbox, a Brazilian technology company. In this chapter, we round up the next largest markets: Argentina, Chile, Colombia, Peru, and Venezuela. We look at how marketers can take advantage of opportunities in these countries.

Spanish-speaking Latin America continues to be a growing market with strong ties to Europe and even more to the United States. Spanish is the most widely spoken language in the world, spoken by close to 500 million people in 23 countries. Most of them live in Latin America. Furthermore, by 2011, Spanish became the second most-used language on Facebook; of 750 million members, 118 million are from Latin America and 14.4 million are from Spain, and there are uncounted numbers in the United States and elsewhere for whom Spanish is their first language.

What opportunities? According to comScore's year-end 2010 study, Latin Americans made more searches per searcher and viewed more search results pages per searcher than any other region in the world. That means Latin Americans searched more often than searchers in the United Kingdom, Europe, or Asia and the United States! Furthermore, search queries grew to 18.5 billion in 2011, which was a 21 percent increase in one year. This was the single highest leap in the world, besting Europe at 1 percent, North America at 10 percent, Asia Pacific at 8 percent, and even the Middle East and Africa at 16 percent. Also according to comScore, this surge in Latin American search queries was driven by a 14 percent increase in the number of unique searchers (see Table 17.1).

Table 17.1 Number of Unique Searchers per Country

	Searches	Visits Per Searcher	Unique Searchers	SERPS Per Searcher	Searches per Searcher
Colombia	1,968,000,000	29.8	11,521,000	228.0	170.8
Venezuela	409,000,000	34.5	2,670,000	214.4	153.2
Peru	511,000,000	36.3	3,511,000	180.8	145.5
Mexico	2,278,000,000	28.4	16,683,000	188.4	136.5
Argentina	1,624,000,000	30.5	12,058,000	194.0	134.7
Chile	898,000,000	29.0	6,772,000	166.4	132.6
Brazil	4,134,000,000	26.7	36,925,000	159.5	112.0

By March 2011, Latin American searches rose to 18.5 billion per month; Chile, more than a billion; Argentina, more than 2 billion; and Colombia, nearly 3 billion, according to comScore. Colombians averaged 233 searches per searcher in March 2011; Peruvians, 232; Argentinians, 175; Brazilians, 150; and Chileans, 148.

Indeed, although the United States has far more searches on search engines overall, because of a much larger population online, Peru, Venezuela, Chile, Colombia, and Argentina all have trended upward to as many or more visits per searcher. Latin Americans use search engines for a portal for their web visits, and the one they use most is Google. This makes for an easy entry for U.S. marketers, at least from the standpoint of using a platform familiar to you.

As with many emerging markets, the markets listed in this profile are likely to bypass old connection types such as dial-up and go straight to broadband. This means multimedia, video, and collaborative content are immediately accessible. Broadband had been slow to develop, with only 6.3 percent penetration in Latin America in 2009 (compared to a world average of 8 percent). The pace has picked up, with top countries showing double-digit gains in 2010. Argentina had the highest broadband rate in the region, followed by Colombia, Chile, and Venezuela. (Venezuela's small penetration might be due to the state-owned CANTV previously holding a monopoly on ASDL.) In Colombia, cable and ASDL began to grow briskly, encouraged by its government eager to reduce the digital divide. Table 17.2 shows the growth of broadband in Latin America.

Table 17.2   Broadband Penetration in Latin America

Country	Broadband Subscribers	Yearly Growth	Penetration
Argentina	5,100,000	19%	12.6%
Chile	1,952,000	13%	11.4%
Colombia	2,400,000	12%	5.3%
Venezuela	1,400,000	13%	4.9%
Peru	935,000	15%	3.1%
Latin American Average	34,645,700	16%	6.8%
World Average	580,000,000		7.25%

Allowing for mobile access is a big factor in search marketing in the Latin American countries covered here because Latin Americans are likely to be online via their mobile devices, and you may be able to reach them more often that way.

Search Media in Latin America

Google has led the search engine market in all Latin American countries, with an average 90.5 percent of the search market (see Table 17.3), more than 16.7 billion searchers on it in March 2011, and 168 queries per searcher. Facebook was the second most-visited property, though trailing in use for search with only 525 million searches.

Table 17.3   Most Visited Web Properties—Latin America

Search Engine	Percentage of Search Market
Google	90.5%
Facebook	2.8%
Yahoo!	1.1%
Ask Network	0.6%

Source: RealTimeStats.com: August 2011

Social media has played a growing role in all of Latin America's engagement online. One in four visited a social media site, according to March 2011 data from comScore. Latin Americans now use search engines and social media more than texting and email, which had been their favored online activities.

Long-time favorite game site Hi5 has remained popular, but YouTube took the lead in 2011 insofar as most time spent at a specific site and volume of users. Facebook's growth across Latin America has been remarkable. Facebook has added 25 million users in the first six months of 2011, almost 45 percent growth, according to SocialBakers. Social media networks and texting (also known as SMS) might be a great addition to your Latin American online marketing campaigns. Latin Americans used instant messaging at a rate twice as high the rest of the world. In August 2010, that number was 7 of every 10 online.

Twitter grew in Latin America to 855,000 Tweeters, 18 percent penetration by March 2011, issuing more than 55 million tweets per day, with 13,000 new registrants per day and 29 million tweets sent per day, 39 percent of them from mobile.

By 2011, group buying sites had caught on in Latin America. One in 10 Internet users there visited Groupon, or one of the local clones, creating a new marketing channel online.

Most Common Mistakes

The most problematic commonly made mistake is using a single site for Spanish language content to target all Spanish-speaking Latin American countries. If you try to use a single domain and a single set of content to target multiple Latin American countries, you pass up the power of country-code top-level domains (ccTLDs) and in-country inbound links to clarify your target market for Google. Worse, if you use the same content on separate domains for each country you are targeting, you risk tripping duplicate content filters in Google's indexing, which can significantly reduce your visibility in your target markets. Placing the identical content on different pages—with different URLs—forces Google to decide what to show where, and such a business decision you wouldn't want to leave to a bot.

There are other problems that a non-native marketer might stumble into when marketing to Latin America. Many of these problems relate to language and demographics, which leads us to another common mistake: treating all Latin American countries as the same. Although all speak Spanish (save for Brazil, which speaks a version of Portuguese), South American countries each have their own distinct history and culture and, yes, variations in the use of their Spanish language.

The South American countries that speak Spanish have backgrounds similar to that of Mexico, in that they were settled by Spanish explorers and now speak Spanish. However, the version of Spanish spoken in each South American country differs insofar as vocabulary and pronunciation are concerned—similar to how American and British English differ.

The subsequent influence of languages of tribes indigenous to each country (as well as the evolution of local terms) made the Spanish spoken in each Latin American country distinctly its own. Although most Latin Americans can likely understand the Spanish their neighbors speak, using a one-size-fits-all language would not be best practice for search marketing. The differences in vocabulary can complicate selecting the best keywords and accurately targeting your messages and calls to action. For example:

- A snack in one country is "marienda," but that means "dinner" in others, which could make a difference if you want to sell a product such as nachos or Tostitos.
- There are nearly 40 different words for popcorn used in Spanish-speaking South American countries.
- In Chile and Peru, a Chinese restaurant is called a "chifa," but not in other countries.

Internet users across South America mostly skew young, though with notable exceptions. Overall, there have been far more younger users online in South America than the worldwide average of 27 percent. In a 2010 study, researchers learned that 30 percent of Latin American users were aged 15–24. If you add in those 25–34, the share of users online leaps to 63%, which is well above the worldwide 53 percent. Think young when you create search ads and landing pages to better target your audience there. The notable exception to the youthful South American market is Chile, where Internet use is distributed more along average global demographics, with twice as many in the middle-aged and older group than its neighbors in the region.

Later we discuss useful tactics to avoid confusing your desired visitors, or Google, but first let's review the five most notable markets in Spanish-speaking South America:

- Argentina
- Colombia
- Venezuela
- Chile
- Peru

Profile of Argentina Online

There were more than 27.5 million people online in Argentina in March 2011, which is 66 percent of the population and enough to make Argentina the second-largest Internet population in South America, after Brazil. Argentina ranks 19th among the top 20 Internet populations in the world. Argentina is the largest Spanish-speaking Internet population on the continent, accounting for 17 percent of all South Americans online. According to a March 2011 comScore study, Argentinians make an average of 47.6 visits to the Internet per month and spend on average 27.4 hours online per month, which is well above the worldwide average of 23 hours per month.

In Argentina, the Internet population skews slightly older than the rest of South America, with 15–24-year-olds representing just 29 percent, which is below the average for the region. The difference is at the other end of the age range where almost twice as many people 55 and older go online than the average for the rest of Latin America. That said, the young folks spend much more time online than any other age group. Males 35 and under spend more time online than their same-age female counterparts. However, women 35 and over spend more time online than men 35 and older.

Those viewing videos reached nearly a billion in 2011. According to comScore, 11.2 million unique visitors in Argentina viewed nearly a billion videos in March of that year—986,753, 000 videos to be exact, watched by 86.5 percent of those online in Argentina, for an average 8.6 hours, and 5.6 minutes per video. Enthusiasm for entertainment sites grew as well. Entertainment sites were visited by 85 percent of Argentinian web users in March 2011—8 percent more than the previous year.

Retail sites received visits from nearly two-thirds of Argentinians online in the first quarter of 2011. In fact, retail sites were as popular in Argentina as they were in Brazil. comScore found that 97 percent of Argentinians online said the Internet was important in making buying decisions. This means the Internet is more important as a shopping tool to Argentinians than to any other country in the region. However, Argentinians have not shown much enthusiasm for purchasing online. You can see this in the way Argentinians visited automotive sites at a rate of 27 percent to research buying cars, more than their neighbors by a wide margin. However, they did not buy much online at travel sites, though this category showed more growth than other e-commerce activity. One of the reasons ecommerce may not be as popular in Argentina as other countries is that many shoppers remain reluctant to pay with credit cards, preferring to use cash at RapiPago or Pagil Facil storefronts where they pay their bills. The debilitating recession and bank failures Argentina endured in 2001 left a lingering distrust of banks and credit.

Meanwhile, a fast-rising new opportunity turned out to be group-discount buying services. Groupon.com launched a successful foray into Argentina in 2010, and was immediately followed with 10 or 12 local lookalikes. All together, coupon sites in Argentina zoomed up in popularity between 2010 and 2011, booming 8,274 percent, much more than the region's average 2,715 percent.

Sports sites drew fans, not surprisingly, at a rate of 38 percent of those online visiting a sports website in March 2011, 8 percent more than the previous year. The top sports site is ole.com.ar, which has the most reach and time spent on site by a wide margin—14.1 percent and 69.6 minutes on average. On the other hand, TyCSPorts.com has a smaller reach—2.2 percent—yet commands a lot of loyal time for such its size (42.6 average minutes per user on average).

Search Media in Argentina

How do you reach Argentinians online? Google, Facebook, YouTube, and SMS are your likeliest paths to get their attention. Although their absolute volume was less than larger populations, Argentinians ranked fourth in the world for the number of visits they make to search engines per searcher, searches per searcher, and SERPs per searcher, according to December 2010 data from comScore. By 2011, Argentina had 12.5 million searchers, 96.7 percent of all online there, averaging 175 searches per searcher for a total of 2.2 billion searches, 2.6 billion search results pages, and 619 million search visits.

As you can see in Table 17.4, Google was the most popular search engine by far with a 96.76 percent share of the market; Bing under 2 percent; Yahoo!, 1 percent; and all others, 1 percent.

Table 17.4   Search Engine Market Share—Argentina

Search Engine	Percentage of Search Market
Google	96.76%
Bing	1.63%
Yahoo!	0.97%
Ask	0.50%
Microsoft Live Search	0.05%
AOL	0.04%
Others	0.05%

Source: RealTimeStats.com: August 2011

However, social media use has been catching up fast. By March 2011, 9 out of 10 Argentinians visited social networking sites, according to comScore data. As you can see in Table 17.5, Argentinians spent more of their online time on social media than anything else, at 29 percent, slightly more than Italy, and third only to the Philippines and Malaysia. In absolute terms, they spent 8.1 hours per month, which ranked them third in the world after Israel and Russia. Social networking flew past email as popular activities in 2010 and 2011.

Table 17.5 Top Categories of Time Spent Online

	January 2010	January 2011	% Change
Portals	38.6%	29%	−9.7%
Social Networking	15.2%	27.8%	12.6%
Instant Messengers	26.2%	19.6%	−6.6%
Entertainment	7.7%	8.1%	0.4%
Email	9.2%	7.1%	−2.1%

Source: comScore Media Matrix, Panel-Only Data. January 2010 versus January 2011; Total Audience Argentina, Age 15+; Home and Work Locations

At 80 percent reach in December 2010, Facebook use in Argentina was well above the Latin American average of 60 percent. By March 2011, Argentina was fifth in reach worldwide for Facebook, and seventh for Twitter. As you can see in Table 17.6, an April 2011 comScore report shows that Argentinians averaged more than 527 minutes (or 8.8 hours) on Facebook, the most in Latin America and the third-highest in the world. By July 2011, there were 15.9 million Argentinian Facebook users, up from 12.5 million in January, 38.53 of the country's population, and 6 of 10 of those online. More of them on Facebook were younger, 18–24 years old and near evenly split between men and women.

Table 17.6 Top Internet Properties By Total Unique Visitors in Argentina

	Total Unique Visitors (in Millions)	% Reach	Average Minutes Per Visitor
Total Internet: Total Audience	12,991	100%	1,614.9
Microsoft Sites	12,253	95.1%	409
Google Sites	12,256	94.3%	181
Facebook.com	11,504	88.6%	527.8
Yahoo! Sites	8,942	68.8%	36.4

	Total Unique Visitors (in Millions)	% Reach	Average Minutes Per Visitor
Grupo Clarin	5,989	46.1%	56.8%
Taringa.net	5,981	46%	26.4
MercadoLibre	5,329	41%	43.2
Wikimedia Foundation Sites	5,319	40.9%	10.3
Terra-Telefonica	4,976	38.3%	10.6
Grupo La Nacion	4,263	32.8%	22.6

Source: comScore Media Matrix. April 2011; Total Argentina Internet Audience, Age 15+; Home and Work Locations.

Despite a shift in time spent on SMS to social media, you were still likely to find Argentinians on Instant Messenger in 2011. Microsoft sites led by a wide margin for time online, because of SMS Instant Messenger, followed by Google sites, including YouTube, and then Facebook and Yahoo!. Of the locals, news site Grupo Clarin is the place where Argentinians went online to get news, and they stay there far longer than other favorites, both local and global.

Profile of Colombia Online

In June 2011, Colombia had the third-largest Internet population in South America with 22.5 million Internet users. This is the first time Colombia's Internet population has exceeded half of its total population. Colombia's online community accounts for 10 percent of all Internet visitors in South America. Growth since 2000 was a whopping 2,352 percent. Colombians spent about 23.9 hours per month online, an hour and a half more than the world average. Close to half of the Internet audience in Colombia was under the age of 24, and more than 70 percent were under 34 years old, comprising a younger population than the rest of Latin America.

According to a September 2010 comScore report, Colombians aged 15–24 spent an of average 28 hours online. Other age groups spent a combined 19 hours online. In middle-aged and older groups women's time online overtook men's, leaping ahead in the 45 to 54 age bracket. Women in this group spent 22.3 hours online and the guys that age 15.5. There were fewer people aged 45+ online, but women in that age group spent much more time online than men.

Search Media in Colombia

How do you reach people online in Colombia? Start with Google. According to comScore, 11 million unique searchers—one of every two online—made 2 billion searches in September 2010. These 2 billion searches created 2.8 billion search results pages and 386 million visits to websites. By March 2011, Colombian searcher activity grew 28 percent. Colombians conducted 2.9 billion searches, becoming the third-largest search market in Latin America, behind Brazil and Mexico.

As you can see in Table 17.7, Google is by far the most popular search media in Colombia. Microsoft's Bing has a small share, but others register barely half a percent or less.

Table 17.7   Search Engine Market Share—Colombia

Search Engine	Percentage of Search Market
Google	96.75%
Bing	2.24%
Yahoo!	0.56%
Ask	0.39%
AOL	0.04%
Others	0.002%

Source: RealTimeStats.com: August 2011

That said, far more of Colombians' online time went to social media sites than search engines. Searching accounted for only 2.7 percent of total minutes online, whereas social networking accounted for 20.3 percent. Colombians spent 2–3 minutes per search engine visit. However, they spent close to 18 minutes on YouTube per visit and 10 minutes on Facebook. On average, Colombians spent 7 hours per month on social networking. According to an April 2011 comScore report, Colombia's social networking usage ranked seventh in the world—higher than the United States, United Kingdom, or Canada.

Search engines are used by 93 percent of the online audience, with social networking trailing just behind at 86.5 percent reach. This is on par with the fact that about 87 percent of Latin America uses social media.

Colombians spend 19.6 percent of their online time sending and receiving instant messages. Time spent using email is only about half that devoted to instant messaging.

Table 17.8 Colombia's Most Visited Sites—April 2011

Sites	Reach	Minutes
Microsoft sites (including Microsoft Instant Messenger)	93.4%	421
Google sites (including YouTube)	91.9%	203
Facebook	83.2%	277
Yahoo! (including email)	48.6%	34.3
Wikimedia	47.6%	12.9
Orange	35.7%	4.7
Terra Telefonica	33.8%	11
VEVO (video)	27.7%	11
Taringa.net	27.5%	11

Source: comScore

Other notable Colombian sites are

- Slideshare—6.9 percent reach
- Sonico.com—11.1 percent reach
- Twitter—10.3 percent reach

Dating site Baddo had a mere 7.3 percent reach but at 52 minutes per month had the fourth-highest average time spent per month (though it is a distant fourth—225 minutes less than Facebook).

By June 2011, one of every three Colombians and two of every three online Colombians were on Facebook—14.6 million in all. Colombia ranked tenth in the world for Facebook reach. Most were young; one-third of Facebook friends in Colombia were 18 to 24, and more than 70 percent were younger than 34, evenly split between men and women. Capital city Bogota had more than 7 million Facebook members in May 2011—the seventh-largest metro network in the world.

Colombia was home to 603,000 Tweeters in 2011, which is 10 percent of the online population. Twitter counts among its Colombian members a shoe model and the country's president, who was second to the model in number of followers.

Colombia was the second most-active market in Latin America for entertainment, particularly music, growing 24 percent in 2010. YouTube led with 64 percent reach and 147 minutes spent on average per month, and music video sites VEVO and Musica followed with 27.7 and 20 percent reach.

Six of 10 Colombians visited a blog in September 2011. However, they proved less interested in reading news at traditional media sites than the rest of Latin America. In terms of media sites, El Tiempo gained the most reach at 27 percent. The other most popular online verticals were technology, retail, downloads, and games and education. Games held users' attention for twice as long as any other category. Such preferences illustrate how Colombia is a "high-context" culture, meaning its people respond more positively to narrative information, unlike other "low-context" countries where more factual information is needed.

Even less interested in ecommerce sites, only one in five Colombians used a travel site in 2011, compared to the Latin American average of one in four. Still, travel sites such as Avianca were growing at 1 or 2 percent each, indicating an opportune trend.

The Interactive Advertising Bureau (IAB) Colombia reported online ad spending levels in Colombia rose 55 percent in 2010, to $41.2 million, with social networks growing the most, at the expense of email marketing, display, and mobile marketing. Ad spend for mobile marketing is likely to change because some experts estimate that Colombia will have 46.8 million mobile subscribers by 2014.

Profile of Venezuela Online

Oil-rich and one of most highly urbanized countries in South America, Venezuela was the fourth-largest Internet market there, with 37.7 percent of its population online in June 2011. Venezuela's online audience is composed of 10.4 million users who spend an average of 26.6 hours per month online, which is more than the world average. During 2010, the Internet population in Venezuela surged 27 percent—the highest increase in Latin America—and nearly double the region's rate overall. The audience online there skews far younger than even the rest of Latin America, with half between 15 and 24 years old, and far fewer 45 and up. According to an April 2011 comScore study, Venezuelans averaged about seven hours online per person, which is more than people in the United States, United Kingdom, or Canada.

Instant messaging reach at 59.6 percent was more than the worldwide average of 34.7 percent, but still less than the Latin American average of 68 percent. Twitter penetration was 21 percent in March 2011. At 1 million-plus, Venezuelans constitute 45 percent of Latin America Twitter traffic. President Hugo Chavez joined in 2010, boosting Twitter use there, and by 2011 online pundits observed he was running the country in 140-character bursts.

More than three-quarters of Venezuelans online visited entertainment, multimedia, music, and television sites, and more than half read news sites and blogs. Banking sites were visited by about 42 percent of Venezuelans online (which is much higher than the Latin American average of 25.7 percent, and the global average of 27 percent). Although 60.3 percent of those online visited retail sites, this number still lags behind both Latin American and worldwide use.

Search Media in Venezuela

Where are you most likely to get your message seen by people online in Venezuela? Searching has been on the rise. In December 2010, 2.7 million unique searchers were making 409 million searches, 153 searchers per searcher. Venezuela's search engine query volume was the fourth-largest in South America. As you can see in Table 17.9, in 2011 search engine query volume rose 31 percent from the year before, a rate second only to Brazil's.

Table 17.9 Search Query Growth in Latin America

	March 2010 (in Millions)	March 2011 (in Millions)	% Change
Latin America	15,293	18,528	21%
Brazil	4,462	5,969	34%
Mexico	2,588	3,171	23%
Colombia	2,232	2,866	28%
Argentina	1,814	2,186	21%
Chile	970	1,041	7%
Venezuela	375	493	31%

Source: comScore

As you can see in Table 17.10, Google had 97.4 percent share of the Venezuelan search market in August 2010, or nearly all of it. The small leftover share was divided among other global media, but none measured much more than around 1 percent.

Table 17.10 Search Engine Market Share—Venezuela

Search Engine	Percentage of Search Market
Google	96.52%
Bing	1.67%
Yahoo	0.92%
Ask	0.374%
AOL	0.05%

Source: Marketshare.Hitslink.com, November 2011

Profile of Chile Online

Chile was the fifth largest Internet population in South America in 2011, but has grown faster than the average for South America for the previous five years and the world overall. Internet World statistics counted 9.2 million Internet users in Chile as of March 2011, a 54.8 percent penetration, and up from 8 million online a year earlier, and 7.3 million in 2007, a growth rate of 27 percent over six years and a leap of 16 percent the last year, much greater than the world average increase of 7.3 percent for the same time frame, and the largest increase among its regional neighbors. Chile is one of the most stable and prosperous nations of South America.

Web visitors in Chile spent some 23.8 hours online, an hour and a half more than the world average in 2010. Like Argentinians, Chileans tended to be older than Internet users across the rest of Latin America, with only 26 percent in the age range of 15–24, just under the world average of 27 percent, whereas in the rest of Latin America, a much larger proportion, 35 percent, are younger users.

Search Media in Chile

Where will you reach Chileans online? Although search engine use at 89 percent followed closely in popularity, people online in Chile were spending more than a quarter of their time online on social network sites by March 2011, according to comScore.

Google is the top search tool in Chile in 2011. Local players have very little reach in Chile, however they may be useful as sources of local links, such as *Buscar.cl,* shown in Table 17.11. By clicking on "AGREGAR URL" in the upper right you can add your site to its index.

Table 17.11   Search Engine Market Share—Chile

Search Engine	Percentage of Search Market
Google	97.45%
Bing	1.28%
Ask	0.8%
Yahoo!	0.38%
AOL	0.01%
Others	0.08%

Source: Marketshare.Hitslink.com, November 2011

Figure 17.1   *Buscar.cl is a local player in Chile, which may be a good source of a local link.*

As you can see in Table 17.12, as in Argentina, more Internet visitors in Chile engaged in social networks and spent more time doing so between 2010 and 2011, trending away from time they used to spend on portals, instant messaging, and email.

Table 17.12   Chile's Top Online Activities

	January 2010	January 2011	% Change
Social Networking	19.6%	28.5%	8.9%
Portals	34.2%	25.2%	−8.9%
Instant Messaging	26%	19.1%	−6.9%
Entertainment	9.3%	10.9%	1.6%
Email	6.6%	5.4%	−1.2%

Social networking was more popular in Chile than in much of the rest of the world in 2010. About 91.1 percent of Chileans use social networks, which is much higher than the worldwide average reach of 69.8 percent, and significantly higher than the average reach across Latin America of 82.7. By April 2011, Chileans spent on average nearly seven hours per month on social media, most often Facebook.

Chile was fourth for Facebook use worldwide in 2010. Though growth slowed the next year, Chile, along with Venezuela, had one of the highest growth rates in the world, and by January 2011, Facebook reached 9 of every 10 Internet visitors in Chile. By the following July 2011, 52 percent of Chile's entire population was on Facebook, the highest penetration in the region. Capital city Santiago had 5.5 million Facebook friends, making it the 12th largest metro network in the world. Chile's Facebook friends are mostly on the younger side, with one-third aged 18–24 and three-quarters younger than 34. Fotolog.com and Windows Live profile were also popular, with nearly a million unique visitors at that time. Photo sharing is popular in Chile, mostly on Facebook.

Instant messaging was popular—68.8 percent reach in 2010, according to com-Score data, with use averaging nine hours per month.

There were 871,000 Tweeters in 2011.

Chileans outpaced their regional neighbors for visits to entertainment sites, including music, movies and TV, entertainment news, and humor. More than 6 million unique viewers watched 562,793,000 videos in March 2011, according to comScore, which was 83.2 percent of the population online, spending 8.6 hours on average per month and 5.6 minutes per video. In April 2011, 8 of 10 users visited entertainment sites, mainly music and video. YouTube is the runaway favorite at nearly 63 percent reach, though local sites Musica.com, VEVO, and Television Nacional De Chile follow, but reach less than 1 in 5 visitors. Games such as Scrabble, Sudoku, and crossword puzzles have drawn a larger following among middle-aged users, mainly women.

Chileans use banking and finance sites much more than other Latin American countries—50.4 percent compared to 37.4 average across the region. Community sites are also much more popular in Chile than other countries in South America.

Like most in Latin America, Chileans have preferred comparison shopping online but making purchases offline.

Profile of Peru Online

Though a smaller Internet market than its neighbors, Peru is worth a look for future opportunities. Enjoying an economic boom in the 2000s and foreign investment in mineral wealth, Peru became one of the world's fastest-growing economies in 2011. Peru had just over 9 million Internet users in 2011, nearly as many as Chile, but they were only 31 percent of the population. According to comScore, Peruvians averaged 24.4 hours online in April 2011, most of the time on major portals, social networks, or instant messaging.

Search Media in Peru

As you can see in Table 17.13, Google enjoyed 97 percent reach among those online in Peru in April 2011, but Peruvians spent more much time on Facebook, staying 5 hours, or 309 minutes as shown in Table 17.14, as opposed to just more than 3 hours searching. Because of the popularity of instant messaging, Microsoft sites clocked the most use at a per person average of 8.4 hours. Much of this was no doubt SMS—Instant Messaging over the Microsoft network. The high "reach" percentages indicate that people in Peru used multiple online media—Google for search, Microsoft for SMS, and Facebook for social networking.

Table 17.13   Search Engine Market Share—Peru

Search Engine	Percentage of Search Market
Google	96.67%
Bing	1.8%
Ask	0.77%
Yahoo!	0.62%
AOL	0.04%
Others	0.1%

Source: RealTimeStats.com: August 2011

Table 17.14   Top Internet Properties in Peru, April 2011

Total Internet Audience	Unique Visitors (000)	% Reach	Time Spent (Minutes)
Total Audience	4,000	100%	1,461.5
Google Sites	3,880	97.0%	226.5
Microsoft Sites	3,566	89.15	504.2
Facebook.com	3,431	85.8%	309.8
Yahoo! Sites	2,587	64.7%	26.8
Empresa Editora El Comerio	2,265	56.6%	49.6
Wikimedia Foundation Sites	1,996	49.9%	13.7
Terra—Telefonica	1,743	43.6%	13.5
Orange Sites	1,709	42.7%	4.6
Grupo RPP	1,444	36.1%	8.0
VEVO, incl. on YouTube	1,334	33.4%	10.8

Source: comScore Media Metrix

By July 2011, 6.4 million Peruvians were on Facebook—22 percent of the entire population and 80 percent of those online. Facebook usage was up significantly (48 percent) from 4.3 million in January 2011. More Peruvian men than women use Facebook, and the largest group were aged 18–24. Nearly half of them were in Lima, ranking that capital 18th in the world. Peru had 256,000 Tweeters in 2011.

Pay-Per-Click (PPC) Advertising in Latin America

Although Google's dominance makes managing paid search campaigns in English relatively easy from your AdWords account, you will have much more success with the help of a native speaker. A native speaker will be able to help select the keywords and compelling ad text that will perform best in each country. Although Spanish is the common language for the countries in this chapter, creating separate campaigns for each country gives you the best opportunity for success. Creating country-specific campaigns allows you to make your ads sensitive to local nuances in language and culture. Country-specific campaigns are also easier to monitor because Google allows you to geo-target specific cities in Chile and Colombia (as well as Brazil and Mexico). However, as of this writing, you can target only regions, not cities, in Argentina.

Microsoft should not be forgotten when it comes to paid search advertising, though your biggest opportunities for success are in SMS texting and marketing through content networks. Microsoft Windows Live Messenger is widely used in Colombia, Chile, Venezuela, and Argentina. Indeed, these countries along with Brazil and Mexico were 7 of the top 10 countries around the world for IM reach in May 2011. Further, Brazil ranks first worldwide in time spent using Instant Messenger. Mexico ranks 3rd; Peru, 6th; Argentina, 8th; and Chile, 10th.

That said, instant messaging appears to have lost share as social media usage has risen. Latin Americans spend as much or more time using social media as they do instant messaging. This is especially true of women who tend to control house-hold spending in the region. You would be wise to consider advertising in Latin America to round out your paid campaigns. Facebook provides geo-targeting in some international regions and cities, as well as advertising assistance in both Spanish and Brazilian Portuguese. Contact the sales team for more information at www.facebook.com/business/contact.php.

Organic Search

With Google unquestionably in the lead in all the Spanish-speaking Latin American countries, your search engine optimization (SEO) might seem an easy task. However, your challenge will be to make it perfectly clear to Google just which Spanish-speaking country's results are the appropriate ones to display your site. To avoid confusion, we recommend you set up a separate site for each country on its own top-level domain. Use .cl for Chile, .com.ar for Argentina, .co.ve for Venezuela, and com.co for Colombia. Next, tweak the Spanish on each to reflect the vernacular and culture in that country. Also, be sure to get inbound links from sites that use top-level domains from the same country. That means if you are getting links for your Venezuelan domain, you want those links to come from sites that use a top-level Venezuelan domain.

Country-specific Spanish language content and inbound links will also help you avoid being filtered out of Google's index as duplicate content. Need we remind you that you have to be included in Google's index to get ranked in searches?

To get links focusing on specific countries, you can start on Dmoz directories for each. As you see in Figure 17.2, you can also find possible link partners on Google by searching for **"web directory site:*.com.ar"** for Argentina, for example. Remember to filter out Google results by using the **"–Google"** operator in your search query.

Figure 17.2   *Use Google to find link partners in individual countries.*

Another source focusing on Latin American countries is Wepa!.com, which provides free access categories of paid links in a variety of categories and may yield useful links partners (see Figure 17.3). However, Wepa!.com's selection is self-limited by those who choose to pay to be listed.

Figure 17.3   *Wepa! provides access to paid-for links in Argentina, Chile, Colombia, Peru, and Venezuela.*

Don't overlook opportunities to appear in universal search results by optimizing your images and YouTube videos with country-specific Spanish language titles and tags (see Figure 17.4).

Figure 17.4   *Note the images and YouTube videos in this SERP from Google Argentina.*

Analytics

With Google as popular as it is in Colombia, Chile, Venezuela, and Argentina, Google Analytics should be a perfect fit for tracking your search marketing there. Of the major paid services, Webtrends serves all of Latin America from its Portland, Oregon, office with concentrations in Argentina, Brazil, and Mexico. In addition, comScore launched its Digital Analytics in Latin America in July 2011.

Online PR

Online PR is kind of a dark horse in South America because it is not as developed as in North America and Europe. We have seen some good results by just antici-pating that reporters in South America will pick up our news using Google Alerts. A low-cost approach is to write a press release in localized Spanish and send it online. To make this "drift-net" approach (as in you throw out the net and see what it brings) work, write original, high-quality, keyword-researched content and send it out optimized for Google universal results pages.

We mentioned that services such as Marketwire and eNewsPR come in handy for direct-to-media distribution. Both Marketwire and eNewsPR offer localized translations and have a good set of online assets that can be used to boost visibility in Spanish-speaking Latin America. Using either, you can reach the inbox of major newspapers, magazines, websites, and news agencies, as well as local, regional, and national television and radio networks in the countries profiled here.

Search Marketing Tips for Latin America

- Use separate sites with localized Spanish content for each country to avoid getting filtered out as duplicate content.
- Geo-target Google AdWords for Chilean and Colombian cities.
- Consider social media such as Facebook, YouTube, and group buying sites such as Groupon in your search marketing plans—all of which have enjoyed rapid growths in popularity.
- Also consider SMS and IM marketing, as South American countries remain among the biggest users of these services in the world.
- When you write content or ad text, keep in mind that the relatively young Internet audiences in South America will respond better to content written to their interests.
- Consider how rising mobile access can be an opportunity for you.

18

Mexico

Online Mexico is truly a land of opportunities, with a fast-growing ecommerce and Internet penetration. Until recently, Internet usage was restricted, a result of dismal socioeconomic conditions and low penetration of personal computers. This has now changed and in 2011's Mexico, 30.6 million people, 27.7 percent of the population, have access to the Internet according to AMIPCI (La Asociación Mexicana de Internet), a rise from 2.7 percent in 2000. Two-thirds of those online are adolescents and young adults, comprising a market that will grow as they do.

Profile of Mexico Online

The number of Mexicans online has been growing by around 15 percent year over year, and comScore released data in May 2010 showing Mexico's online population soared 20 percent in 2009. Only the United States and Spain have as many Spanish speakers online. The growth potential in Mexico appears to be greater than any Spanish-speaking nation. According to the U.S. Census Bureau, there were around 112 million Hispanics in Mexico and 32 million more in the USA in 2010.

Mexican Internet users spend more time online than ever before. Around 33 percent of users spent five hours or more online in 2010, a big jump from 22 percent in 2009. An important finding in this survey was the volume of users coming from Internet cafes, especially people from lower middle class and below, that gained some economic power in the previous decade. This number had grown to 32 percent in 2010 from 29 percent in 2009.

In Mexico, Spanish is the language commonly spoken, though Mexican authorities do not legislate it as an official language. The second article of the 1917 Mexican constitution defines the country as multicultural and recognizes the right of the indigenous peoples to "preserve and enrich their languages" promoting "bilingual and intercultural education."

Mexicans all learn a standardized version of Spanish, but they use different words and accents according to where they live. The INEGI Organization in Mexico reports approximately 5.4 percent of the Mexican population speak an indigenous language and 1.2 percent do not speak Spanish at all.

According to the third edition of the *Survey of Consumer Digital Media* study done by the Interactive Advertising Bureau Mexico, Internet users there spend 79 percent more time online than on broadcast TV, spending more than 4 hours on average online against only 2.29 hours watching television.

The growth of connectivity through mobile, both cell phones and smartphones, and WiFi networks has had a major impact on Internet access and retention. The IAB Mexico Consumer Digital Media study found moms with children 0–12 years old often access the Internet on their cell phones and are more likely to halt and look at online advertisements than other Mexicans. Only 4 percent of all Mexicans online say they always notice online advertisements, whereas 7 percent of moms do. In the category of "sometimes seeing online advertisements," 70 percent of moms say they do, more than the national average of 63 percent.

Worth noting is that of those who did not notice advertisements or click on them, 48 percent said they lost time if they clicked. This highlights a bandwidth issue in Mexico. The penetration of high-speed Internet connections through landlines is far from as widespread as in the United States, for example, and capacity is normally shared. What might sound like a fast Internet connection is actually much slower due to the volume of people sharing it.

Worldwide, there were 18,013,789,836 ad requests through cell phones on the AdMob network worldwide according to the AdMob Mobile Metrics Report in April 2010. Of those, some 357,012,217, or 2 percent of the total, came from Mexico, giving them a place on the top 10 list (see Figure 18.1). This is a rise from 1.7 percent the month before.

Country	Requests	% of Requests	% Share Change
United States	7,489,183,337	41.6%	-4.4%
India	1,705,752,157	9.5%	2.1%
Indonesia	792,762,749	4.4%	0.0%
United Kingdom	585,487,190	3.3%	-0.5%
Canada	440,661,500	2.4%	-0.9%
France	357,828,344	2.0%	-0.1%
Mexico	357,012,217	2.0%	0.3%
China	333,671,744	1.9%	0.1%
Japan	327,072,385	1.8%	0.0%
Australia	252,697,001	1.4%	0.1%
Other Countries [1][2]	5,371,661,212	29.8%	
Total	18,013,789,836	100.0%	

Figure 18.1   *Ad Requests by Geography—April 2010, taken from the AdMob Mobile Metrics Report.*

This information underscores the importance of using mobile-friendly sites and remembering that not everybody has a fast broadband connection.

Ecommerce in Mexico has been growing by 70 percent every year according to Innopay, a global online transaction consulting firm, fueled by the adolescents and young adults who make up two-thirds of those online there. Popular payment methods are cash or debit, offline bank transfers, and the prepaid Todito card.

According to a comScore report, Microsoft Sites ranked as the top online property in Mexico, reaching more than 90 percent of the online population, followed by Google Sites, Yahoo! Sites, and Facebook (see Table 18.1).

Table 18.1   Top 10 Web Properties in Mexico—Millions of Unique Visitors

Site	September 2009 (in Millions)	September 2010 (in Millions)	% Change
Total Internet Audience	12,914	15,462	20%
Microsoft Sites	11,084	14,268	29%
Google Sites	10,738	14,218	32%
Yahoo! Sites	7,311	9,003	23%
Facebook.com	2,696	8,736	224%
Wikimedia Foundation Sites	5,427	7,312	35%
WordPress	3,606	5,222	45%
MercadoLibre	6,154	5,044	−18%
Batanga	4,508	4,975	10%
Tarringa.net	2,296	4,669	103%
HI5.com	4,100	4,197	2%

Source: comScore, Total Mexican Audience, Home and Work, Ages 15 and Up, March 2009 vs. March 2010

The popularity of Instant Messenger and email are the main reasons Microsoft Sites tops the chart in Mexico. Google is by far the dominant search engine, used by more than 90 percent of Mexican Internet users. With YouTube's popularity, Google Sites has been gaining fast and overtook Microsoft in late 2011.

Search Media in Mexico

Google has been rolling out its algorithmic changes fast to the Latin market as well as other innovations such as the voice search app that was released to Latin America, including Mexico, in March 2011. As you can see in Table 18.2, Google has a firm grasp on the search market in Mexico. Google Universal search results are firmly embedded, as you can see in Figure 18.2.

Table 18.2   Search Engine Market Share—Mexico

Search Engine	Percentage of Search Market
Google	92.67%
Bing	4.18%
Yahoo!	2.57%
Ask	0.38%
AOL	0.10%
Others	0.10%

Source: marketshare.hitslink.com

Figure 18.2   *Google.com.mx returns news, videos, and images in search results.*

Social media usage in Mexico has taken off with more than 85 percent of Internet users using at least one social network. Both Facebook and Twitter recorded outstanding growth in 2010. Mexico's Facebook population increased 94.2 percent from 2010 to 2011, nearly doubling to rank sixth in the world in May 2011. More than two-thirds of Mexicans online use Facebook. According to IAB Mexico, Hi5 and YouTube also stand out as places to share photos and video.

Most Common Mistakes

Equating Spanish Spanish to Mexican Spanish could be the first mistake a marketer would make, but as Mexican Spanish is quite widespread in the United States, it is likely that the person translating and/or localizing is actually a native speaker. Even so, running through a Spanish translation without addressing any possible differences in dialect in your targeted area could cause you to miss your mark as well.

Like Brazilian Portuguese, around 15 percent of the Mexican Spanish is different from the original spoken on the other side of the Atlantic. You can find words like "car" that would be "carro" in Mexico but "coche" in Spain. Another example is "jacket," which would be "chamarra" in Mexico but "jersey" in Spain.

Don't count too much on high-speed connections, and use a lot of slow-loading content on your sites. Though the infrastructure for landlines is in good shape, there are far more people using cell phones than landlines. The GSM sector is booming with 79 percent of the Mexican nation on mobile, and of that, around 4 percent are estimated to be using smartphones, some 3.5 million users.

> "Don't count too much on high-speed connections, and use a lot of slow-loading content on your sites."

Pay-Per-Click

Google AdWords is your main opportunity. You can run your PPC campaigns from your Google AdWords account, setting up separate campaigns for Mexico. In February 2011, Google rolled out city targeting for Mexico, allowing marketers to target not only regional levels but also down to cities (see Figure 18.3). However, as of this writing, Google does not provide the capability to target on a metro level within a city. This capability is available only in the United States.

Bing and Yahoo! enjoy some popularity in Mexico and allow you to geo-target in Mexico from your account as well.

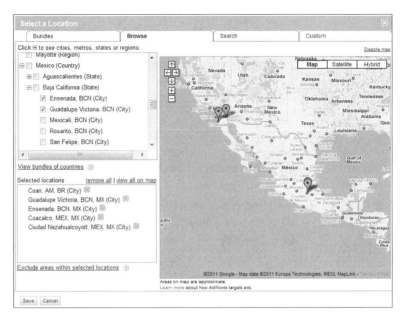

Figure 18.3   *Google rolled out city targeting for Mexico in February 2011.*

Organic Search

With Google as the leading search engine, it is important to implement all organic optimization according to Google's Webmaster guidelines, just as you would in the United States. Make sure you keep up to date with best practices because Google is likely to start rolling out algorithmic changes in Spanish-speaking markets soon after it does in the United States.

Be sure to take advantage of Google's Universal search results in Mexico as you would in the U.S. market. You can do this by optimizing your images, videos, and news releases.

For local visibility, it is important to get local links, focusing on .com.mx domains and localized Spanish. Combining these two elements with good, unique quality content is likely to help you gain organic visibility.

Google.com.mx is a great starting place for finding links, and you can even start by using English. Enter this search string: **"web directory" site:*.com.mx –google** (see Figure 18.4). By doing this we found some 445 results and of them at least 10–15 were link partners we could use.

Figure 18.4   *Finding possible directories in Mexico through Google.*

Other good directories are Dmoz (the Open Directory Project), pagina.com.mx, Mexicoonline.com, and directory.com.mx (see Figure 18.5). To use pagina.com. mx, use Google Translate to find and go to your category; then click on the Add Link tab within and follow the directions to add a link to your site.

Figure 18.5   *Pagina.com.mx is a link directory.*

Analytics

As with all markets where Google leads the way, using Google Analytics for your campaign management can be quite useful, and it's free. Another tool worth noting for the Mexican market is Yahoo! Web Analytics. It is also free and can give great insight into how your visitors are behaving, sorting by age and gender and even interests (see Figure 18.6). Yahoo! Web Analytics is available to Yahoo! Store merchants or through the Yahoo! Web Analytics Consultant Network.

Age	Female			Male		
	Visit %	Visitor %	Conversion %	Visit %	Visitor %	Conversion %
0-17	2.30%	3.38%	0.00%	1.00%	1.40%	0.00%
18-24	8.29%	10.81%	0.00%	13.47%	13.99%	0.00%
25-34	24.42%	31.08%	0.00%	32.92%	31.47%	0.00%
35-54	39.63%	35.14%	0.00%	34.66%	32.87%	0.00%
55+	25.35%	19.59%	0.00%	17.96%	20.28%	0.00%
Total	100.00%	100.00%	0.00%	100.00%	100.00%	0.00%

CROSS-REFERENCE FILTERS — Visiting Countries: Mexico

Figure 18.6   *Being able to see age and gender of those visiting your site can be really helpful (Yahoo! Web Analytics).*

Webtrends and Omniture are a available as elsewhere for a fee.

Online Public Relations

You can use online PR services such as Marketwire to reach major newspapers, magazines, websites, and news agencies, as well as local, regional, and national television and radio networks in Mexico (see Figure 18.7).

Figure 18.7   *Marketwire has proven to be a good resource when sending press releases online to Mexico.*

Marketwire includes translation into Spanish. Other similar services are PR Newswire and eNewsPR. In all cases you need to sign up for an account.

Be sure to have your press release written in localized Spanish for maximum impact.

One important issue to have in mind when sending out press releases to Mexican media is the possibility of its being picked up in other Latin American countries. Mexican media and culture are widely recognized across the regions, mainly because of the virtual monopoly exercised by Mexican media conglomerates in literally every country in the Spanish-speaking world. One of the many examples of this is Grupo Televisa (revenue in 2009 was $4.0 billion US), a Mexican multimedia conglomerate and the largest media company in the Spanish-speaking world. It is a major international entertainment business and broadcast media online, with much of its programming airing in the United States on Univision.

Tips for Search Marketing in Mexico

- Do keyword research in Mexican Spanish and in a regional dialect where appropriate.
- Keep in mind high-speed connections in Mexico may be shared by many and make sure your site and landing pages load quickly.
- Moms of small and school-age children are likely to use their cell phones to access the Internet.
- Target your PPC campaigns to the city level in your Google AdWords account.
- Universal search is in full swing on Google Mexico; be sure to optimize your images, videos, and news releases.
- Marketwire is your best source for press release distribution in Mexico.

19

Singapore

Just over 44 percent of the world's online population resides in Asia, according to Internet World Stats. Although Singapore is far from the largest country in Asia, it is among the best and most well connected of all, with a whopping rate of 77.8 percent Internet penetration, and steadily rising.[1] Only South Korea, Japan, and Brunei have more of their population online. This percentage amounts to more than 3.6 million Internet users on the little island itself. What's more, Singaporeans online have made U.S. retail sites their number-one online shopping destination.

According to Singapore Internet Statistics and Telecommunications data collected in June 2010, Singapore showed considerable growth in its average number of Internet users in the past decade. In 2000, Singapore had 1,200,000 users—merely 36.8 percent of its population being Internet savvy. However, Singapore recorded an increase of connected users of 77.8 percent by the end of 2010. For those doing the math, that's 3,658,400 connected users.

1. International Telecommunications Union

Profile of Singapore Online

The way Singapore has embraced the Internet is inspiring. The government of Singapore has been promoting the use of the Internet as part of its Intelligent Nation 2015 (iN2015) master plan. Singapore was the first global country to deploy high-speed Internet at a commercial level. Sing Tel launched its high-speed Magix service in November 1997. Since then, the country has constructed an extensive infrastructure of broadband services. By 2011, this small island nation had ready access to the Internet and a connectivity of more than 99 percent. Of course, this connectivity presents massive opportunities for external marketers focusing on local users. Singapore was second only to the United States in its share of web traffic from noncomputer devices. Specifically, 5.9 percent of all web traffic received came through mobile phones, smartphones, tablets, and other handheld web-enabled devices. That number is astounding when compared to 6.2 percent in the United States, 5.3 percent in the United Kingdom, 4.6 percent in Japan, and 4.3 percent in Australia.

Singapore is the fourth-strongest mobile market in the world with more than 1,310 mobile phone subscriptions per 1,000 people (some people have more than one phone) and a fast expanding high-speed mobile market. These numbers forecast a large population of mobile Internet users in Singapore in the coming years. Furthermore, 4 out of 10 online shoppers made purchases from mobile phones in 2010. The composition of devices that contribute to traffic also varies between the two. Although the United States has a higher share of total traffic coming from mobile phones (at 4.2 percent), Singapore has more of its traffic coming from tablets (at 1.6 percent).

Moreover, Singapore is gaining prominence in the world as an optimal destination for shared services such as IT, finance, and logistics that provide investors with key benefits such as lower operating costs, reliable service, and enhanced productivity. These figures and statistics reflect how unique the reach of the Internet is in Singapore when compared to other countries in South East Asia, where search engines still maintain an upper hand over social networking.

Singapore provides big opportunity for global businesses that want to reach out to a growing community of users. Indeed, the following data resembles some of the online usage trends in Western countries:

- More than 77 percent Internet penetration rate.
- More than 13 percent of those online use Twitter, putting Singapore in the top 10 countries worldwide.
- More than 55 percent of the entire population use Facebook.
- While at home 34 percent access the Internet from their mobile phones.

Furthermore, online advertising competition has not been as fierce in Singapore as in many other countries discussed in this book. In 2010, Singaporean marketers spent only around 6 percent of their budgets, equivalent to $12.2 million (USD) online even though the average visitor there spends more than 22 hours per month online. The exodus from traditional offline ways of marketing to modern online marketing efforts in Singapore has been slow to start. However, online spending has been estimated to grow about 15 percent each year.[2] This growth forecasts a great future for this small country over a span of the next five years, as well as growing competition for those targeting it.

Trends further pointed to an early mover advantage in 2011 for those targeting locals from abroad because many local companies had not caught on and were still stuck in the old way of doing things. Although Singapore is one of the most developed markets in the world when it comes to Internet penetration and usage, it is also an underdeveloped market when it comes to using the Internet as a marketing medium; the native competition is not as strong as it is in other markets. As you can imagine, this means marketers outside Singapore have some tremendous marketing opportunities in front of them.

According to research done by PayPal in 2011, the size of the Singapore online shopping market reached $1.1 billion (Singapore dollars or SGD) in 2010 and is forecasted to hit $4.4 billion SGD in 2015. Of these numbers, fashion, beauty, and lifestyle have a 26 percent share of the total categories, as you can see in Table 19.1. In 2007, the online shopping rate among Internet users in Singapore was at a whopping 35 percent, compared to only 6 percent in the United States during the same time period. In 2011, online shopping rose to 40 percent of all sales in Singapore. Singaporeans spent a significant amount on domestic websites but were increasingly drawn to foreign websites as a result of greater availability and selection of merchandise, as well as favorable pricing due to the strength of the Singapore dollar. In 2010, 1.2 million shoppers in Singapore spent an average of $1,492 SGD. Two-thirds of the spending was from people in middle and higher income brackets ($4,001 SGD or more in personal annual earnings).

More than a quarter of all spending was on fashion and entertainment, according to a market study done by PayPal. Travel accounted for more than 28 percent of online spending. Two U.S. retail sites, Amazon and Apple, together accounted for nearly a billion unique visitors. The number of Amazon and Apple visitors totaled more than the remaining top 10 retail sites combined.

---

2. *Digital Marketing Yearbook of 2011,* published by the Asian Digital Marketing Association

Table 19.1   Online Spending in Singapore by Category

Shopping Category	Spending in Singapore Dollars (SGD)	Share
Travel	307 Million	28%
Fashion and Beauty	146 Million	13%
Entertainment and Lifestyle	143 Million	13%
IT and Electronics	117 Million	11%
General Insurance	83 Million	8%
Gifts and Collectibles	75 Million	7%

Source: PayPal

Singapore's appetite for online videos is quite large; the average Singaporean watches 11.5 hours of video per month (145.7 videos). Residents watched most of those videos (63.3 percent) on YouTube. Only residents of China and Australia watch more online video (13.4 and 14.3 hours per user per month, respectively). Compared to the world averages, Singaporeans use travel sites and instant messaging significantly more but visit auction sites less often. Though online gaming is popular, use in Singapore is about the same as worldwide averages.

Although shopping is popular online, the top Internet activities in Singapore are work-related, as you can see in Table 19.2.

Table 19.2   Top Five Online Activities in Singapore

Rank	Online Activity	Percentage Who Value It
1	Research for work	54.3%
2	Research how to do things	52.2%
3	Find products to buy	49.5%
4	Access news and events	48.7%
5	Stay in touch with friends	42.5%

Source: ADMA 2011 Yearbook

Search Media in Singapore

Google Singapore (see Figure 19.1) led the search field in 2011 with 146 million searches and just shy of 73 percent search market share. Google Singapore was followed by Yahoo! with 39 million searches and 11 percent of the search market share (see Figure 19.2). Baidu.com trailed Google and Yahoo!, with 8 million searches and less than half a percent of search market share. The searches conducted on Google were the most prolific, with more than 79 searches per single user per month.

Table 19.3 shows the percentage of the search market owned by each of the search players in Singapore.

Table 19.3 Search Engine Market Share—Singapore

Search Engine	Percentage of Search Market
Google	72.95%
Yahoo!	22.66%
Bing	4.13%
Ask	0.15%
Baidu	0.04%
AOL	0.01%

Source: http://marketshar.hitslink.com

Figure 19.1 *Google Singapore comes in four languages, displaying results depending on the language used for the query.*

Figure 19.2   *Yahoo! Singapore is English only.*

Hitwise data from July 2011 puts Google on top with more than 86.5 percent of the total search engine share. Yahoo! and Bing follow with a combined share of 11.9 percent. In this context, not much share is left over for local search engines. However, on the local level, Singapore's own website, www.insing.com, has earned quite a name for itself as a place to search for premium lifestyle, business, entertainment, and shopping.

Internet users in Singapore are not untouched by the massive growth of Facebook, which has attracted the highest number of visits among all the websites visited by users in the country. In addition to Facebook, two other social networking sites appear in the top 10 list of websites visited by online users in Singapore: Twitter and its predecessor, Plurk (see Figure 19.3). Twitter in Singapore has a 13.3 percent penetration rate, making Singapore one of the top 10 countries insofar as Twitter penetration is concerned. As you can imagine, Twitter is a formidable force when marketing to Singaporean consumers.

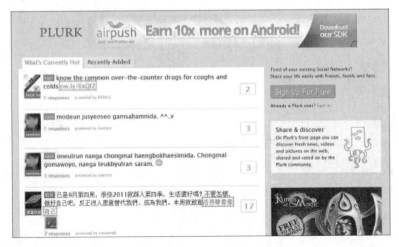

Figure 19.3   *Plurk.com was big in Singapore before Twitter and Facebook.*

Social networking in Singapore skews older than in other parts of Asia. More than half of those on social networks are older than 35. According to comScore, nearly 9 out of 10 people online there visited a social network site in 2010, spending on average 4.4 hours per month. This number is higher than the regional average of 2.8 hours per month in 2010.

Most Common Mistakes

The first and biggest mistake often made stems from the very cultural diversity that makes Singapore exciting—a population comprising people from different nation-alities, with different customs and varied needs and wants. Education policy in Singapore is bilingual; that is, to teach English, an official language, in addition to a "mother tongue," which is one of the other three official languages: Mandarin (also known as Modern Standard) Chinese, Malay, or Tamil (a derivation of Indian). Even though the majority of Singaporeans speak English as a first or second lan-guage, assuming that marketing to them exclusively in English is as effective as doing so in their native language is a mistake. You need to determine which lan-guage the customers you want to reach customers are speaking and use that.

Another common mistake is to lump Singapore, Hong Kong, and Taiwan together. Even though they are all smallish island city-states, and even though they share at least one common language, Mandarin Chinese, each country has its own identity, culture, and customs (as do the Nordic countries, covered in Chapter 10) and the differences among them should be of keen interest to marketers.

A third and related issue is that Google returns results to searchers in Singapore in the language the query was written in, but Yahoo! Singapore provides results only in English. if you are using Yahoo! to advertise, your ads will be most effective among the Singaporeans for whom English is a first language, a good thing to keep in mind as you plan your search ad budget.

Pay-Per-Click

Google AdWords is your primary source of pay-per-click advertising in Singapore, and you can assign your campaign to Singapore within your AdWords account. As with all the countries in this book, best practices include setting and tracking Key Performance Indicators (KPIs). Be sure to match your search terms and ad text in the language you choose because that is how Google will display the results.

And remember your ads for Yahoo! will be in in English only.

Organic Search

According to a January 2011 comScore study, 304 million searches were conducted in Singapore that month, averaging 115.4 searches per searcher. This was a 43 percent increase from the year before. Given that general SEO research has shown 80 percent of clicks to be organic, this translates to around 175 million clicks. You can tap into this activity by leveraging the four main languages spoken in Singapore (English, Mandarin Chinese, Malay, and Tamil). The bottom line is localization and, even more so, localization with Google as the main focus. As we have mentioned throughout the book, similar SEO fundamentals apply everywhere Google is the dominant search engine (such as in the United Kingdom, Iceland, and France). However, Singapore is set apart by the fact that you can target different audiences through different languages. In our experience, those marketing in Singapore have not on the whole taken advantage of all the opportunities presented by multiple languages. Instead, many marketers choose to stick to English or Chinese alone. This leaves a large space for those who determine the language to best reach their audiences and optimize their websites for that individual language. Also, you'll find that some marketing opportunities only exist among people who speak one of the four languages.

Online PR

Table 19.2 underlines the opportunity for using articles to endorse products and services, when it comes to online PR and distributing content. Researching purchases and networking for work are two of the biggest reasons Singaporeans go online. For purchases, 48.4 percent use the Internet to research and/or find products to buy. Some 36.8 percent use the Internet to be inspired and/or get gift ideas. One good way to reach this market is to target marketing and advertising trade publications because there is a limited number of them in Singapore and they are often looking for articles.

Web Analytics

When tracking your Singapore campaigns, you must be sure to set your KPIs according to which of the four languages you are targeting. These are likely to be heavily based on the languages you are targeting within the market. Track the languages used by those entering your site and use that information to identify your target audience. As of this writing, the most popular analytic tools in Singapore are Google, Omniture, and and WebTrends.[3]

---

3. Facebook profile—Singaporean Web Analytics Wednesday

Tips for Search Engine Marketing in Singapore

- Identify which of the four official languages your target audience uses—English, Modern Standard Chinese (also known as Mandarin), Malay, or Tamil—to use in your content, search terms, ad text, and links.

- Set up separate campaigns for each language.

- Take advantage of wide availability of high-speed mobile, smartphones, and tablets for mobile campaigns.

- Use your Google AdWords account for your paid advertising and Google Analytics to track it.

20

Middle Eastern and North African Countries

The term MENA, short for "Middle East and North Africa,"
is a region that extends from Morocco in northwest
Africa to Iran in southwest Asia and generally includes
all the countries of the Middle East and North Africa.
This includes the Gulf Cooperation Council (GCC) bor-
dering the Gulf of Arabia, and those with shores on the
Mediterranean often referred to as the Levant. Sometimes
Turkey is included even though it's technically an associate
member of the European Union. Turkey borders three Middle
East countries and shares cultures and some language.

Profile of MENA Online

As you can see in Table 20.1, Arabic Internet use is largely concentrated among Turkey, Egypt, and Saudi Arabia. Other than Israel, Syria, and the United Arab Emirates, the remaining MENA countries represent less than one percent of the region's online population.

Table 20.1   MENA Internet Usage

MENA Country	People Online	% of Population	Growth Since 2000	Share of Region
Turkey	35,000,000	44%	1,650%	27.4%
Egypt	20,136,000	24.5%	4,375%	15.8%
Saudi Arabia	11,400,000	43.6%	5,600%	8.9%
Israel	5,263,146	70.4%	314%	5.7%
Syria	4,469,000	19.8%	14,796%	3.5%
UAE	3,555,100	69%	384%	2.8%
Region	127,633,466	33.84%	2,126%	100%

Source: Internet World Stats Data 2011

Internet usage in the MENA region grew more than 2,000 percent between 2000 and 2010, and represented 6 percent of the world's Internet population in 2011. With the exception of Israel, all MENA countries use either an Arabic dialect as their main language (Egypt, Saudi Arabia, Tunisia, and Morocco) or are heavily influenced by Arabic and other languages (for example, Turkish, Persian, English, and French). Turkey is a fast-growing market of 35 million people online, which represents 44 percent of the entire population. Turkey's Internet usage grew 1,650 percent from 2000 to 2010 and leapt from 14th to 12th place among Internet users worldwide in 2010. In Turkey, the Arabic language is secondary to Turkish, though Arabic is widely spoken.

Slightly more than one in five Internet users in MENA live in Egypt; more than 20 million people are online. Egypt's online usage is up from 16 million users in 2009, which is a 16 percent hike.

Though Iran has many more Internet users, we chose to omit that country because U.S. commerce there is mostly restricted by U.S. government sanctions.

In 2011, Saudi Arabia had 11.4 million people online, up from 7.7 million in 2009, and almost 44 percent of all the people living there. Saudi Arabia's online community represents 9 percent of the MENA region.

Israel with 5.2 million users had 6 percent of the region's use and a high penetration among its population—70 percent, more than twice the world's. Although Israel's official language is Hebrew, Arabic is used officially for the minority Arab population. With 70 percent of its population already on the Internet, Israel's subsequent growth has been much slower than Saudi Arabia, Egypt, and Turkey. That said, Israel grew to rank first in the world among average hours spent per visitor on social networking sites in 2011.

As you can see in Table 20.2 Arabic-speaking countries make up the fastest-growing online community in the world. Though far from reaching full potential, they are on a fast track toward it, growing 2,500 percent from 2000 to 2011, far more than the world average of 480 percent. Their common language, Arabic, is spoken by 65 million people online around the globe, making Arabic the seventh-largest of all online languages, and 3.4 percent of the overall Internet population, ahead of French, Russian, and Korean.

Table 20.2   Top 10 Languages Online, by Number of Users

Top 10 Languages	Number of Users	Growth 2000–2011	Share of All Users	World Population for This Language
1. English	565,004,126	301%	26.8%	1,302,275,670
2. Chinese	509,965,013	1479%	24.2%	1,372,226,042
3. Spanish	164,968,742	807%	7.8%	423,085,806
4. Japanese	99,182,000	111%	4.7%	126,475,664
5. Portuguese	82,586,600	990%	3.9%	253,947,594
6. German	75,422,674	174%	3.6%	94,842,656
7. Arabic	65,365,400	2501%	3.3%	347,002,991
8. French	59,779,525	398%	3.0%	347,932,305
9. Russian	59,700,000	1826%	3.0%	139,390,205
10. Korean	39,440,000	107%	2.0%	71,393,343
Top 10 Languages	1,615,957,333	421%	82%	4,442,056,069

Source: Internet World Stats, May 2011

According to a May 2011 study by Internet World Stats, there were approximately 347 million Arabic speakers in the world, representing 5 percent of the global population and 65.3 million online. That means Arabic speakers represent

3.3 percent of the world's Internet users. Arabic has 26 main dialects and is the official language in 23 countries. Despite many dialects, only one version is taught in schools and used by the media across the Arab world. Arabic was the fastest-growing language online between 2000 and 2011.

Although you might think the Arabic language is spoken only in the Middle East and North Africa, it's important to note that there is a huge Arabic population in the United States and a far-flung diaspora in countries such as Germany, France, Spain, Sweden, and the United Kingdom. When marketing

> "When marketing on search engines in the Arabic language, you could find yourself targeting across multiple regions and cultures to reach Arabic-speaking Internet users living far from the MENA region."

on search engines in the Arabic language, you could find yourself targeting across multiple regions and cultures to reach Arabic-speaking Internet users living far from the MENA region. For this book, we focused this chapter on the Middle East region countries. You can apply what you learn here to target Arabic speakers in other countries also, although the media you work with may vary from country to country.

According to 2011 comScore and Google data, going online has recently become more popular than watching television in GCC and North African countries. In GCC countries, Internet visitors average 126 minutes a day online from their desktops and PCs, plus another 58 minutes from mobile devices, largely phones, while watching an average of only 117 minutes of television per day.

In North Africa, TV watching remained slightly more popular than going online (177 minutes per day watching television as opposed to 162 minutes per day online) but if we add mobile Internet access (41 minutes per day on average), going online is pulling ahead. Note that, although mobile use was robust, this was mostly by "feature" phones instead of smartphones. Smartphones were less popular because of the high cost of data plans to support their use in countries such as Egypt.

Internet purchases in the United Arab Emirates (UAE) rose 42 percent in 2010, according to a Mastercard survey. The 25–44 age group led in the number of online shoppers, but 35- to 44-year-olds purchased more items more often. Purchases by women rose to 40 percent from 33 percent the year before.

Twenty-three percent used a mobile phone to shop, which is in line with the rest of the Gulf region. What did they buy online? Airline tickets, 74 percent; hotel room bookings, 66 percent; movie tickets, 48 percent; music and arts event tickets, 60 percent up from 47 percent; but music downloads were down 19 percent. Yet even with all this activity, the survey revealed that 45 percent of UAE consumers do not feel safe shopping online.

Forty percent of Turkish users visited retail clothing sites in 2010. Altogether visits to retail sites increased 22 percent from the year before, while visits to travel sites increased 40 percent. What's more, just 5 percent of all Turkish users do NOT use social media. Furthermore, in Turkey, video is as popular as elsewhere in the region. According to comScore, online engagement in Turkey matched the top markets in the world in 2010.

Group buying platforms were on the rise in 2011, with Groupon operating in Turkey, the UAE, and Israel. In Egypt, local startup Offerna.com (literally "our offer") launched in 2011, as did GoNabit in Dubai the year before to take on the import—or perhaps hoping to be acquired in Groupon's global expansion. According to The Next Web (http://thenextweb.com/), there were about a dozen group buying sites across the Arabic-speaking Middle East in December 2010.

According to a 2011 ClickMarketing Summit study on digital marketing trends in the Middle East, 56 percent of companies increased their online ad budgets 20 to 50 percent, and a third of companies increased their budgets but less than 20 percent. The advertisers surveyed reported spending more of the increase on social media marketing (27 percent) than Google AdWords (10 percent). Ten percent of the increase went to SMS marketing. However, the largest beneficiary of the increased funding was good old email marketing. Among the companies surveyed, 28 percent reported spending more on email marketing. The majority of respondents (56 percent) named social media their most favored channel, followed by email (17.5 percent). SEO and Mobile marketing were each named by 12.5 percent of the respondents.

In terms of online ad growth, eMarketer reported that overall spending in the MENA region was just 0.3 percent of worldwide spending in 2009, but more than doubled to 0.7 percent in 2011. This number is projected to double again by 2014. This is a small share of total worldwide spending, but it's a much faster growth rate than we're seeing in established markets. In U.S. dollars, this share of the growing worldwide spending totaled $200 million in 2009, half a billion in 2011, and was projected to grow to $1.5 billion in 2014.

Search Marketing Media in the Middle East and North Africa

As you can see in Table 20.3, Google was the dominant search engine in the MENA region in 2010, ranging from 84.5 percent share in Saudi Arabia to 96 percent in Egypt and Turkey. Yahoo! and Microsoft's Bing captured small shares where Google was used less often. Local players have very little of the market.

Table 20.3 Search Engine Market Share—MENA Region

Search Engine	Percentage of the Search Market
Turkey	
Google	96%
Bing	2.65%
Yahoo!	0.85%
Ask	0.31%
AOL	0.11%
Egypt	
Google	95.82%
Yahoo!	2.23%
Bing	1.77%
Ask	0.10%
AOL	0.05%
Others	0.03%
UAE	
Google	93.18%
Yahoo!	4.56%
Bing	1.79%
Ask	0.29%
AVG	0.11%
Others	0.07%

Search Engine	Percentage of the Search Market
Saudi Arabia	
Google	85.95%
Bing	6.63%
Yahoo!	6.55%
Ask	0.59%
AOL	0.04%
Excite	0.02%

Source: NetMarketShare, marketshare.hitslink.com

Google provides English as an alternate language in key markets, such as Egypt and Saudi Arabia (see Figure 20.1). This will make it easier to find your way around Google in those countries, and indeed you might attract attention from English speakers in the region. However, the Middle East market is largely Arabic speaking, and they will understand and respond better to your messaging if you speak to them in their own language and provide a right-to-left interface, which is what Arabic-speaking people are accustomed to seeing.

Figure 20.1   *Google Morocco offers Arabic and French as main languages.*

Global search engines have been making targeted efforts to reach Arabic-speaking Internet users. Yahoo! acquired Maktoob in 2009 to strengthen its status in the Arabic-speaking countries (see Figure 20.2). In April 2011, Google launched localized domains for Iraq and Tunisia. However, at that time, Google was still not allowed to display sites from domains in Iran, Syria, and Yemen because of ongoing U.S. government-imposed trade sanctions.

"...Google was still not allowed to display sites from domains in Iran, Syria, and Yemen because of ongoing U.S. government-imposed trade sanctions."

Figure 20.2   *Yahoo! combined Maktoob into its interface for Arabic speakers.*

Despite the prominence of Google and presence of the usual suspects Bing and Yahoo! in the region, we cannot ignore a locally created search engine (see Figure 20.3). Ayna (www.ayna.com), which means "where" in Arabic, was the first search engine native to that language. Ayna, launched in 1997, is based in Jordan and opened an office in the United States in 2010.

Figure 20.3   *Ayna, the first Arabic search engine, provides SERPs in English and French; searchers can switch between these languages within the same search.*

Ayna further provides news and widgets for weather and other popular topics, and also provides a virtual Arabic keyboard to improve usability for Arabic searchers, as well as those trying to reach them.

YouTube made notable progress in the MENA region (see Figure 20.4). In 2009, Arab Advisors Telecom executives observed 40 percent of Arab Internet traffic was going to YouTube instead of regional startups iKbis and D1G. Between 2009 and 2011, YouTube made strategic forays into the MENA market, first offering Arabic as a language choice and then launching localized versions in eight countries, including Egypt, Saudi Arabia, Jordan, Morocco, Tunisia, Algeria, and Yemen. Later in 2011, Saudi Telecom partnered with Google Saudi Arabia to distribute YouTube directly onto televisions there. It is not surprising that by mid 2011, 100 million Arabs—that is, 40 percent of the region's online population—were watching YouTube.

Figure 20.4 *Arabic YouTube.*

However, more Turkish people watched videos on Facebook in 2010 than they did on YouTube. Facebook's Turkish population numbers 29.6 million, making it the fifth-largest Facebook population in the world. Even more remarkable, usage of YouTube.com in Turkey was in third place behind Dailymotion.com out of Paris, and Turkey-based Izlesene.com (see Figure 20.5).[1] Izlesene means "YouTube" in Turkish.

1. Source: comScore

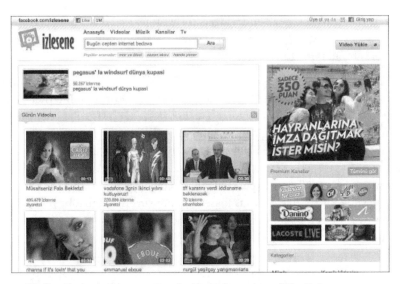

Figure 20.5   *Turkey's Izlesene site, the Turkish version of YouTube.*

Facebook use in April 2011 totaled 27.7 million, doubling from the year before and up 6.4 million since January. This amounted to a 30 percent increase in the first quarter of 2011. Egypt was home to one-fourth of the Facebook users in the region. Arabic was expected to surpass English as the most-used language on Facebook in the region by 2012. Youths 15–29 made up 70 percent of Arabic speakers on Facebook. Women were only one in three, significantly less than the global average of 61 percent in the first quarter of 2011.

In June 2011, there were 7.3 million Egyptians, 4 million in Saudi Arabians, 3.4 million Israelis, and 2.3 million UAE Facebook users.[2] A study done by the *MENA Facebook Digest* showed that 56 percent of Facebook subscribers in Egypt used the Arabic interface. The same study showed that an average of 41 percent of people in GCC countries used the Arabic interface, although its use was much higher in Saudi Arabia (61 percent). Only in the UAE was the situation reversed, with just 10 percent using Facebook in Arabic—most likely because of its very large English speaking ex-pat population.

Across the MENA region, Facebook saw 19 million new subscribers between 2010 and 2011, a 51 percent increase. LinkedIn grew in the Middle East by 140 percent between March 2010 and March 2011. Looming on the horizon in 2011 was China's Baidu, poised with a fresh multilanguage platform and a deal with Microsoft to funnel English-language queries to the Bing search engine.

---

2. Source: www.internetworldstats.com

Most Common Mistakes

The main mistake that marketers make about the MENA region is relying too heavily on the expectation that those online will respond to English. Even though English is quite widely spoken in the region and on some platforms used more, Arabic has the most potential for reaching the widest audience in the region. In the past, the majority of global companies were observed to be importing English-only keywords to target the Arab world on the assumption that customers there could easily search on Arabic language sites and find what they wanted in English. This assumption was disproved in subsequent research showing that Arab Internet users prefer to search using keywords in Arabic. Using Arabic is especially important if you are targeting users with localized issues, such as culture, news, local events, and regional products or services.

Besides English, French is a widely spoken alternate language in Morocco, Algeria, and Tunisia. In Turkey, Arabic is widely spoken, but the official language is Turkish, which has roots closer to Hungarian and Finnish than to Arabic.

Arabic presents challenges in both character set and page layout. Arabic-keyboard. org and Yamli.com both provide browser-based keyboards that translate English, and French as well, into Arabic as you type (see Figure 20.6). As you will see if you start typing onto one of these keyboards, they read right to left. One place this layout is routinely overlooked by Western marketers is on calendars, such as travel booking websites targeting Arabic speakers.

Figure 20.6   *The site www.arabic-keyboard.org allows you to type in Arabic.*

Pay-Per-Click

Because Google is the main contender for PPC marketing in the MENA region, you will be able to manage your campaigns in the English interface on your AdWords account, creating separate campaigns for your Arabic keywords and ads, and geo-targeting them from within AdWords. As we mentioned previously, Google does not allow geo-targeting in some MENA countries that are under sanction by the U.S. Office of Foreign Assets Control (OFAC).

> Google does not allow geo-targeting in some MENA countries that are under sanction by the U.S. Office of Foreign Assets Control (OFAC).

From Google's AdWords forum:

> Google's policy is that people in these countries that are under OFAC sanctions are not able to create an AdWords/AdSense account. Also, we don't allow users to advertise for landing pages that end in an OFAC sanctioned domain (that is, you can't advertise for a page that ends in .ir, for Iran).

In June 2009, these countries included Iran, Syria, Iraq, and Sudan. However, Google launched domains in Iraq and Tunisia in 2011.

Google is the tool of choice for keyword research. As the leading search engine, it draws from the largest pool of search terms, providing the most accurate results. When working with any language based on a non-Latin alphabet, you might find it hard to understand what you see. Google Translate might give you some insight, but do not rely solely on such translations to create your campaigns. Instead, get help from someone on the ground in the country, preferable a native speaker. Google also provides an AdWords blog (http://google-arabia.blogspot.com/) to assist advertisers targeting Arabic speakers (see Figure 20.7). The blog can be read in English.

Figure 20.7   *Google provides an AdWords blog in Arabic, with a link to read the posts in English.*

You can also use the arabic-keyboard.org tool to refine keywords. Though the arabic-keyboard.org tool is not a keyword research tool as such, it can be a valuable part of your initial research when you are looking for types of Arabic words for your PPC campaign and organic search optimization.

Ayna.com is the first regional search engine that has demographically and geo-targeted advertising options through hybrid text advertisements combined with images (see Figure 20.8). Ayna's growing list of more than 3,500 regional sites in the Ayna content network provides pay-per-click advertising opportunities to gain the kind of targeted leads and brand awareness usually available only in display advertising.

Figure 20.8   *Ayna.com has a local content network of over 3,500 sites (Ayna Shareek Network).*

Organic Search

When searching on Google's Arabic sites, you will notice that the layout goes from right to left, not left to right (see Figure 20.9). Google might not have adapted its look and feel for many other languages, but it did for its Arabic sites. This change underscores the importance of incorporating cultural differences when marketing online in this language.

Figure 20.9   *Things go from right to left on Google, when searching in the Arabic region.*

In general the same SEO practices apply to Arabic as with any other market where Google, Bing, and Yahoo! are dominant. If your target is the whole of the Arabic-speaking region, you need to optimize the core Arabic language as it is taught in schools and used by media, and skip any dialects that might be in the way.

If you are targeting a specific country within the region, let's say Egypt, you need to alert Google by using Google Webmaster Tools to identify your selected region if you are using a .COM site and attract inbound links from sites with Egypt ccTLD (".eg") or hosted in Egypt. Doing so will also help you avoid the risk of tripping Google's duplicate content filters, as we explained in Chapter 2, "Common Territory: Search Marketing Without Borders."

Google's universal search results pages are also evident across the region, so take advantage of optimizing your images and videos (see Figure 20.10).

Figure 20.10   *Google Egypt universal search results page.*

Analytics

Both Google Analytics and Yahoo! Analytics are free tools that can be used in the Arabic market. Your challenge will be working in the Arabic language, and interpreting user behavior on your site in the Arabic right-to-left page layout. Here again it is best to find assistance from someone who is both fluent in Arabic, and familiar with search marketing analytics.

Online PR

There are not many options for online PR focusing on the Arabic region. Marketwire distributes press releases to the region and includes translation in its services. Marketwire's main strength is direct access to media services. You should be able to reach out to general and business newspapers, magazines, newswires, and broadcast media in Bahrain, Egypt, Iraq, Jordan, Kuwait, Lebanon, Oman, Qatar, Saudi Arabia, Syria, United Arab Emirates, and Yemen. In many cases, a translation into Arabic is included.

If you want to send out press releases online only in the Arabic language, you might want to consider either NewsCertain or the eNewsPr network. It's best if you send out your press releases in the local language because doing so will improve your appearance in Google search results.

Search Marketing Tips in MENA

- Focus your marketing throughout the region on Google and find advice on the AdWords blog, where you can also read posts in English.

- Use Arabic keywords and content to reach most of this market, but be prepared to use French, Turkish, and English in selected markets.

- Besides Google's keyword tool, use www.arabic-keyboard.org or Yamli.com to refine your search phrases.

- If you are targeting the Arabic region, focus on the core language as taught in schools and skip regional dialects.

- Make sure your content and ads are in the Arabic layout of right to left.

- Leverage YouTube in Arabic markets with video content optimized for search.

- Consider Facebook and other social media for marketing, to youth in particular.

- Keep in mind Google is prevented from displaying ads or search results from some MENA countries because of government trade sanctions aimed at them. In 2011, they were Iran, Syria, Sudan, and Yemen.

A

SEO/SEM Resources

Finding the right resources—whether you are learning the basics or want to keep current with international search marketing—can be a barrier, and understanding where and how to search for such resources is fundamental. For the authors of this book, tools such as Twitter and Google are important, but meeting people at conferences and sharing information are even more important. Indeed, from the beginning, all of us in the search marketing industry have learned most of what we know from sharing experiences with each other.

In this appendix, we list books, conferences, websites, tools, and other resources we rely on. Although we have not tried every resource available out there, we have used all the resources in this appendix and have tested all the tools here. (Kindly note, website addresses change from time to time; if any of the ones we list here don't work, try searching online for the name of the resource.)

In our experience, there is no one tool that does it all, so expect to mix and match when it comes to realizing your potential online...and worldwide.

Books

- *Search Engine Visibility* (Second Edition)—An excellent foundational book by Shari Thurow that teaches you the basics and also provides insight into how design and content can affect your site's visibility in search engines. New Riders, 2008. ISBN-13: 978-0-321-50324-4.

- *Search Marketing Inc.* (Second Edition)—A comprehensive guide to everything you need to know to plan and execute search marketing campaigns. Written by Bill Hunt and Mike Moran from extensive experience in international marketing and large companies. The second edition includes mobile marketing. Pearson plc, publishing as IBM Press, 2009. ISBN-10: 0-13-606868-5.

- *Winning Results with Google AdWords* (Second Edition)—The definitive guide to PPC advertising on Google. Written by Andrew Goodman, longtime expert search engine marketer. McGraw-Hill, 2009. ISBN-13: 978-0-07-149656-8.

- *The Truth About Search Engine Optimization*—The title says it all. Written by Rebecca Lieb. Que Publishing, 2009. ISBN-10: 0-7897-3831-7.

- *Mobile Marketing: Finding Your Customers No Matter Where They Are*—The first and most comprehensive guide to marketing on mobile devices. Written by Cindy Krum. Que Publishing, 2010. ISBN-10: 0-7897-3976-3.

- *Outlook Country Reports*—These econometric studies are expensive but give good insight into the individual markets that they cover. They address the latent demand outlook for search engine optimization (SEO) and Internet marketing in general across the prefectures and cities they cover. Written by the Icon Group International. www.icongrouponline.com/countries.asp.

- *YouTube and Video Marketing: An Hour A Day*—Written by Greg Jarboe, this is the first and most comprehensive guide to search marketing for video, updated in the new edition. 2011.

Websites

- **Multilingual-search.com**—This is a site edited by Andy Atkins Kruger, one of the world's most knowledgeable people about international multilingual search marketing, and written by close to 50 experienced contributing editors from around the world (see Figure A.1).

Figure A.1   *Multilingual-search.com focuses exclusively on the topic of multilingual search marketing.*

- **Searchenginewatch.com**—This site is full of tips from by experienced search engine marketing writers who cover a broad range of topics that have to do with search engines. It also offers a good newsletter that we recommend (see Figure A.2).

Figure A.2   *Search Engine Watch covers many SEO and SEM topics.*

- **Searchengineland.com**—A good source of wisdom from experienced writers.
- **Searchcowboys.com**—Europe's most popular blog about search engine marketing.
- **Stateofsearch.com**—Another good blog based out of Europe.
- **ajpr.com/wordpress/**—A blog by Motoko Hunt, expert on Japan and other Asian markets—the go-to source if you are targeting Japan.
- **Websitetestingtools.com**—The Online Marketer's Toolbox by Bryan Eisenberg, author and online marketer. It's a collection of great tools, some that fit directly with the topic of this book. So far, he has collected more than 150 tools and counting. www.websitetestingtools.com/.

Tools

- **KeywordSpy**—A tool that helps you track and understand search engine visibility in close to 30 languages. The tool shows both your position and that of your competitors. www.keywordspy.com.

- **Google Keyword Tool**—In short, *the* global keyword tool, and there are no other tools that show as many languages. www.googlekeywordtool.com.

- **Google AdWords**—Online advertising by Google. http://adwords. google.com.

- **Google Webmaster Central**—Your best connection to Google, where you will find data about Google's crawling, indexing, and search traffic to your site, and receive alerts if there are problems with it. www.google.com/webmasters.

- **Yandex Keyword Tool Wordstat**—Great for those focusing on the Russian market, this tool shows impressions per month but does not give clicks. We recommend mixing Google data and Yandex data together. wordstat.yandex.com (English) and wordstat.yandex.ru (Russian).

- **Yandex Webmaster Tools**—In English. webmaster.yandex.com/.

- **Yandex Direct Search Advertising**—In English. http://direct.yandex.com/.

- **Baidu Keyword Tool**—A Baidu tool that you can use to see search volume, but you need to be logged in to your Baidu Phoenix Nest account to use it. Also, it does not show numbers, but instead shows a graph that indicates search volume. http://is.baidu.com/keyword_tool.html (English).

- **Baidu Paid Search**—In English. http://is.baidu.com/paidsearch.html.

- Baidu Webmaster Platform—In Chinese (Simplified) and in public beta at this writing, here is where Baidu provides tools to optimize websites. http://zhanzhang.baidu.com/.

- **Linkdex**—Good all-around tool that has an option for those who want to test visibility in countries outside their own and want to do it so that it looks as though they are at specific location. www.linkdex.com.

- **MajesticSEO**—One our favorite tools, Majestic provides competitor backlink intelligence to SEO specialists. We have not found any markets for which the tool does not give valuable data. www.majesticseo.com.

- **SpyFu**—Good PPC and Organic competitive analysis tool. It works only in the United Kingdom and United States. It gives good insights if you are targeting the UK. www.spyfu.com.

- **SEMRush**—Similar to SpyFu, the tool gives good PPC and organic competitive analysis. The main difference is that SEMRush shows data from nine markets and, on top of that, has U.S. Bing data (see Figure A.3). www.semrush.com.

Figure A.3   *SEMRush shows data from nine countries.*

- **AddThis Social Media Service Country Comparison**—AddThis is a social media sharing widget maker that gives access to its data, providing trends in how people share their data through social interaction (see Figure A.4). http://www.addthis.com/services.

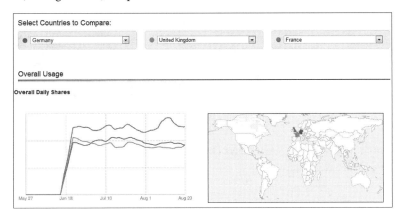

Figure A.4   *AddThis data can show some good insights into the usage of social media by country, or by service, such as comparing Facebook, email, or Twitter.*

- **SEOMoz**—A comprehensive suite of tools for search engine optimization, including OpenSite Explorer for backlink data, rank checking, keyword analysis and competitive intelligence, plus a basic guide to getting started in search engine optimization, and a forum where you can ask questions. Works in Russian and you can specify Yandex as a search engine you want to track in it. www.seomoz.org.

Figure A.5   *PressPort offers international press release services.*

Online PR

- **Marketwire.com**—Great for worldwide distribution of PR, normally gets great pick-up and audience engagement.

- **NewsCertain.com**—Search engine friendly multilingual, multimedia news distribution. NewsCertain.com sits at the center of a network of international news sites in the world's major languages.

- **eNewsPR.com**—Similar to NewsCertain, eNewsPR is a network of sites that accept multilingual press releases with good international reach.

- **Pressport**—Another international online press and news release service. In this case, PressPort has shown some good results in the Scandinavian market (see Figure A.6). www.pressport.us.

Figure A.6   *PressPort offers international press release services.*

- **mynewsdesk.com**—My News Desk is a news exchange site headquartered in Sweden, but with great international reach.

Conferences

As we mentioned, in the search marketing industry we learn from each other, and one of the best ways to do that is to immerse yourself in a conference. Here are a few we have found useful.

- **SES Conference**—The longest-running search marketing event, held in many locations around the world. These conferences have long been proven to be of great value for those getting started, as well those seeking more advanced information. www.searchenginestrategies.com.

- **Search Marketing Expo Conferences**—A great source for advanced information and for those who want to go international because they are in 11 locations around the world. http://searchmarketingexpo.com/.

- **International Search Summit (Conference)**—ISS is the only search marketing event focusing exclusively on international SEO and social media. These conferences are held in worldwide locations and bring in a great set of international speakers. www.internationalsearchsummit.com.

- **RIMC (Conference)**—This conference is in Reykjavik, Iceland, midway between America and mainland Europe. It is small but very personal and attracts speakers from around the world. www.rimc.is/en.

Google Countries and Domains

How to Find Google Domains Around the World

Google domains vary from country to country and are not always "Google.(country extension). We have listed them all here. As they may change from time to time, the fastest way to find the correct URL in a given country is to Google the term listed for it in the column at the far right, and Google will take you there.

Countries	Languages	Google Interface
Andorra	Catalan	Google Català
Anguilla	English	Google Anguilla
Antigua and Barbuda	English	Google Antigua & Barbuda
Argentina	Spanish	Google Argentina
	Guarani	Google Guarani
Armenia	Armenian	Google Armenian
	Kurdish	Google Kurdish
Austria	German	Google Österreich
Albania, Kosovo	Albanian/Tosk	Google Shqiptar
Arabia (Saudi), Emirates, Maghreb, Egypt, Lebanon, Syria, Jordan, Kuwait, Oman, Sudan, Iraq, Bahrain...	Arabic	Google Arabic
		Google Saudi Arabia
Australia	English	Google Australia
Azerbaijan (and Iran, Georgia)	Azeri, Russian	Google Azerbaijan

Countries	Languages	Google Interface
	Azerbaijani	Google Azerbaijani
Belgium	French, Dutch, German, English	Google Belgium
Belize	English, Spanish	Google Belize
Bangladesh	Bengali (Bengla)	Google Bangla
Belarus	Byelorussian	Google Byelorussian
Bolivia	Spanish	Google Bolivia
Bosnia & Herzegovina (Federation)	Bosnian	Google Bosanski
	Serbian	Google Srpski
	Croatian	Google Hrvatski
Brazil	Portuguese	Google Brasil
	Guarani	Google Guarani
Burundi	French	Google Burundi
Bulgaria	Bulgarian	Google Bulgarian
Canada	French, English	Google Canada
Chad	French	Google Tchad
Chile	Spanish	Google Chile
China	Chinese simplified	Google Simple Chinese
	Chinese traditional	Google Traditional Chinese
	Mongolian	Google Mongolian
	Uighur	Google Uighur
Colombia	Spanish	Google Colombia
Congo (Republic of the)	French	Google Rép. du Congo
Congo (Democratic Republic of the)former Zaïre	French	Google R.D. du Congo
Cook (Islands)	English	Google Cook Islands
Czech (Republic)	Czech	Google Cesky
Cocos (Keeling) Islands-Asia [Australia]	English	Google Cocos (Keeling) Islands
Costa Rica	Spanish	Google Costa Rica
	English (spoken around Puerto Limon)	
Cote D'Ivoire	French	Google Côte d'Ivoire
Croatia	Croatian	Google Hrvatski
	Serbo-Croatian	Google Serbo-Croatian

Countries	Languages	Google Interface
Cuba	Spanish	Google Cuba
Denmark	Danish	Google Danmark
	Faroese	Google Dansk
Djibouti	French, Arabic	Google Djibouti
Dominican Republic	Spanish	Google Rep. Dominicana
Ecuador	Spanish	Google Ecuador
El Salvador	Spanish	Google El Salvador
Erytrea, Ethiopia (north)	Tigrinya	Google Tigrinya
Estonia	Estonian	Google Eesti
Ethiopia (south)	Amharic	Google Amharic
Faroe Islands [Denmark]— east of Iceland	Faroese	Google Faroese
	Danish	Google Dansk
Fiji (Islands)	English	Google Fiji
France	French	Google France
Bretagne	Breton	Google Brezhoneg
Languedoc Roussillon, Midi-Pyrénées	Occitan	Google Occitan
Basque country	Catalan	Google Català
French, Berrichon...	Basque	Google Euskara
Finland	Finnish	Google Suomi
	Swedish	Google Svenska
Gambia (The)	English	Google The Gambia
Georgia (and Azerbaïdjan, Turkey, Iran)	Georgian	Google Georgian
Germany	German	Google Deutschland
Schleswig-Holstein	Frisian	Google Frysk
Ghana	Twi	Google Twi
Gibraltar	English, Spanish, Italian, and Portuguese	Google Gibraltar
Greece	Greek	Google Greek
		Google Greece
Greenland	English, Danish	Google Grønlands
Guatemala	Spanish	Google Guatemala
Guam, Saipan (Islands)— Oceania [USA]	Chamorro	Google Gujarati

Countries	Languages	Google Interface
Guernsey (Island)—Normandy [GB]	French, English	Google Guernsey
Honduras	Spanish	Google Honduras
Hong Kong	Chinese (trad.), English	Google Hong Kong
Hungary, Vojvodina	Hungarian	Google Magyarország
		Google Magyar
Korea	Korean	Google Korea
India	English, Bengali, Hindimarathi, Telugu	Google India
	Hindi	Google Hindi
	Kannada	Google Kannada
	Marathi	Google Marathi
	Oriya	Google Oriya
	Punjabi	Google Punjabi
	Tamil	Google Tamil
	Telegu	Google Telugu
	Urdu	Google Urdu
	Bengali (Bengla)	Google Bangla
	Bihari	Google Bhojpuri
	Malayalam	Google Malayalam
	Uighur	Google Uighur
	Sindhi	Google Sindhi
Indonesia	Bahasa Indonesia	Google Indonesia, Google Bahasa Indonesia
	Sundanese	Google Basa Sunda
Indonesia-Java Island	Javanese	Google Jawa
Iran, Iraq, United Arab Emirates...	Perse (Farsi)	Google Persian (Farsi)
	Kurdish	Google Kurdish
Ireland	English	Google Ireland
	Gaelic Irish	Google Gaeilge
Iceland	Icelandic	Google Íslensku
Israel	Hebrew	Google Israel
	Arabic	Google Arabic
	Yiddish	Google Yiddish
Italy	Italian	Google Italia

Countries	Languages	Google Interface
Piemonte, Liguria, Calabria...	Occitan	Google Occitan
Sardinia	Catalan	Google Català
Jamaica	English	Google Jamaica
Japan	Japanese	Google Japan
Jersey (Island)—Normandy [GB]	French, English	Google Jersey
Kazakhstan	Kazakh	Google Kazakhstan
	Uighur	Google Uighur
Kenya	English	Google Kenya
	Kiswahili	Google Kiswahili
Kyrgyzstan (Republic of)	Kyrgyz	Google Kirghizstan, Google Kyrgyz
	Uighur	Google Uighur
Laos	Laothian	Google Lao
Latvia	Latvian	Google Latvija
Lesotho	English, Zulu	Google Lesotho
	Sesotho	Google Sesotho
Libya	Arabic, Italian, English	Google Libya
Liechtenstein	German	Google Liechtenstein
Lituania	Lithuanian	Google Lietuvos
Luxembourg	German	Google Luxemburg
Macedonia (former Yugoslav, Republic of)	Macedonian	Google Makedonski
	Serbian	Google Srpski
	Croatian	Google Hrvatski
Malaysia	Bahasa Melayu, English	Google Malaysia
	Bahasa Melayu	Google Bahasa Melayu
	Tamil	Google Tamil
	Malayalam	Google Malayalam
Malawi (République)	English	Google Malawi
Malta (Island)	Maltese	Google Malti
		Google Malta
Mauritius	French, English	Google Mauritius
Mexico	Spanish	Google Mexico
Micronesia (Federated States of)—Oceania	English	Google Micronesia

Countries	Languages	Google Interface
Mongolia	Mongolian	Google Mongolian
		Google Mongolia
Montserrat (Island)— Caribbean [GB]	English	Google Montserrat
Mozambique	Zulu	Google Zulu
Portugal	Google Português	
Namibia	English, Afrikaans	Google Namibia
Nepal	Nepali	Google Nepali
		Google Nepal
Netherlands	Dutch	Google Nederland
Friesland/Fryslan Province and Islands	Frisian	Google Frysk
New Zealand	English	Google Newzealand
Nicaragua	Spanish	Google Nicaragua
Norfolk (Island)—(Pacific, Est of Australia) [Australia]	English	Google Norfolk Island
Norway	Norwegian (Bokmål)	Google Norway, Google Norsk
	Norwegian (Nynorsk)	Google Nynorsk
Pakistan	Punjabi	Google Pwiksqwn
	Sindhi	Google Sindhi
	Uighur	Google Uighur
Panama	Spanish, English	Google Panama
Paraguay	Spanish	Google Paraguay
	Guarani	Google Guarani
Peru	Spanish	Google Perú
Philippines	Filipino Tagalog	Google Pilipinas
		Google Filipino
Pitcairn (Islands)	English	Google Pitcairn Islands
Poland, Lituania...	Polish	Google Polska
Portugal, Brazil, Angola, Mozambique..	Portuguese	Google Português
		Google Português (Portugal)
		Google Portugal
Puerto Rico	Spanish	Google Puerto Rico

Countries	Languages	Google Interface
Romania, Moldova, Vojvodina...	Hungarian	Google România
		Google Româna
Russia (Federation), ex-USSR...	Russian	Google Russia
		Google Russian
Rwanda (Ruanda)	French, Swahili, English	Google Rwanda
Saint-Helana (Island)—Atlantic, west of Angola [GB]	English	Google Saint-Helena
Saint Vincent and the Grenadines	English	Google Saint-Vincent and the Grenadines
Samoa (American)	English	Google American Samoa
San-Marino	Italian	Google San-Marino
Scotland (UK)	Scots Gaelic	Google Gàidhlig
Seychelles	French, English	Google Seychelles
Serbia (part of former Yugoslavia)	Serbian	Google Srpski
	Serbo-Croatian	Google Serbo-Croatian
Singapore		Google Singapore
	Tamoul	Google Tamil
	Malay Bahasa	Google Bahasa Melayu
Slovakia (Republic of), Vojvodina	Slovak, Hungarian	Slovenskej Republiky
		Google Slovensky
Slovenia	Slovenian	Google Slovenščina
Somalia	Somalia	Google Somali
South Africa	English	Google South Africa
	Afrikaans	Google Afrikaans
	Xhosa	Google Xhosa
	Zulu	Google Zulu
	Sesotho	Google Sesotho
Spain	Spanish, Basque, Catalan, Galician	Google Spain, Google Español
Basque Country	Basque	Google Euskara
Cataluna	Catalan	Google Català
Galicia	Galician	Google Galego

Countries	Languages	Google Interface
Val D'Aran	Occitan	Google Occitan
Sweden	Swedish	Google Sverige
		Google Svenska
Sri Lanka (former Ceylon)	Tamil	Google Tamil
	Sinhalese	Google Sinhala
Switzerland	German, Italian	Google Suisse
	Romanche	Google Romanche
Taiwan	Traditional Chinese	Google Taiwan
Tajikistan	Tajik	Google Tadjikistan
Tanzania	Kiswahili	Google Kiswahili
Thailand, Vietnam	Thai	Google Thaï
		Google Thailand
Tonga (Kingdom of)	English	Google Tonga
Trinidad and Tobago	English, Spanish, Chinese,	Google Trinité-et-Tobago
Turkey	Turkish	Google Türkçe
	Turkish	Google Türkiye
	Kurdish	Google Kurdish
	Uighur	Google Uighur
Turkmenistan (Republic)	Turkmen	Google Turkmen
		Google Turkmenistan
Uganda	English	Google Uganda
Ukraine	Ukrainian	Google Ukrainian
		Google Ukraine
United Arab Emirates	Arabic	Google Arab Emirates
United States of America	English	Google.com
	Spanish	Google Español
	Yiddish	Google Yiddish
Uruguay	Spanish	Google Uruguay
Uzbekistan (and Afghanistan, Kazakhstan, Kyrgyzstan, Tajikistan, Turkmenistan)	Uzbek	Google Uzbek
	Uighur	Google O'zbekiston
		Google Uighur
United Kingdom/Great Britain/ England	English	Google UK

Countries	Languages	Google Interface
Scotland	Scots Gaelic	Google Gàidhlig
		Google Gaeilge
Wales	Welsh	Google Cymraeg
Ukraine	Ukrainian	Google Ukrainian
		Google Ukraine
Vietnam, Cambodia, Laos	Vietnamese, French Chinese (trad.)	Google Viêt Nam
		Google Viet
Virgin Islands (British/ American)—Caribbean	English	Google British Virgin Islands
		Google US Virgin Islands
Wales (UK)	Welsh	Google Cymraeg
	Esperanto	Google Esperanta
Yugoslavia (former): Kosovo, Montenegro, Serbia, Vojvodina	Serbian, Montenegrin, Albanian, Hungarian, Slovak, Romanian, Serbo-Croatian	Google Srpski
		Google Shqiptar
		Google Magyar
		Google Slovensky
		Google Româna
		Google Serbo-Croatian

Index

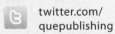
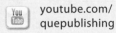

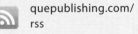

que®

Biz-Tech Series

Straightforward Strategies and Tactics for Business Today

The **Que Biz-Tech series** is designed for the legions of executives and marketers out there trying to come to grips with emerging technologies that can make or break their business. These books help the reader know what's important, what isn't, and provide deep inside know-how for entering the brave new world of business technology, covering topics such as mobile marketing, microblogging, and iPhone and iPad app marketing.

- Straightforward strategies and tactics for companies who are either using or will be using a new technology/product or way of thinking/ doing business

- Written by well-known industry experts in their respective fields— and designed to be an open platform for the author to teach a topic in the way he or she believes the audience will learn best

- Covers new technologies that companies must embrace to remain competitive in the marketplace and shows them how to maximize those technologies for profit

- Written with the marketing and business user in mind—these books meld solid technical know-how with corporate-savvy advice for improving the bottom line

Visit **quepublishing.com/biztech** to learn more about the **Que Biz-Tech series**